Joseph Henry Allen

Christian History in Its Three Great Periods

Vol. 2

Joseph Henry Allen

Christian History in Its Three Great Periods
Vol. 2

ISBN/EAN: 9783337263034

Printed in Europe, USA, Canada, Australia, Japan

Cover: Foto ©ninafisch / pixelio.de

More available books at **www.hansebooks.com**

CHRISTIAN HISTORY

IN ITS

THREE GREAT PERIODS

Second Period

THE MIDDLE AGE

BY

JOSEPH HENRY ALLEN

AUTHOR OF "HEBREW MEN AND TIMES," "OUR LIBERAL
MOVEMENT IN THEOLOGY," &c.

Porro subesse Romano Pontifici omni humanæ creaturæ declaramus dicimus definimus et pronuntiamus omnino esse de necessitate salutis. — *Bull " Unam Sanctam " of* BONIFACE VIII.

BOSTON

ROBERTS BROTHERS

1883

CONTENTS.

THE MIDDLE AGE.

I.

THE ECCLESIASTICAL SYSTEM.

SEVEN centuries, dating from the time of Charlemagne, include the Catholic system of the Middle Age. Strictly speaking, the great era of ecclesiastical power covers only two centuries and a half, beginning (about 1050) with the work of Hildebrand, and ending with the Jubilee of the year 1300. In a broader sense, however, the Middle Age extends from the founding of the Empire of the West in 800 to the dawn of the Protestant Reformation.

Again, it will be convenient to take the exact middle point of the period thus defined (1150), as the moment when the spiritual power, properly so called, culminates. The Papacy reached its greatest political splendor and strength a little later; but reasons will appear for taking the above date as marking the time of highest vigor in the system as a whole.

Mr. Bryce, in his "Holy Roman Empire," has made familiar to students of history the theory of Sovereignty on which the Mediæval system was built. It is, shortly, something like this. The ideal government, divinely appointed for all mankind, is of two sorts, spiritual and temporal. The first (including worship, morals, and education) is represented by the Holy Church Universal, whose head is the vicegerent of God on earth. The second (including political government, civil order, and military authority) is embodied in the Holy Roman Empire, which is, in theory, alike universal, and inherits direct from that of Rome as established by the Cæsars.

Ideally conceived, the two are co-extensive and co-ordinate; but the first has the greater dignity. The Empire is to the Church as body is to soul, or (in the phrase addressed by Gregory VII. to William the Conqueror) as moon to sun, shining only by its reflected light.

When we speak, then, of the spiritual power of the Church, we speak not only of its authority over men's conscience and belief, but of its divine right to assert that authority, at will, through the " secular arm " of any state-government the world over; nay, to control and overrule all political authority, or to abolish any which shall not exactly execute its will.

First of all, in dealing with the theory of the Catholic Church, it is important to bear in mind that it regards men — theoretically, every individual of the human race — not simply as the Objects of its instruction, discipline, or charity, which Protestant churches do, but as the Subjects of its government, which Protestant churches do not. The submission it requires is first of all obedience to its authority, as to that of a government. To question this is not merely heresy, but rebellion. Assent of reason and conscience is well also; but submission to the sovereign must be had first. Believe: but first, Obey.

Bearing this in mind, what now is the nature of this spiritual or ecclesiastical power in itself? Instead of discussing its theory in the abstract, I will present a few familiar aspects of it as they meet our eye.

We see a Church which, after a thousand years of various fortune, has reached at length a height of power, the like of which was never held in human hands, nor, it is likely, conceived in human thought, elsewhere. It is a power resting on the invisible foundations of conscience, conviction, and religious fear. To the popular belief, it holds literally the keys of heaven and hell. It spans like an arch the dreadful gulf between the worlds seen and unseen. Its priesthood rules by express divine appointment; and its chief is addressed in language such as it seems impious to address to any other than to Almighty God.*

We see this Church, in the person of its Priesthood, present absolutely everywhere. It carries in its hand the threads that govern every province of human life. It enters every house. It is a guest at every board, a companion at every hearth. It adopts every new-born babe by its mystic rite of baptism, or else consigns it, unblest, to endless limbo, that dreary twilight of hell. It watches over and teaches every growing child. It regulates the marriage-contract, and the solemn rites of burial. It guides through the confessional every scruple of conscience, every

* The Pope is *alter Deus*, according to the expression of Paul II.

impulse of devotion, every affection of the heart. It offers or withholds, on its own terms, the soul's peace on earth, and its salvation in eternity.

We see it, in the person of its Pontiffs, maintaining conflict or alliance, on equal terms, with the powers of the world. At its will it lifts up the lowly, or tramples on the proud. To haughty feudal chiefs it dictates its haughtier counsel or command. A sovereign who (like the Emperor Frederick II.) defies its authority it punishes by its doom of excommunication. A stubborn and proud realm (like England) it lays under the awful shadow of its interdict. It is a party to all treaties, an accomplice in all political intrigues, a power behind the throne mightier than the throne itself. It allies itself with sovereign, nobles, or people, as its policy requires: here warily concedes, there imperiously commands; gives its license of conquest to the Norman William, or sets its foot on the proud neck of the German Barbarossa; protests against an English *Magna Charta*, and defies a French States-General; refuses to own allegiance to any earthly sovereign, and asserts, in the name of God, its authority to make or unmake kings.

We see it, in the person of its Religious Orders, penetrating to every nook and hamlet, ruling the popular passion and imagination no less than the counsel of courts by its imperious word. It stirs men's minds by its enthusiastic appeal, — sending forth its enormous hosts under the banner of the Cross to battle in the Holy Land, or defending the fastnesses of its empire by the fanatic hate it breathes against heretic and infidel. By the same insidious, ubiquitous control it arms the invincible valor of its military monks to war with Turk and Saracen, and the implacable fanaticism of its mendicant monks to hunt down heresy at home. With its right hand it upholds the glorious Orders of the Temple and St. John; with its left it guides the merciless police of the "Holy Office" of Inquisition.

We see its matchless skill and power employed in the accumulation of enormous wealth. The terrors of a death-bed, the popular fear of the approaching Day of Judgment, the enthusiasm that equips the ranks of the Crusaders, and the disorders of their impoverished estates,—all are skilfully wrought upon to fill the treasuries of the Church. It turns its doctrine of Purgatory into a source of profit, and sets a fixed price on its Masses for the dead. It makes a traffic of penance and indulgences. It seizes lands under forged charters and deeds, and claims the administration of intestate estates. It owns half the landed property of England, a nearly like proportion of France and Germany. It profits even by the violence of robbers and plunderers. "Those very men," says Hallam, "who in the hour of sickness and impending death showered the gifts of expiatory devotion upon its altars, had passed the sunshine of their lives in sacrilegious plunder." Thus its power is extended and increased in a thousand hidden ways, aiming, apparently, at an absolute monopoly of men's temporal as well as spiritual estate : a power employed often in behalf of the enslaved and poor, to loose the heavy burden and let the oppressed go free; often to feed the vices and pride of some bishop-sovereign of Bamberg or Cologne, and to strengthen upon the kingdoms the grasp of the heavy hand of Rome.

We see its pomp of Priests, with chant and lighted taper and silver bell, striking the rude mind of barbaric ignorance with awe, as some holy spell or oracle. We see its Hermits, in their austere seclusion; its trains of Pilgrims, with bead and cockle-shell; its Palmers, journeying from shrine to shrine, and bearing the fragrant memory of the Holy Land; its barefoot Friars, sworn to beggary, and wrangling whether Jesus and his disciples held in common any goods at all. We see its secluded Abbey, in some smiling valley by the waterside, — where its ruins stand yet, as at Tintern, Holyrood, or Melrose, — a centre of culture, peace, and religious veneration, almost under the very shadow of the frowning castle of some feudal lord; its stately Cathedral, looming large, as at Strasburg or Milan, amid the dark and lowly dwellings of the city, — the daring and vast proportions, the intricate perfection of workmanship, challenging all modern rivalry; its statuary and painting, as in Parma, Florence, Rome, that from rude beginnings reach gradually the topmost height of sacred Art. We see its Universities, at Padua, Paris, Oxford, thronged by great armies of young men, as many as twenty thousand at once, it is said, in a single place: first the fond care, then the arbiter, at last the invincible rival of the Church itself in the realm of intellect. To these we add the troubled yet stirring story of Feudalism as it slowly shaped itself towards modern Monarchy; the gorgeous associations of Chivalry, throwing its fitful grace over the barbarism of perpetual strife; the thrilling adventure of the Crusades; the stern devotion and fatal pride of the Military Orders, which from champions became at length the victims of ecclesiastical and civil policy.

Lastly, we see its monstrous engine of despotic power, exercised through Inquisition, Excommunication, and Interdict. By its secret spies, by the ambush of its Confessional, it seeks to lay bare every private thought or chance breath of opinion hostile to its imperious claim. No husband, father, brother, is safe from the betrayal that may become the pious duty of sister, daughter, bride. No place of hiding is sufficiently close, · or far enough away, to escape its ubiquitous, stealthy, masked police. No soldierly valor, no public service, no nobility of intellect, no purity of heart, is a defence from that most terrible of tribunals, which mocks the suspected heretic with a show of investigation, which wrenches his limbs on the rack or bursts his veins with the torturing wedge, and under a hideous mask of mercy — since the Church may shed no blood—delivers him over to the secular arm to be "dealt with gently" as his flesh crackles and his blood simmers at the accursed stake. That is the Inquisition, the Church's remedy for free thought.

For simple disobedience, it has in its hand the threat of Excommunication. Shut out from all church privilege; shunned like a leper by servants, family, and friends; incapable of giving testimony, or of claiming any rights before a court (so to this day, or till very lately, by the common law of England);

the very meats he has touched thrown away as pollution; a bier sometimes set at his door, and stones thrown in at his casement; his dead body cast out unburied, incapable (as was thought) of decay, but kept whole to bear everlasting testimony against his guilt, — emperor, prince, priest, or peasant, the excommunicated man is met every moment, at every hand, by the shadow of a Curse that is worse than death.

The Interdict excommunicates a whole people for the guilt of a sovereign's rebellion. No church may be opened, no bell tolled. The dead lie unburied; no pious rite can be performed but baptism of babes and absolution of the dying. The gloom of an awful Fear hangs over the silent street and the sombre home; and not till the Church's ban is taken off can the people, in these "ages of faith," be free from the ghastly apparitions of supernatural horror. Nay, more. The Interdict, in the last resort, "dissolved all law, annulled all privilege, abrogated all rights, rescinded all obligations, and reduced society to a chaos, until it should please the high-priest of Rome to reinstate order on the terms most conducive to his own glory and the pecuniary profit of the chief and his agents." * These are the *ultima ratio*, the final appeal of ecclesiastical sway. "From the moment these interdicts and excommunications had been tried," says Hallam, "the powers of the earth may be said to have existed only by sufferance."

The steps by which this vast ecclesiastical empire had been won, through a campaign of some six cen-

* Greenwood: *Cathedra Petri*, vol. v. p. 622.

turies, we have briefly traced already:* The period of conquest being passed, we come now to that of organization.

The historical fact before us, early in the ninth century, is the strict alliance between the Roman Church and the Empire of Charles and his descendants, together with the temporal power of the Pope founded on that alliance. The historical fact had been wrought up into a myth, — as in a rude time all significant facts are apt to be, — which at the date we are approaching had already taken distinct form as accepted history.†

This mythical account reports that Constantine, when at Rome after his triumph over Maxentius, suffering with incurable leprosy, had been directed to bathe in innocent blood; and to that end had gathered many young children, to be slain for the healing bath. His compassion, however, did not suffer the sacrifice, and the infants, with their weeping mothers, were dismissed with gifts. He was then rewarded by a vision of the apostles Peter and Paul, who directed him where to find the Christian bishop Sylvester, hiding from persecution, who should heal him of his malady. Converted, and healed by the water of baptism (that is, the blood of Christ), he bestowed on Sylvester and his successors, to the end of time, all

* See "Early Christianity," especially the chapters on "Leo the Great" and "The Holy Roman Empire."

† In a document of the year 1152 it is called "a falsehood and an heretical fable." Greenwood (*Cathedra Petri*) quotes Fleury as saying that it was first cited by Ratramnus, about 875 ; but gives, himself (vol. v. p. 327), 776, as the date when it was first notified by Pope Adrian I. to King Charles (Charlemagne).

the imperial power, dignity, and authority over the regions of the West, transferring his own seat of empire to Byzantium; for it was not meet (he said) that any earthly sovereign should reign where the Lord himself had appointed to be the head of his kingdom upon earth.*

This celebrated fiction of the Donation of Constantine — on which the whole theory of papal sovereignty has rested since—is to be taken as the mythical form in which an age at once unscrupulous and uncritical had clothed the historical fact with which we are already familiar. But in the process that fact was exaggerated to an enormous falsehood, which made the Pope real Emperor of the West, and all sovereigns mere delegates acting under his authority. We shall see, in due time, what this was sure to lead to.

The moment of the perfect coincidence of the two powers, spiritual and temporal, was the founding of the Christian Empire in the person of Charlemagne. In fact, during this period and that immediately following, the two overlapped each other. Under Charlemagne, we may even say that the two were not so much allied, as fused and blended into one. Something to Adrian's surprise, it is likely, Charles had not only presided at the church-council in Frankfort (794), but had taken in hand to discuss the theological points at issue, — the heresy of the Adoptians, and the worship of images. In the latter, particularly, he was quite in advance of the average church feeling

* The tale is given in full in Migne's " Patrologia," vol. cxxx., col. 245–251.

then, in the clear good sense with which he distinguishes between religious homage of images and their use as pious memorials; and one is struck, in the books put forth under his name,* with the ease and confidence of handling the Scripture argument. Of his Capitularies, or Imperial Laws, also—particularly the earlier ones — fully half may be set down as dealing with matters that, by every fair line of division, belong purely to the spiritual power. So plainly he asserted his own authority, in Church as well as State.

On the other hand, this frank assuming or combining of both hemispheres of authority went in the long run to the clear benefit of the Church as against the State. Not only the Pope could claim that he had conferred the imperial crown by his own hand, and so, that the spiritual power was the real source of the political and above it; but the very tenure of power worked to weaken the one and confirm the other. The Pope was head of a spiritual body, which kept its identity without change. The line of ecclesiastical tradition was unbroken. A weak Head of the Church might waver, a profligate one would cause scandal; but nothing would be permanently lost. The next man of intelligence and vigor would by a single turn of the helm put the ship into her old channel.

It was no such thing with a temporal sovereign, — least of all with such a monarchy as that of Charles, however strong in his own person. The turbulent traditions, the disorderly household, the shifting frontiers, the degeneracy of descendants, dissensions

* The *Libri Carolini*, composed, probably enough, by Alcuin.

among brothers or cousins only to be settled by force of arms, — these were seeds of weakness and division always ; and against them was the steady, powerful pressure of an authority which knew its own mind, kept its own counsel, and chose its own Head as the policy of the moment seemed to demand. So that, within two generations, the royal councils were controlled by churchmen, and the able, clear-headed, and ambitious prelate Hincmar, of Rheims, was the real sovereign of France.

Thus, in the division and decay that so quickly overtook the empire of Charlemagne, the Church was able to assert its independent authority as it had never done before. I shall not attempt to trace the steps of the revolution. It is sufficient to connect it with the name of one of the three or four Popes who have been called "great," — Nicholas I. (858–867),— and to note the three main acts, or causes of policy, which have made his brief term memorable.*

In the first of these, Nicholas tried to assert the jurisdiction of Rome over all the East, and he carried great weight in the decision ; but, a few years later (879), a Council at Constantinople definitely rejected that jurisdiction, and made the separation of East and West complete. The policy of Nicholas failed

---

* These were : 1. The steady support of Ignatius, the banished and persecuted Patriarch of Constantinople, against Photius, an accomplished and able statesman put in his place by the Eastern emperor. 2. The firm maintaining of the rights of Theutberga the divorced queen of Lothaire, a grandson of Louis, King of Lorraine in the divided Empire. 3. Enforcing the claim of Rome to supremacy over the feudalized and secularized church of France and Germany, as against the powerful and able Hincmar.

here, exactly as that of Leo had failed before him.*
In the second, the case of the divorced Queen of Lorraine led to one of the most extraordinary ecclesiastical trials on record; and fairly established the Church of Rome as a court of appeal, to control the lawless will of kings — this time, as perhaps generally, in favor of humanity and morals. In the third, the case of Hincmar, the decision turned on what may be called a point of ecclesiastical Constitutional Law; and of this it remains now to say a word.

I have already told, in brief, the myth of the Donation of Constantine, which was assumed at this time as the real ground of the temporal authority claimed by the Church. Now a myth is the vivid and imaginative picture of a forgotten fact. The legend about Constantine here is pure invention; very probably a wilful fraud. But the thing which it signifies was real. In fact, and by co-operation of the imperial government, church power had grown to what it was, because it was a needed thing in the long social evolution. Here are the steps : —

1. The accepted Creed must have its recognized expounder : Theodosius had forbidden all but the clergy even to discuss theology.

2. That privilege must be respected : to dispute it, even, was declared heresy by Arcadius.

---

* The grounds of the jealousy of the Greeks are thus stated by Nicholas (Ep. 152) : 1. The affair of Photius. 2. The Latin claim to Bulgaria. 3. The addition of *Filioque* to the Creed. 4. Celibacy required of the Latin clergy. 5. Certain laxities in the observance of Lent. 6. The false charge of placing a lamb on the paschal altar. 7. The shaving of beards by the Latin clergy. 8. That a deacon may be made bishop without having first been presbyter.

3. Unity of administration must be had : the decree of Valentinian (445) had put Gaul in direct subordination to Rome in the person of Leo; declaring the Pope "director and governor," and that "whatever he ordained should be as law."

4. The spiritual Head must be chosen by those most competent, — in the interest, that is to say, of the spiritual order : hence the body of clergy became self-elective and independent.

5. As the old order of things decayed, the duties of civil magistrate were forced more and more upon the church-officers : a ruler of secular rank, with genius and courage for command, would be compelled (as Ambrose was) to become a bishop,—a fighting bishop, perhaps, as often happened in the barbarous times that followed.

Piety took refuge in the Monastery; and monks were in demand for offices of administration, however honestly reluctant. Of such a one a certain bishop writes : "We seized him unawares, stopped his mouth close, lest he should adjure us in Christ's name, and made him deacon; when we appealed to him by his fear of God to fulfil the duties of his office. When he had done this, again with great difficulty we held his mouth and made him priest." The burden so imposed must be borne, — how bravely and well sometimes, we have seen in the compulsory pontificate of Gregory the Great.

The services of some of these men have been recounted by Guizot. Thus Hilary of Arles — the same stern ecclesiastic who crossed the Alps to dispute with Leo, and who went barefooted summer or winter on his parish rounds — "rose early; received on rising whoever wished to speak with him; heard complaints, settled disputes, and was in short a local judge of circuit; taught daily, as well as served and preached at church; worked with his hands in carding wool for the poor or cultivating his plot of ground, and had some useful task for every hour." Of St. Lupus such was the reputation for sanctity, that Attila the Hun took him with his army to the Rhone, thinking no harm could come to him while the saint was near. Of cultivated mind also, he was a patron and defender of that learning which was in danger of being swallowed up in the universal wreck.

Thus, for generations, the real tasks of administration had come to be assumed by officers of the Church, — sometimes reluctantly, sometimes unconsciously, sometimes (no doubt) with a definite policy, and an increasing corporate ambition. The theory or ideal of the Church shaped itself more and more to that of *a constitutional rule over obedient subjects*, rather than a mere method of converting the souls and instructing the minds and guiding the moral conduct of men. It was in recognition of an accomplished fact, that Pepin made (755) the formal grant which fiction ascribed to Constantine; and that Charlemagne confirmed it, and made it effective by appointing tithes as the Church's legitimate revenue. Under his successors (as we have seen) ecclesiastical power grew steadily at the expense of the State. In the abject humiliation of his son Louis "the Pious," while the Empire was yet whole, the Church was by contrast arrogant and encroaching. When the Empire was divided, the Church remained the only tribunal of authority and appeal.

This is the point of view from which we should try to understand that most famous document of this time, the Forged Decretals that pass under the name of Isidore.* Two things are very remarkable in these Decretals: one, that they appeared and were accepted without challenge, not in a time of obscurity, as is sometimes said, but in the middle of a century illustrious for a group of eminent theologians and able disputants;† the other, what we may call the frank and childlike simplicity of their fabrication.

It is some three hundred years since there has been any question or pretence as to their genuineness. Indeed, a document which contains the manifest fable I have already told of Constantine, which begins by setting forth as of the first or second century an ecclesiastical code in the very spirit of the eighth; which states in full the enormous assumptions of the Roman See in long epistles of the most didactic and patronizing cast addressed by Clement as successor of Peter to James "the Lord's brother," bishop of Jerusalem,—does not need to have its claims seriously discussed. The time of its composition is pretty clearly limited between the years 829 and 845; the date of its first citation in an official paper was in

---

* That is, *Isidorus Mercator*, the assumed name of their compiler. They are understood to be an amplifying of genuine decretals compiled by Isidore, Archbishop of Seville, who died in 636, — a series being forged to fill the gap of the first three centuries, and many being interpolated farther down.

† See "Early Christianity," pp. 261–273.

865, towards the end of the term of Nicholas.* Its authorship is an unanswered riddle.† Its motive is perfectly plain and simple, — to legitimate the authority of the priesthood, to make the Church independent of secular control, and to vindicate the claims of Rome. It only remains to say a word of the circumstances that called it out, and to tell briefly what it is.

It appears to me fairest to regard the Forged Decretals as a challenge, or counter-assertion, on the part of the Church, seriously alarmed at the encroachment of the State on its spiritual domain. The boundaries, which it required three centuries to define, — which in fact are not determined even now, — were as yet only beginning to be traced. Pope Leo III. exercised then, as Pope Leo XIII. desires to exercise to-day, actual sovereignty over the territories and the police of Rome. The Emperor Charles, in entire simplicity and good faith, lays down the law of morals and conduct for the clergy of his dominion, and engages frankly, with a certain tone of authority, in theological disputes. The Roman Emperors, from whom in theory he inherits, had a sacred as well as secular function; they were the official chief priests of the Pagan ritual, nay, were held to be gods in their lifetime.‡ We have seen with what revering acclaim Constantine was received, when he took his seat as

---

* Its authority is argued at length by Nicolas I. (Ep. 75, "ad Universos Episcopos Galliæ," Migne Patrol. cxix. 899–908.)

† Unless we accept the evidence that points to the Abbot Wala and the theologian Radbert. See *Cathedra Petri*, vol. iii. p. 178.

‡ The same Theodosius who abolished Paganism was deified in the pagan pantheon after his death by the Roman Senate.

official head of a Christian Council. Who should say how far those sanctities were inherited with the office? Or, now that the powers, secular and spiritual, were clearly seen to be two, not one, who should adjust the boundary-line between them? Should the Church, which had been glad to lean on the strong arm of Charlemagne, and trust his loyal heart, be at the mercy of any violent will, or any unscrupulous policy, of the man who might happen to be his successor? Or, on the other hand, in the chaos of disorder, moral as well as political, that threatened in the impending break-up of that loose-jointed Empire, how could society itself be saved, except one central authority should be established on the basis of whatever sanctity could be recognized or invented at such a time?

So much for the circumstances. The motive, so far, was honest and legitimate. Three things were evidently to be secured: first, the independence of the Church upon the State within its own hemisphere of power; second, a stricter definition of the character, immunities, and discipline of the Priesthood; third, the recognition of a supreme Authority, or the appointment of an ecclesiastical tribunal of final appeal. These three motives may be traced in the "Forged Decretals of Isidore," though with no attempt at orderly or systematic setting-forth. The Decretals may, accordingly, be regarded in three characters: first, as a declaration of constitutional right, or privilege; second, as a code of ecclesiastical or canon law; third, as an authoritative or official assertion of the claims of Rome.

In form and bulk, the Decretals may be compared to a "blue-book," or body of statutes, of about one thousand pages. In substance, they consist of the records of fifty-one Councils, beginning with that of Nicæa, preceded and followed by the decrees and epistles of sixty-five popes, beginning with Clement, as immediate successor of Peter. Two thirds of the collection, perhaps more, are no doubt genuine; but the whole mass of documents prior to Constantine is most likely pure fabrication, — made to order, as it were, to give a fictitious completeness and antiquity to the Code. A very large part consists of the formal and reiterated statement of the church creed and the refutation of heresies, — a task always requiring to be done over again, as if it had never been done before. Much, too, is made up of what we might call Rules of Order, or the parliamentary law of Ecclesiastical Assemblies.

The first object, the independence of the religious body from secular control, is covered by a large amount of provisions, or assertions, which there is no need of reciting here. A word must be said, however, of that most daring appeal to the credulous imagination, on which it finally rests. The appeal lies in the assertion — never before so frankly made as now — of the central mystery of the sacerdotal faith. God (that creed declares) is corporeally present in the Eucharist, or daily sacrifice. The priest " makes with his own lips the body of the Lord "* and delivers it to the people. This body of the Lord in the Sacra-

* "Qui proprio ore corpus Domini conficiunt." — *Decretal of Pontianus.*

ment is " that same body," argues Radbert, " which was born of the Virgin Mary, suffered upon the cross, arose from the tomb, and sits at the right hand of God."

The theological conception on which the doctrine of transubstantiation rests will come to be reviewed hereafter, when we deal with the theology of the Schoolmen. At present, we have only to consider its appeal to the mind of the time. That craved something more tangible than the allegorizing of Origen, or the pious symbolism of Cyprian and Augustine. " Those pagans," says Peyrat,* " who forsook their bloody sacrifices, did not comprehend the Eucharist without a victim literally sacrificed upon the altar. Those barbarians who had eaten the flesh and drunk the blood of men, thought they could soothe the remorse of their hearts by nothing less than feeding in reality on the flesh and blood of the god-man." †

Now can the Priest, the word of whose mouth can effect this awful mystery, who in fact works daily this stupendous miracle, be subject to any tribunal of this world ?   Nay, " for those who with their own lips make the Lord's body must be obeyed and feared by all."‡   " It was too execrable," says Southey,§ "that

* Les Réformateurs au douziéme Siècle.

† How definite this demand was is shown by the story, so often occurring, that the consecrated wafer was seen as a piece of bleeding flesh. Tales equally wild are inserted by Radbert in his treatise on the subject. A pagan, whom Rabanus met in south-east Germany, proposes a health to " the god who turns wine into his own blood." How far the idolatrous feeling attached itself to the visible emblems may be seen in the arguments and defence used before the Council of Basel respecting the use of the Cup : Mansi, xxviii. 1182.

‡ Decretal of Telesphorus.   § Book of the Church.

hands which could create the Creator, and offer him to the Father as a redeeming sacrifice, should become the servants of those which were constantly polluted with impure contacts, with rapine, and with blood."

Besides, the consecrated bread, being literally the Lord's body, became in the believer the actual nucleus, the physical germ (so to speak) of the "celestial body" in which he must rise again.* To withhold the sacrament, then, was to take away his one chance of immortal joys. It was to inflict the dreaded penalty of annihilation; or, at least, to leave the soul naked before the eternal wrath. In all these ways the Church thus defends its supremacy, above all human control, by what we may call the logic of the imagination.

The second object is to establish a Code of Ecclesiastical and Canon Law.† In this, as found in the Decretals, we may note two things : first, that it guards by numerous provisions the persons, property, and privileges of the Priesthood, while laying down a rigid code of character and official duty; second, that it frankly assumes the control of the marriage-law,

---

* The point here stated will be found admirably expounded in Froude's "Short Studies," vol. i. pp. 161–163, article "Philosophy of Catholicism." (See Note below.) The most distinct announcement of it that I have been able to find is in Albertus Magnus (*De Eucharistiâ*, Dist. iii. Tr. 1, c. 5) : "Confert immortalitatem, immortalitatis radicem, . . . radix est immortalitatis . . . *germen immortalitatis surgit ex ipso, sicut ex vineâ surgunt novi surculi*, ferentes fructum æternorum gaudiorum." Thomas Aquinas says, simply, "Hoc sacramentum . . . dat nobis virtutem perveniendi ad gloriam" (*Summa Theol.* Qu. 79, 2). See also Anselm, Epist. 107.

† These two are not the same thing. The first signifies the law *concerning* the Church ; the second, the rule *within* the Church.

and the rules respecting consanguinity and inheritance, along with all matters of education and morality. In this last regard, it is simply the re-assertion of that code of morals — in some points technical or overstrained, perhaps, but in the main right and wholesome — which it had been the main task of the Church to inculcate from the first.*

It is hard to think of anything more hopeless, as material to work on, than the decayed and decrepit society of the old Pagan world; unless it were the brutish and ferocious manners of the barbarian hordes that came to take its place. And no work in the development of doctrine or polity does the Church half so much honor as the courage, patience, and faith with which it so labored to plant and enforce its moral rule. Something of this code is doubtless hard and overstrained; something of it is repugnant to and discarded by our modern manners. But, in far larger part, it may be fairly called the real basis of our social morality and Christian family life.

Much of it, again, is purely professional, or technical, — as where ecclesiastics are forbidden to trade for gain, or let out money at interest; or to visit women unattended, or admit them (except nearest of kin) † as members of their households; or to keep hawks and hounds, or indulge in rich food or costly furniture or unseemly jesting; or to frequent public houses, or haunt the market-place idly, or " cultivate

---

* Found, in its earliest developed form, in the " Apostolical Constitutions and Canons."

† These, too, are forbidden by Capit. Theodulf. c. 12 (Migne, cxix. 711).

their hair;" or to take fees for sacraments; or to pray
with heretics and schismatics; or to mutilate themselves, on penalty of exclusion from church offices.*
But it includes, besides, many rules of morals and
decency in living, — many, in fact, which could not
be applied except by a regular system of Confession,
and for which the only penalty is longer or shorter
exclusion from church sacraments; so that these
are assumed to be a high privilege, and the control
of them a real instrument of power, as just shown
already.

Being rules of ecclesiastical morality, they are especially rigid as to sins of wantonness, infanticide,
living carnally "like the brutes" (for which, twenty-
five years' penance), and gross forms of licentious-
ness, with the contagious distempers resulting, — " for
which one should pray as for men exposed to storm
at sea." It is also forbidden to keep the Jewish
Sabbath; or to wear the dress of the other sex; or to
marry cousins; or for a married woman to correspond
with another man than her husband; or for actors, or
drivers on a race-course, to commune while actually
employed in their vocation. Many of these rules, in
short, simply testify to the incessant, assiduous, daily
care, by which — line upon line, precept upon precept
— the accepted Christian code of domestic morality
was built up.

The supremacy of Rome, and of the Pope as official
Head, is not only asserted, in the dogmatic fashion

* It is provided, however, that accidental mutilation — as for instance the loss of a finger while engaged in farm work — shall not
operate to disqualify, nor mutilation inflicted by barbarian enemies.

adopted ever since Leo the Great, but is suggested in the very form given to this collection, and expressed in its name, *Decretals*. A "decretal" is simply the official letter of a pope, conveying his personal opinion and authority. To include a long series of such missives —some genuine ; many forged outright, or at best copied out from arguments current at the time and backed by the sanctity of venerable names — among official Acts of Councils and recognized Codes of Law ; and to cite such a compilation (as is incessantly done afterwards) with the cool assumption of its equal weight throughout,—such was the easy and effectual device by which this prodigious fabrication was made to play into the hands and sustain the policy of Rome.

From this time forth we find it held in reserve, as a magazine of proofs ready for all emergencies, and equal to all assumptions of the spiritual power. We find the name "decretalist," as late as Dante, to designate the party that upheld the autocracy of the Pope. And the bold forgery of the ninth century becomes the basis of a recognized Code in the twelfth.*

In these documents, then, we have the Constitutional Law and the Code of Statutes which made the basis of the spiritual power during the Middle Age. The historical foundation it professes to rest on is manifestly, we might almost say frankly and unsophistically, false. Its plump assertions, its naïve pretensions, make one of the most curious riddles of history. For many centuries — at least six or seven — these glaring forgeries were asserted without hesi-

* The *Decretum* of Gratian, first published in 1151.

tation by an ambitious Priesthood; were accepted without criticism, apparently without question, by the "ages of faith." One would almost think them fabricated less as a conscious fraud, to back up a power ill got and in danger of being lost, but rather because they met the want and the mood of the time, and gave a theoretical completeness and finish to an authority which was honestly held to be both legitimate and indispensable.

For the empire-church is hereafter, as that name implies, to be judged as a form of established government. In this view it may claim, if not pardon, at least some indulgence for its monstrous forgery. A "pious fraud" is neither better nor worse than a diplomatic fraud. The papal government of that day probably told no more lies and no worse lies than have been told by high dignitaries on the Eastern Question in the last two years.* Few existing cabinets can afford to throw the first stone at the Forged Decretals. The great guilt and mischief, as well as craft, that lay in them, could not be known till they were made the text to justify the enormous pretensions, the inexorable policy, the wanton and extravagant usurpations, of a later age. The acts of the ninth century waited for their fit comment till the eleventh or twelfth.

Like other forms of government, the Mediæval Papacy has had its mixed good and evil, and must submit to be judged by the good it has done or attempted, by the evil it has harbored or admitted. Like other forms of government, it had its day of

* Written in 1878.

essential service to mankind; and the time came to it, as to them, when the evil began slowly to overbalance the good. Its duration I have reckoned, roughly, at seven hundred years. Speaking in the large way in which such general statements must be made, I think it may be said, broadly, that for half this period its real aim was the service and instruction of mankind, the building up and defence of Christian civilization; and that in the other half it was reduced to the hard, the ignominious, the corrupting task of maintaining its own existence against new intellectual forces that were coming into the field, and that had the promise of the future in them.

A line drawn to divide midway the period indicated would cross the field somewhere about the middle of the twelfth century. This time shows us the height of the armed struggle between Church and Empire. It is the time of Alexander III. and Barbarossa, of Henry II. and Thomas Becket. The new intellectual forces in the field are signified to us by the controversies that rage about the daring speculations of Abelard, and by the newly revived study of Roman Law, which must slowly sap the foundations of the Decretal system. The vindictive and for a time triumphant resolution of the Church declares itself in the ferocious persecution already preparing against the Waldenses and Albigenses, — the pious heretics and the bold free-thinkers of the Middle Age.

NOTE.

[See page 21.]

"The carnal doctrine of the Sacraments . . . has long been the stumbling-block to modern thought. It was the very essence of the original creed. Unless the body could be purified, the soul could not be saved; because, from the beginning, soul and flesh were one man, and inseparable. Without his flesh man was not, or would cease to be. But the natural organization of the flesh was infected with evil; and unless organization could begin again from a new original, no pure material substance could exist at all. He, therefore, by whom God had first made the world, entered into the womb of the Virgin in the form (if I may with reverence say so) of a new organic cell; and around it, through the virtue of his creative energy, a material body grew again of the substance of his mother, pure of taint, and clean as the body of the first man was clean when it passed out under his hand in the beginning of all things. In Him, thus wonderfully born, was the virtue which was to restore the lost power of mankind. He came to redeem man; and therefore he took a human body; and He kept it pure through a human life, till the time came when it could be applied to its marvellous purpose. He died; and then appeared what was the nature of a material human body, when freed from the limitations of sin. The grave could not hold it, neither was it possible that it should see corruption. It was real, for the disciples were allowed to feel and handle it. He ate and drank with them, to assure their senses. But space had no power over it, nor any of the material obstacles which limit an ordinary power. He willed, and his body obeyed. He was here, he was there; he was visible, he was invisible; he was in the midst of his disciples, and they saw him, and then he was gone — whither who could tell? At last he passed away to heaven; but, while in heaven, he was still on earth. His body became the body of his Church on earth, not in metaphor, but in fact! — his very material body, in which by and by the faithful would be saved. His flesh and blood were thenceforth to be their food. They were to eat it as they would eat ordinary meat; they were to take it into their system, a pure, material substance, to leaven the old natural substance and assimilate it to itself. As they fed upon it, it would grow into them, and it would become their own real body. Flesh grown in the old way was the body of death; but the flesh of Christ was the life of the world, over which death had no power. . . . Death, which till Christ had died had been the last victory of evil, in virtue of his submission to it became its own destroyer; for it had power only over the tainted particles of the old substance; and there was nothing needed but that these should be washed away, and the elect would stand out at once, pure and holy, clothed in immortal bodies, like refined gold, the redeemed of God." *

* Froude's "Short Studies," vol. i. pp. 161–163.

II.

FEUDAL SOCIETY.

FEUDALISM appears in history as a natural makeweight against the dangers to which Society was especially exposed at the time of its appearing. That time was just after the founding of the Western Empire under Charlemagne; and the period of Feudal Society—at least, of the predominance of Feudalism over every other force in society — may be put, roughly, as the two centuries just before the era of the Crusades. The field it occupied was almost exactly that of the Empire itself, — that is, the western half of Europe. Its roots were in the manners and customs of the Barbarian tribes, meaning in particular those of German blood. It was set face to face against the Ecclesiastical system, which feared, hated, checked, and to a great degree mastered it; and it was finally absorbed in the growth of modern Monarchy, which found in it first a rival, then an ally, and at length (as in France before the Revolution) an ornamental but hateful and dangerous appendage.

The dangers against which Feudalism served as a counterpoise were these three: —

The first was the loss of manhood and courage that followed the period of Roman conquest and the establishing of the Empire. As the price it had to pay for the "peace of the Empire" (*pax Romana*), the population was disarmed. The man, the town, the province, was not trusted for the necessary business of self-defence, but was systematically made helpless and jealously watched by an Authority which kept all military force in its own hands. Even that had seemed not too dear a price to pay for peace, after the incessant and exterminating conflicts of the ancient commonwealths. But a non-resistant population is pretty sure to be a population of cowards, imbeciles, and slaves. There was no such thing as modern science to train the intelligence, or modern industry to develop the peaceful energies of men. And for this condition of things the fierce temper of barbaric independence was the only apparent remedy.

Again, this danger was only increased by the first effect of barbarian conquest. Conquest means at best an irresponsible and most likely a cruel despotism. Conquest over the abject and helpless mass of Roman subjects would inevitably add contempt to cruelty. What the danger was in Europe we see by what continually befalls under the military despotisms of Asia. That is what even the humane and enlightened centralism of Charlemagne, or of his son Louis " the Pious," must lead to in so rude a time. And though the disorder and the tragedy—as they showed to the Christian mind of the period — seemed the very wreck of society itself, yet it was for the gain of humanity when that centralism was roughly broken, and the new Empire went to fragments within sixty years of its founder's death ; when the private citizen, lost in the great imperial system, became visible and ponderable once more in the petty feudal estate.

Again, despotism of the Church over mind and con-science — which might seem the only counterpoise — menaced a condition even worse than that under the despotism of Empire. The two together threatened to extinguish the very faculty of self-assertion, and make anything like free manhood impossible. Now, as Feudal Aristocracy made the deliverance from the one, so Feudal Society was in some degree an emanci-pation from the other. The stubborn pride that runs in barbarian and aristocratic blood was never quite subdued by ecclesiastical spells. How hateful a thing Ecclesiasticism can become, we see in the stifling of free thought, the enslaving of conscience, and the horrible machinery of persecution which came in play as soon as the Church had definitely gained upon its rival in the race for dominion. What it would have been if the only antagonist had been an imperial system which in theory was a portion and an agent of the same authority, — if a universal Em-pire had been by turns rival and tool of a sacerdotal Caste, — we can only guess. The check to both was found in that system of individual force and pride which we call Feudalism, — a system resting on strength of arm, force of will, and pride of life; of temper essentially barbaric; under a rule aristocratic, turbulent, haughty, cruel, and domineering; a condi-tion of society easily moved by great waves of passion and imagination; easily stirred by the enthusiasm of military adventure; in which what we call humanity and justice are all but absolutely unknown. This formidable state of things made (as it were) the bridge over which Society had to pass, to reach the better conditions and larger possibilities of modern life.

Leaving aside all antiquarian questions as to the roots of Feudalism in barbarous times, it is easiest to see it as it comes before us at the time where we are now arrived.

In a view of the whole ground, there are two distinct things to be considered, — the feudal *hierarchy*, or gradation of ranks, as in an army ; and the feudal *tenure*, or the system of property-right, including the social structure attached to it. As to the first, the feudal Hierarchy, it belongs to an earlier time, and is implied in the drill and discipline by which the forces of Barbarism overcame the Roman world. As a military movement, that invasion could not have been conducted, or have held together a month, without some sort of rigid army organization. The second, the feudal Tenure, including all that is really meant by Feudalism as an order of society, is the great historical fact with which we have now to deal.

This order of society may be briefly described to the imagination as the *arrest* of that broad, tumultuous movement of the nations which we call the barbarian invasion, and the fixing of its restless waters in a rigid mould,—as we sometimes see a sheet of water chilled so suddenly, under a high wind, that it is turned into a meadow of frozen waves. To our thought the process is a sudden one, like that operation of frosty wind. In fact, like all great organic changes, it was slow, painful, continuous, durable. It was, in a sense,

the outcome of the long process of disintegration —
disordered, chaotic, and very painful — by which the
premature Christian Empire of Charles had gone to
pieces. The battle of Fontenoy, fought among his
grandsons twenty-seven years after his death, had
destroyed, it was said, the manhood of the Franks.
Forty thousand of their warriors were slain on that
disastrous field. Divisions and subdivisions of territory which followed weakened more and more the
bonds of central authority. More and more, men
were free to choose their military chief; more and
more, they were free to revolt from him. Not to
dwell upon the process, we easily see to what it led.
Its upshot was, that each man became lord of so much
ground as he could actually hold by the strength of
his own arm, or win by the cunning of his own craft;
that each man must choose for his sovereign, or military chief, or feudal lord, whoever could best help
maintain him in his right. Petty as his estate might
be, he had the sovereign right of JURISDICTION as an
independent Prince. In the main, the same grada-
tions of rank would remain, as of officers in an army;
while, instead of the incessant change and shifting of
power, as in an actual campaign, the system became
a fixed Social Order, and fastened its roots in the soil
everywhere. Thus a rigidity and stability, as of frozen
arrested waves, is the first feature by which we begin
to understand the new order of things now getting
fixed throughout Western Europe.

It is shown to us, farther, by what is sometimes
called the one distinguishing thing that made Feudalism what it was. Not only property-rights, but

office, title, and rank of every sort, were made hereditary. The tenure was settled in the person. No man could be deprived of office or rank, except by process as deliberate and formal as that which stripped him of his estate. This personal tenure was extorted from the sovereign in his weakness and . distress; it became the foundation of an aristocracy more permanent and often far stronger than monarchy itself. Titles of rank were originally names of military office. Duke, Earl, or Count, meant no more than General, Captain, or Adjutant; and, like these posts of service in an army, the title might be given or taken away at the pleasure of the Commander-in-Chief, or Sovereign. Now, they became the absolute right of the holder of them; and, like any other property-right, went to his heir, — who, again, in an age just seeking fixity and repose after a long armed struggle, would generally be the eldest son. Thus, as a second feature of Feudalism, we have an aristocracy of birth along with an aristocracy of rank, — this aristocracy descending, by sharply marked and definite steps, from the sovereign to the serf.

The new order of society, it will thus be seen, means an immense strengthening of the family bond, as the real foundation of the political structure. The old republics of Greece and Rome — whatever the weight of certain great families in them — recognized only two political entities, the Citizen and the State; and all the rights of the citizen were absorbed in the authority of the State. In later time, the sacred and sovereign person of the State was identified with the

Emperor himself, who by a fiction of law was held to own in fee simple the estate of every man; so that the most pitiless exactions of the imperial exchequer were only claiming a part, more or less, of what he might call his own, outright. Nay, so sharply was this claim enforced, that Roman citizens actually migrated sometimes beyond the frontiers of the Empire, that they might find among barbarous tribes the personal rights denied them at home. These imperial traditions had been adopted, along with the Roman Law, into the theory and practice of the new Christian Empire; and the revolt against them was a re-assertion of barbaric independence. The system now coming to take its place thus implies an immense social revolution. It was, in fact, a reversal of the fundamental idea on which the State itself was founded. For the turbulent equality of the old Republics, for the dead level of Imperial despotism, it established the rights of Family, making them everywhere dominant and supreme. And so the dominion of great families, the feudal Nobility, came to be what it was, — a dominion established on personal force or cunning, and handed down through generations as a family estate; engendering class pride and family pride in an extraordinary degree; and, along with some very great and noble qualities, breeding often an insolent cruelty of rule which has probably never been surpassed.

This rule, however, never became quite intolerable. It never blighted the prosperity of districts, or crushed out the national life, like an Oriental despotism, or showed such ghastly corruption on so large a scale

as in the decaying Empire of Constantinople. For
several centuries, it was on the whole a defence not
only of social order, but even of such rights and liberties as could then be had. The rage of the revolt
against the corrupt remnant of it in France, a hundred years ago, need not blind us to its real service a
thousand years ago. It was a step forward in the
march, not a step backward. That it was so, resulted
from two things, — the fixed and limited local rights
which I have already spoken of; and the close mutual
ties that bound class and class. Each class depended
directly on *that next above*, not on the large and impersonal abstraction called the State. Not only each
feudal proprietor was lord of his own estate : he was
joint-owner of it, so to speak, with numerous dependants. Their fixed rights in it were as good as his.*
He was not simply landlord, and they tenants at
will, — as the cruel fictions of law long afterwards
interpreted the relation. He was Sovereign, not
merely owner; and owed the duties of a sovereign, as
well as held the powers of one. His tenants were
theoretically his army, as well as his subjects. Each
estate must furnish its quota to his military force.
As his subjects, he had no more right to thrust them
off, than any government has to drive its citizens
beyond its frontier at the point of the bayonet. As
his army, he was quite as dependent on them as they

* It is the tradition of this state of things, differing not much
from the early communism of the Tribe, which makes so impracticable and hopeless the state of things in Ireland to-day. The
Tenantry hold themselves to have an older right in the soil than
that of the Landlord class, which they regard as resting merely on
conquest or usurpation.

on him. If he must be their leader, so they must
fight his battles. In the absence of any moral bond,
this rude tie of mutual dependence at any rate would
not fail. Even the lowest rank of all, the serf or
" villein," must share at least the security of that
fixed rule. Words can hardly tell the brutal inso-
lence of feudal pride or lust towards its humbler
subjects, — expressed sometimes in acts of ferocious
cruelty and wantonness, sometimes in words that
goaded almost as keenly.* Rights of service on one
part, enforced with deliberate brutality, and proverbs
or ballads of plaintive misery on the other, tell too
plainly this dark side of Feudalism. But, take it at
its worst, it is something altogether different from
that wild elder time, when every man's hand is
against every other man; — and not so much worse,
either, than that later condition of so-called "indus-
trial feudalism," where no relation is recognized on
either side but the relation of work and wages; where
the ruined craftsman becomes a pauper, and the dis-
charged operative a tramp.

One other thing, to complete this outline of feudal
society. It not only rested at bottom on personal
force, but it gave immense field and development to
personal force. The phrase " sovereignty of the individual " never could have been fully explained to us,
if it had not been for the illustration given of it in
Feudalism. The highest and best known types of it,
perhaps, are those two valiant contemporaries, Richard of England and Frederick Barbarossa, greatest of

* See, for example, the piteous account of the condition of a
peasant-woman given by Michelet in *La Sorcière*.

the Germans. But the innumerable illustrations are far more impressive than the most brilliant typical two or three. That personal vigor, planting itself everywhere directly upon the soil, is seen most effectively in that exhibition of it which is also most picturesque, — the numberless Castles, which sprang as it were from the soil like trees of a great forest eight or nine hundred years ago, and still cover with their ruins almost every spot of advantage in provincial England or along the Rhine. These castles, with the rude, turbulent, freebooting, hospitable life grouped about them, crowded as many of them are with romantic or tragic memories, are what remain in our imagination often as the only vivid picture of feudal times. They are monuments of the personal force which showed itself then, oftenest, as sheer brute strength and violence. Hate and fear, not any romantic or admiring association, made up the feeling of the bondman or of the churchman who looked up from below to those frowning battlements. " The wicked and the rich," they said, " piled about them these vast masses of stones and earth, as if to make themselves safe before God as well as man." To us, the terror is forgotten ; the strength and the service are what we remember now. The picturesque ruins are not only the type of the rude strength that built them up and made its fastness of them ; they remind us that the real task of Feudalism was not a task of destruction, but one of building up. Society was to be reconstructed on a new foundation with new elements of durability and power.

We shall perhaps conceive the spirit of Feudalism most vividly, if we think of that most characteristic expression of itself, which it has left in the institution of Heraldry. I hardly know whether to call it a science, an art, or a mere arbitrary decoration. At any rate, the very type and temper of that time are in it. The shield, the crest, the motto, the symbolic figure emblazoned on the banner and wrought in the coat-of-arms, are the express image and likeness of that haughty strength, that family pride, that fierce courage, that temper clinging to warlike memory and tradition, which we associate closest with the name. The crest or the device may have been copied from the wild equipment of tribes that delighted, like our Indians, in head of wolf or horns of buffalo for decoration in battle. At least, a new meaning was given them when they were made to carry the memory and the pride of a noble house down through generations; so that a leopard or an eagle or an ostrich-plume literally testifies to-day to some incident of a battle-field or tournament or court-festival of four or five centuries ago. This singular creation, absolutely unlike anything we know of ancient art, — with the intricate pedigrees it records, and the strange conventional science built upon it, — is the perfect reflex of the intensely aristocratic temper, the inordinate family pride, the love of turbulent adventure, which are the very spirit of Feudalism.

I have not tried in this brief sketch to picture to the imagination feudal society as a whole, or to give an account of it as an institution. Romancers and historians must divide that task between them. For

the one, we turn to Walter Scott; for the other, to
Mr. Hallam. What we want just now is to see how
it came in contact with the Christian Church, and to
trace as clearly as we can against it the lines of influence and the lines of contrast which define the working of the Church as a spiritual power.

When we try to see the way of that working, it
will be fairest not to dwell so much on the obvious
and glaring faults of either,—the violence of one, the
bigotry of the other. That contrast would be easy
enough, but neither very instructive nor very just.
What we should do rather, is to take each at its best
and strongest; to look at its ideal aim, as well as
its actual result; and to see not merely where they
are in contrast, but how they are also counterparts.
Society tends to the realizing of its ideals, and could
in fact hardly subsist if they were lost. Either of
the two is one-sided and imperfect; but each has
developed something which, if we could understand
it, we should find quite indispensable to the larger
life of to-day.

The most obvious point of the contrast is the intensely individual and local character of Feudalism,
compared with the spiritual and universal theory of
the Church. Feudalism is a system of separation
and division. It not only broke that bondage and
spell of Empire, which had come to be too galling for
its restless independence. It threatened to undo the
painful work of centuries; to destroy the unity which
had been attained by long and very costly struggle;
to bring society back into the condition of local, petty,
jealous sovereignties, bound by absolutely no political

tie, such as had made the long misery and political death of Greece.*

It did in fact go even farther than that. It made war legitimate between nearest neighbors and next of kin, where each was sovereign of his own petty estate. Its very pride of family had to be kept up by primogeniture : hence jealousies and galling inequalities and fraternal feud, — such as we see in the tragic history of the sons of William the Conqueror and of Henry II., or, on a larger scale, in the English " War of Roses." Devoid of any general code of justice, it could decide a disputed claim only by armed quarrel and the wager of battle.† The time of its supremacy was a time of incessant private war. It was only by reluctant submission to church authority that it consented to keep the peace for half of every week,‡ by what was called " the Truce of God." It chose contention and despised quiet; called no death honorable

* Pro rege est regulus ; pro regno, fragmina regni ;
  Cassatur generale bonum, sua quisque tuetur.
—*Lament of* FLORUS DIACONUS *at the Division of the Empire after the death of Louis the Pious* (A.D. 840).

† Thus in the tenth century, under Otho the Great, the difficult question whether a nephew can inherit as his uncle's representative was determined by wager of battle, in which the champion of the nephew conquered. In Spain, the choice of liturgies was decided in the same way in favor of the Mozarabic as against that of Rome. (Laurent.) Lothaire proposes, in 867, to try the fidelity of his wife Theutberga by combat of champions,—" *pro hoc hominem suum et hominem Theutbergæ ad monomachiam impellere, et si homo ipsius reginæ ceciderit, disponit hanc sine dilatione perimere.*" Nicolai Papæ Ep. 148 (col. 1144). This is naturally resisted by the spiritual order. The judicial combat is "a tempting of God." Ibid. App. xx.

‡ Namely, the four " passion-days," from Thursday morning to Sunday evening.

unless upon the field of conflict; and held it a point of personal dignity that every free man should go fully armed.*

The traditions of the Church, on the other hand, were all of unity and peace. If it could not stop the fighting, at least it did something to define the objects men fought for. The object of the Crusades, for instance, was ideal, not personal. In a time of universal violence and contention, when all notion of a central authority was in danger of being lost, it alone preserved the tradition of such an authority. Its creed was one for all. Its ritual was the same everywhere. Its moral code, incessantly proclaimed, was uniform, through all local diversities. Its priesthood was one body corporate, bound together by one allegiance, sharing the inheritance of a common culture, using everywhere the same phrases of speech, clothed in the one language they knew,—the ancient, sacred, majestic tongue of Rome.

And then, this ideal unity had its visible type in the one sovereign Pontiff, whom all Western Christendom acknowledged; victorious over all heresy and schism, or attempts of able men (like Hincmar) to establish a separate national authority; recognized alike by all classes, nationalities, and estates as the one potentate, supreme over all the Christian world. The range of his power was not very wide, — not a third as large as the territory of the United States.

* The sword, which was the ordinary distinction of a gentleman a century ago, is still a feature of court dress; and to this day the hat-buckle must be worn on the left, because the plume which it replaces would have interfered with the sword-arm if worn on the right side of the head.

But, local as men's interests were then, ignorant and disdainful as they were of everything beyond their narrow bound, it was to their imagination as if the Catholic Empire were indeed as broad as the universe itself, which it claimed to be.   And so the sense of a unity in diversity was never lost.*

Again, feudal society was built upon pride of family and pride of rank.   Every grade—social, political, military — was guarded with a jealousy vigilant and intense.   Rules of intercourse and precedence were rigidly defined.   The sharp boundary of noble and common, of freeman and serf, was practically impassable, — guarded not only by its own traditions and rules, but by intense contempt on one side, profound even if angry and vindictive humiliation on the other.   The popular proverbs tell of pitiless disdain matched against sullen hate.   On one side it was: "My man is mine, to boil or roast him if I will;" "The villein is dull-witted, without pity, fidelity, or love;" "Humor a villein and he will beat you; beat him and he will humor you."   On the other side it was: "The lords would fain tax our fresh air, rain, and sunshine;" "Never villein loved a lord; his only thought is to cast lordship down;" "Who can count the sorrows of the serfs? to their tears there is no end;" "Thistles are the villein's food."†

Over against this hard animosity of rank, these rigid barriers of class and class, the Church set its

---

* From the ceiling of the papal palace at Avignon I copied the following inscriptions: IN ARMIS CONCORDIA EX BELLO.   EX PLURIBUS UNUM.   TERRORE HOSTIUM, CIVIUM SECURITAS.

† See Laurent's *Histoire de l'Humanité*, vol. iii. *passim*.

ideal, in which all such distinctions were absolutely ignored. The equality it declared was an equality which literally put prince and peasant on the same level. Louis the Pious, son of Charlemagne, set the example for sovereigns of all coming time, when he "prostrated himself three times at full length on the ground" before Stephen IV. It was a later custom for emperor or king to help the Pope mount, or hold his bridle-rein like a groom. A pope who was himself of a noble or reigning family might be (and in fact was, in 1261) succeeded by a cobbler's son. A Duke of Burgundy, who would look down infinite degrees on his own body-servant, used to grease the shoes of monks. This theory of equality, on a level absolutely independent of family or rank, was vividly presented to the eye, when a weak old man, little of stature, lean with long fasting, claiming to own not a farthing of worldly wealth, forbidden the use of weapons or any act of violence, saw at his feet the proudest of feudal lords, — as Hildebrand saw Henry of Germany at Canossa.

Again, this social equality was not only asserted by the Church, but was insured by its rule, which made impossible the building up of a sacred family or a sacerdotal caste. I say nothing now of the wisdom of its rule of celibacy, or its success in carrying out its theory of ascetic morals in the body of the clergy. The bitter and difficult struggle by which it was finally established as a universal rule belongs to the story of the eleventh century, and need not come before us now. Morally it failed, no doubt; but in its social effect it was all-important. What we have to see is, how the Church's ideal, which repudiated all family ties for its priesthood, not only secured their absolute devotion and exclusive loyalty, but became a powerful check on the feudal aristocracy, striking the theory it was built on at the very heart.

When we think of the enormous assumption of the spiritual Order, the incredible arrogance of Alexander III. or Boniface VIII., of a Becket or a Wolsey, we have to remember the price paid in advance for that ecclesiastical absolutism. It was, the complete renunciation of the one great aim of feudal ambition, — the hope of founding a noble name, or the building up of a family estate. At his first step in that career, the ecclesiastic must debar himself once and forever of the passionate pride and hope that were the most distinctive things in Feudalism. At the last step and the highest, his very birth and baptismal name must be forgotten. The son of the Italian house Aldobrandini is no longer the monk Hildebrand, but Pope Gregory ; Cardinal Lothario is known in history as Innocent III. ; Nicholas Breakspear, as Adrian IV., does not recognize his own mother, even by a gift of alms to her poverty ; a Fiesco becomes Innocent IV., and a Medici, Leo X. ; or, if a Borgia seeks out of family pride to perpetuate a noble house, the name itself becomes infamous in the crimes of Alexander VI. In no one thing, perhaps, is the Church set over against feudal society so sharply as in this. Nothing helps us to see more clearly both why ecclesiastical power was tolerated in that age, and how it was prevented from becoming an unmitigated curse. In its most arrogant days it offered no remotest possibility of growing into that most hateful of all institutions, a ruling sacred Caste.

In one other thing the Church ideal was strongly contrasted with that of Feudalism, though the practice of the Church might seem to give its ideal the lie. And yet, I would think, a theory of what is really the best and highest thing in life is never quite without its effect on character and conduct. When Jesus said, "Take no thought for the morrow;" "Sell all that thou hast and give to the poor," — he fixed an ideal which, under whatever change of circumstance, has its distinct effect on us to-day. We can never be quite so frank in our worship of wealth, quite so cynical in our scorn of misery, as if those words had never been spoken.

Now the Church was never permitted to forget that contempt of riches was, if not its practice, at least its theory and its pledge. The lesson was enforced and reiterated at every turn. To divest oneself of individual property, of whatever sort, was not only the tradition — dignified by such examples as St. Ambrose and Gregory the Great — but the rule, on entering the sacred Order. All church maxims and morals run that way. "Our Lord Jesus Christ," says St. Francis, "was born in poverty, lived in poverty, enjoined poverty, and died in poverty. . . . Know, dear brethren, that poverty is queen of all the virtues." "Wealth is the most detestable of vices," says St. Benedict. A monk who called anything his own was excommunicated, was not prayed for on his death-bed, and was buried in a dung-hill. Only by a series of bulls, from different popes, could the nice rules of casuistry be laid down, which defined how far the goods of this world could be held, — in trust, and not in ownership.

The extreme theory asserted that all human ownership is absolutely forbidden, and planted itself on the assumed " poverty of Christ ; " and this theory had been sanctioned by the highest church authority. When it was found impossible to carry this out, there were two devices to reconcile it with the exigencies of life. According to the first, Nicholas III. claims that, as " the earth is the Lord's and the fulness thereof," the Pope, as God's vicegerent, is the real owner ; and all use of church property must be held to be a trust from him. The other — unable to deny that the food in a man's mouth, or the clothes on his back, are in some sense his — declared it a use *de facto* but not *de jure;* which John XXII. again condemns as bad in law. On the whole, the real church theory of property was a certain regulated communism, the most absolute contrast conceivable to the rigidity of feudal tenure.

Of course, we understand that human practice never squares with moral theory. As matter of fact, we know that mere ostentation and luxury of wealth were never carried farther than in so-called religious Orders and religious Houses. Still, the theory had a definite effect. The strongest temptations of wealth were removed by the mere fact that it could not be made hereditary. This mere fact gave some color to the assertion that wealth was held only for pious uses. It is true that avarice is a vice not seldom characteristic of a childless priesthood. Still, it could not strike its roots quite so deep in the soul, when the one motive of it which seems almost generous is struck away. At least ecclesiastical tenure went, so far as it went at all, to discourage personal hoarding, — just as the feudal tenure was precisely what gave the desire of wealth most tenacious strength. The oldest and the most sumptuous private properties to-day are feudal properties, — as of the Marquis of Westminster and the Duke of Argyll. The enormous church estates — enormous as they at length grew to be — were at least held by the " dead hand," and by no living one. They ministered in theory not to enhance personal indulgence or gain, but to teach the ignorant and feed the poor; to build and decorate gorgeous temples for public use; to give splendor and effect to a public ceremony; to make a great estate productive, beautiful, and rich. Tenants of Church or Abbey were a privileged class, compared with tenants of a feudal lord. And the breaking up of the English monasteries by Henry VIII., who made them the property of his feudal nobles, set adrift that great army of paupers and tramps, that have been the despair of legislation ever since.

Once more, the ideal of the Church was charity; while the temper — almost we might say the ideal — of Feudalism was merciless cruelty. It is not worth while to multiply illustrations of this.* One or two will suffice to show what the assertion means. Richard *Cœur-de-lion* sends to Philip of France fifteen prisoners whom he has blinded, giving them for guide

* Such as may be found in Laurent, *La Féodalité et l'Église* (pp. 246–257).

one to whom he has spared a single eye ; to which Philip retorts by a like procession of English captives. Robert of Belesme, for a jest (*quasi ludens*), gouges out with his thumbs the eyes of a little godchild, in spite to the infant's father. The orders ascribed to Henry II. in an invasion are, "Spare not one farm, set fire to the houses, wrap the whole country in ruin ; " and he "shivers with joy" to see the wreaths of smoke and blasted fields. The atrocious cruelties of Barbarossa, and of his grandson Frederick II., will appear farther on.

Feudalism had, it is true, another ideal, which was Chivalry ; that is, courtesy and humanity such as one Knight might show another, — an ideal as well realized, perhaps, as that of the Church's poverty. But that the temper of the religious classes towards poverty and suffering was tender and merciful in the main, there is not the least reason to doubt. Everything led that way. The dealings of the humbler clergy were closest and oftenest with the poor, so that the kinder sympathies would be drawn out. They were mostly themselves from the ranks of the poor, where the chief suffering was, and felt nearest to them. The higher clergy had often risen from the same mean rank ; and the corporate feeling must have been strong to check any pride of birth. Their official duties, too, among the sick or near the dead, were in their essence offices of sympathy. That, in fact, has always been the best side and the strong side of the Roman Catholic priesthood, whose charities in all ages have covered a multitude of sins, — always tender and pitiful, whatever other fault it might be guilty of, or whatever harm might come to industry and thrift from the alms-giving, which was then the only way of humanity and mercy.

Again and again, by correspondence or personal appeal, priest and monk would try to forbid the cruelty of torture, or save a criminal from the death penalty. It is true that when the Church once began to tremble for her own authority, she borrowed and even improved upon the horrors of feudal dungeon and torture-chamber; that whatever debt she might claim on the score of mercy was wiped out at St. Bartholomew. But these later horrors were against her own tradition, which was of tenderness and mercy.

In these features, then, we may notice what will serve us best for comparison between the two great counterparts in Mediæval society — Feudalism and the Church. I have tried to see fairly what were the strong and necessary points of both; to see each in its own genuine ideal, not in the haze which is so apt to transfigure it into an ideal of our own. Considering the general development of history, we may say, accurately enough, that the first was inevitable, the second providential. Translated into stricter phrase, this would mean that Feudalism — its personal courage and force, its family pride, its spirit of adventure — was the one form possible for society to take, in that time of wreck and disorganization, if secular society was to continue to exist at all. It would mean, on the other part, that the forces which shaped out the Church's theory, and defined its work, and adjusted it to such human needs as it was fit to meet, were moral forces. Below all else, they had their source in the Conscience, — that is, in a real desire to know the right and to do it.   The agents to do that task were very imperfect, often wilful, domineering, corrupt.   In time they had adopted, some of them, the worst vices of Feudalism, and rivalled its most enormous cruelties.   Even for these it may be pleaded, perhaps, that the dungeon of the Castle was before the torture-chamber of the Inquisition ; that the barbarities of Eccelino were earlier if not worse than the fires of Torquemada ; that the crusade in Palestine was as ferocious, after all, as the crusade in Languedoc.   Let these poor apologies go for what they are worth.   At least, we shall see how essential it was that the hard regimen of Feudal Society should be confronted by so opposite a temper and ideal in the Christian Church.   At least, the comparison will help us to understand how greatly more beautiful, rich, noble, and strong our modern life is, than it could possibly have been if either of the two had been wanting them.

One other thing.   The long process which came to its term in the Empire of Charlemagne was a constructive process throughout, and may be said to have been steadily, consciously, and successfully directed by the policy of the Western Church.   The great Emperor himself was only in part its creator.   I have endeavored to show how events worked with him to bring that result to pass.   It is commonly said that he left no one behind him strong enough to sustain the fabric he had built.   This is true.   But it is also true that neither he nor any other man would have been able to do the same thing, fifty years later.   Not even he could have made it or saved it then. At that stage of society, the dissolving process of Feudalism was as inevitable as the work of Charlemagne had been indispensable.

That dissolving process, like a spring thaw on some mighty river, set everything afloat. Not politics and society alone, but apparently morals and religion as well, went all adrift. Feudalism took possession of the Church as well as of the State. "Priests and deacons," wrote Abbot Desiderius,* about 1050, "took to themselves wives after the manner of the laity; they left families behind them, and bequeathed their ill-gotten wealth to their children. Yea, even bishops, in contempt of all shame and decency, dwelt with their wives under the same roof,—a nefarious and execrable custom, prevailing, alas! most commonly in that city where the laws, thus shamefully set at naught, first issued from the sacred lips of the Prince of the Apostles and his holy successors."

Fighting and hunting bishops are matched with riotous monks and lower clergy. Great lords claim the right of ecclesiastical preferment, and exact feudal service of the incumbent. Hungry younger sons, or collateral heirs, are thrust into high places of church preferment. Last of all, the Papacy itself is made the prize of unseemly struggle; is held at times by mere boys; and for more than fifty years is controlled by female politicians, infamous in history, because the Head of the Church could enter into no canonical marriage, or have lawful heirs of his blood.

These are what we find in wading through the

* Afterwards Pope Victor III.

dreary interval of the tenth century. But the rigid ecclesiastical theory only lay in abeyance. The German Otho, the first great feudal monarch, came into Italy like a hero of romance, to the rescue of the noble Adelaide; and the century went out, the year 1000 of the Christian Era came in, under the reign of that bright idealist the third Otho, — the worthy and noble restorer, it was hoped, of the work of Charlemagne, — whose early death left the task of reform to be taken up more vigorously, half a century later, by that brave champion of priestly rule, the monk Hildebrand.

III.

THE WORK OF HILDEBRAND.

IN the long campaign — of years or it may be of
centuries — by which a feeble power fights its
way to empire and dominion, our sympathy runs
along with its efforts and its fortunes, as in the un-
folding of a drama. The cruelty, the craft, the narrow vindictive patriotism, the lust of conquest, which
enter into the passion of the play, we allow for as
human motives in the actors, and as necessities in the
plot. They do not touch us half so nearly as the
valor and self-devotion that have won the victory.

And this, even in the rude, unscrupulous, implacable career of pagan and imperial Rome. Far more,
when the aim all along is not *mere* conquest, but to
give victory to ideal justice and truth. Something of
the halo of that motive will invest its most obstinate
struggles and its most questionable acts.

Up to the founding of the Christian Empire, and
the attempt to fix the boundaries of temporal and
spiritual power, our sympathies go justly with the
leaders in that long campaign against a corrupt Paganism and a rude Barbarism. It is different, now
that society is nominally Christian. Now, the power
has been got; and the question is, How shall it be
used? We have gone through the period of con-

quest and the period of establishment; we come now to the period of administration. We deal no longer with an army and a campaign, but with the acts of a recognized and lawful government. How will the Church employ the authority it has won?

It must be confessed that the answer to be given to this question, for more than two hundred years after the founding of the Christian Empire, was about as disheartening as it is possible to imagine. I have already traced some of the leading features of Feudalism, whose ideal was in so many points the opposite of that of the Church; and have hinted at the moral chaos which engulfed the Church during the tenth century, in the collision of those hostile principles.

During this period the Papacy was at its lowest degradation, subject to licentious priests or imbecile boys or insolent nobles; so that, for very scandal, the strong arm of the Saxon Otho had interfered, and Rome had become an appendage to the German throne.

With the Clergy, as a class, it was hardly better. Many, of the higher ranks, were mere feudal lords and barons,—fighting, tyrannizing, hunting, revelling, after the manner of those half-barbaric chiefs. The Priesthood had become a refuge for landless lords and younger sons. Against the spirit if not the strict letter of canon rule, church properties were fast coming to be held as family estates. A bishopric would descend by birthright to the eldest son; a benefice would be given as dowry with a daughter on her bridal. Church offices were openly bought and sold.

A child of five or six would be installed in the sacred chair, and, "stammering two words of his catechism for response," be invested with the charge of souls; while in the lower clerical orders the ignorance was such, that many a priest "scarce knew A from B."

Meanwhile, the piety of the Othos (936–1002), — especially the extravagant and feverish temper of the boy-Emperor Otho III.,—and, at the same time, terror of the approaching end of the world, which became in some quarters a sort of epidemic frenzy towards the year 1000,* made the case more formidable, by heaping gifts and gratuities upon the Church, enormously exaggerating its wealth and its claim of holding by a higher than any human tenure. In the social revolution that was thus playing into its hands, the wildest pretensions of the Forged Decretals, on which its theory of sovereignty rested, passed without any question. Its actual power was thus prodigiously increased, just when it showed itself most glaringly unfit to hold any power at all. And even the virtues of Henry II. (1003–1024), emperor and saint, but more monk than monarch, had only made things worse.

Two directly opposite arguments have been built on this state of things. Cardinal Baronius, a zealous Catholic, argues that nothing less than a Divine commission and a special miracle could have lifted the Church out of that mud-pit and put it on its feet again. The heavenly pilot was asleep (he says) while the ship drove before the storm, but was sure to wa-

* Very far, however, from being common or universal, as is often represented.

ken in due time. The average mind infers that both the fall and the recovery lay in the range of human motives. It finds the sufficient reason in the circumstances of the age, particularly in the temper of Feudalism, which brought the rudest passions to the front. It justifies itself by the fact that the second fall, five hundred years later, was followed not by recovery, but by the destruction of the Catholic unity itself. I do not enter into the argument; only try to present the fact.

The crisis of that long disease may be set at from 1040 to 1050. A few years before, in 1033, a child ten years old, son of one of the noble houses, had been put on the papal throne, under the name of Benedict IX.; and was restored to it by force of arms, five years later, when he had grown into a lewd, violent, and wilful boy of fifteen. At the age of twenty-one he was weary of the struggle, and sold out, for a large sum of money paid down, to a rich purchaser, — first plundering the papal treasury of all the funds he could lay his hands on.

His successor, Gregory VI., naturally complained of his hard bargain, which was made harder by another claimant (Sylvester III.), elected by a different party; while no law that could possibly be quoted or invented would make valid the purchase and sale of the spiritual sovereignty of the world, which in theory the Papacy still was. Gregory appears to have been a respectable and even conscientious magistrate, by the standard of that evil time. But his open purchase of the dignity not only gave a shock to whatever right feeling there was left, but it made the extraordinary dilemma and scandal of three popes at once,— a knot which the German king, now Emperor, was called in to cut.

Henry III. (1038–1056) was, as sovereign, able, upright, and resolute ; and his early death — for his reign was cut short by disasters that preyed upon his health — is one of the calamities of history. The cause of the Roman Court he judged with vigor and good sense. His strong hand, more than any man's, dragged the Church out of the slough it had fallen into. The worthless Benedict was dismissed, as having betrayed his charge. The impotent Sylvester was not recognized at all. The respectable Gregory was duly convinced of his deep guilt of Simony, — because he had " thought that the gift of God could be purchased with money," — and was suffered as a penitent to end his days in peace. A fourth, a German ecclesiastic, who was clean of all these intrigues, was set in the chair of Peter, where he reigned righteously for two years, under the name of Clement II.

And so we come to the year 1048, to the moment of the revolution which determined all the later features of the Church, — the revolution associated with the name of Hildebrand.

Here it is necessary to look a moment at the situation. By the events just referred to the chief office in the Church had come, by general consent, to be the express grant of the German king, taking the titles Patrician, and Emperor of the Romans. Theoretically, on the other hand, these titles could be given only by the Pope, who was thus the political superior, while made personally — as it were, feudally — dependent on his temporal sovereign.

The political difficulty need not detain us now. But, from the point of view already familiar to us, it is easy to conceive the humiliation, the galling dishonor, that must be felt by any one who had kept true to the theory of sacerdotal dominion in the Church. I will not restate that theory; the main points of it will become sharply prominent as we go on. But I will recall to mind, just here, how completely that theory had been worked out in the great body of constitutional law accepted in the ninth century under the name "Decretals of Isidore." This, along with the monstrous forgeries that a good part of it rested on, we have to keep in mind. Whether or not that ecclesiastical code was honestly thought to be genuine throughout, is a question which we cannot answer, and which need not trouble us.* At any rate, it had been assumed as genuine for now two centuries. It had been appealed to without dispute in the several grants made by the Othos to the Roman See. It might, without much blame, at any rate without much misgiving, be assumed as the accepted code of Christian law by any one, of either party, who had a point to make by it.

Again, we must bear in mind that there would certainly be within the Church a strong party, however baffled and obscure, which would brood upon that theory all the more intently because of its pres-

* The special portion of it called "the Donation of Constantine," sometimes referred to the age of Pepin, is also confidently said to belong to the time of Hildebrand.

ent eclipse. Such a party would chafe and rebel, in bitterness of spirit, at anything that made against it; would train a multitude of sectaries, if need were, to a fanatical devotion to it; would watch its chance of any practicable time and way of putting it into force. Such a party would certainly find its leader in the most daring, the most resolute, at need the most unscrupulous, of those who should ally their fortunes with it; and he would most likely be the sincerest of partisans as well. If such a man were able as well as resolute, and favored not thwarted by events, he would be sure to effect a great revolution, perhaps achieve a great success. All these conditions are found in the character and life of the remarkable man whose career for the next thirty-seven years is the history of the time.

Hildebrand was a carpenter's son of the little Tuscan town Saona. He went in his youth to Rome, where he became private chaplain and fast friend of Gregory VI., the same who bought his office, repented of it, and went into exile. At Gregory's death Hildebrand became a monk, and joined the famous religious house of Cluny in France, waiting events.

Meanwhile Clement, installed by Henry III., had died; and a successor, Damasus, after only a few months' reign, also died. This was looked upon by many as a divine judgment; and the high Church party — those who demanded complete emancipation from the State — may be understood as gaining strength fast, only wanting a leader. So, when Henry for the third time offered the papal throne to his old friend and instructor Bruno, bishop of Toul, he ac-

cepted, reluctantly, only on condition that the choice
should be ratified by the clergy and people of Rome.

According to the story so often repeated since, it
was by Hildebrand's firm counsel that Bruno refused
to accept the papacy as the Emperor's gift. They
undertook the long journey together as pilgrims and
on foot. And when in town or village men looked
for the pompous procession that should attend the
new Pope to Rome, they beheld, instead, two barefoot
monks, humblest of wayfarers, journeying to the
shrine of Peter, to lay the choice before the clergy
of the sacred city.

Whether or not this is the true tale unvarnished, it
is true that Bruno went up to Rome as a pilgrim on
foot; where he was at once elected, without contest,
as by the original choice of the clergy, and assumed
the robes and style of office as Leo IX. (1048–1055).
It is also true that Hildebrand was speedily promoted
to a post of chief trust under him, and was known as
the ruling spirit of the papal court, — "lord of our
lord the pope," to copy the half-jealous, half-admiring
phrase of the day.

For twenty-five years — through the restless and
indefatigable pontificate of Leo and those of his four
successors * — the hand of Hildebrand still kept the
helm. And at length his own time came.

A council held at Rome, in 1059, among its other
acts to secure the discipline and independence of the
Church, had carefully provided that a pope must be
first nominated by the free act of an inner circle of

* These were Victor II. (1055), Stephen IX. (1057), Nicholas II.
(1058), Alexander II. (1061–1073).

seven "cardinal-bishops." It was an awkward comment — and so Hildebrand felt it to be — when fourteen years later, as he returned from the burial of Alexander II., the street crowds saluted him with shouts, declared that no other was worthy or fit to rule, and fairly forced him, would he or not, into the chair of state. "Suddenly," he says, "there rose a great tumult and shouting among the crowd. They rushed upon me like madmen, giving me no time to speak or take thought. They dragged me with rough hands to the place of apostolic rule, to which I am far from equal, so that I may say with the prophet: *I am come into deep waters, where the floods overflow me ; I am weary of my crying, my throat is dried up. Fearfulness and trembling are come upon me, and horror hath overwhelmed me.*"

It is most likely that the recoil of spirit was real. The resolute ambition was also real, which would have been heavily cast down by any different result. At any rate, whatever was lacking in the form must be made good in the fact.

The whole body of clergy met in the Church of St. Peter *ad Vincula*, and hastily went through the forms of election ; then put the vote as follows to the throng: *Placet vobis ? Placet.—Vultis eum ? Volumus. — Laudatis eum ? Laudamus.* And so he was installed under the title of Gregory VII. on the 22d of April, 1073. From this time for twelve years he bore himself in office so firmly, energetically, and boldly, that the Church of Rome feels the strong pressure of his hand to this day.

The new Pope had before him two distinct tasks:

first, to confirm the independence of the Church in its own sphere, as against the Empire, the feudal lords, and the "ring" of Roman nobles; second, to secure the absolute devotion of its priesthood, and, as essential to this, their strict subjection to canon law, particularly in the matter of the marriage of the clergy.

To secure these two objects had long been the aim of what may be called the party of Reform within the Church. In this party, again, were two sections, .the "disciplinarians" and the "politicians." The first aimed simply at moral reformation; that is, to bring Church and Society under ecclesiastical rule — which meant, in practice, monastic rule — in all matters of social and personal morality. The theory of the second would be content with nothing less than the absolute sovereignty and supremacy of the Church in every department of human life, including politics.

The Disciplinarian party was represented by the archdeacon Peter Damian, a man fanatic and indefatigable, whose numerous writings, apparently sincere and often incredibly coarse, give us the clearest notion of the monastic code of the day. All matters pertaining to marriage, it will be remembered, the Church claimed for its own control, regarding marriage not as a civil contract but a Sacrament. Canon law had barred it about by strict rules of kindred; and these were so rigidly interpreted, by the Council before spoken of, as to forbid alliance between any who had a common ancestor within seven generations, "*or as far as consanguinity can be traced.*" We may easily imagine the hostility this must rouse in the family pride of Feudalism, and the confusions of property it must cause when estates were so often to be united or strengthened by family alliances. The mere statement of the point throws light on the interference of the Church in many a State affair of the Middle Age.*

The Political party, led by Hildebrand, had availed itself of the honest fanaticism of the other to kindle the enthusiasm necessary to carry out its broader plan. It is not easy to separate the political motive from the religious or ecclesiastical motive. We are to think of the work of Hildebrand not as the work of a saint, but of a statesman. He comes before us not especially as a good man, but as a determined, inexorable, and very strong man. It is by the ordinary maxims of politicians that we must often vindicate his acts, if at all. It is by these that we must justify, if at all, his uncompromising severity, his subtle and double-dealing craft, his implacable cruelty at need, his deference to the strong, his vindictive arrogance to the defeated and weak. In the battle in which he found himself engaged, he doubtless believed with all his heart that his first duty was success. Complete and overwhelming victory was the only condition of success.

The first fruit of that victory must be *a celibate priesthood.* I have already hinted at the abuses he

---

* Thus the act which dissolved the marriage of Henry VIII. followed accurately a precedent which we find in a letter of Gregory VII., prescribing that one cannot lawfully marry the *betrothed* of a deceased brother (Ep. vii. 9).

would correct. Gravest of perils, then, was family interest, building up a despotic clerical Caste on the basis of feudal power and pride. Even now, in England, the most decent and best-ordered of countries, we see the scandal: worldly living, family influence, the building up of private fortunes from church endowments, the open sale of benefices, or, if not that, at least speculating on the lives of those who hold them.

We must remember the far greater and grosser dangers then, — not to justify, but to pardon, the acts to which Hildebrand was led. As "war-minister" of Alexander II. he had given full support to the most violent of the monkish party. With his own hand he gave a consecrated banner to the veteran warrior Herlimbald, who enlisted in a ferocious crusade to expel by force of arms the married clergy of Milan, — a war in which the bishops of Northern Italy were "driven to Rome like a herd of cattle;" a war in which the old ecclesiastical liberties of Lombardy, cherished with extreme local pride and consecrated by the great name of Ambrose, perished in fire and blood. So implacable, indeed, was the spirit of this crusade, that once (it is said), when a certain abbot had torn out the tongue and eyes of a non-conforming priest, Hildebrand approved, upheld, and promoted him for it.

From a very early time, spite of Peter's example and Paul's advice, the marriage of the clergy had been held a scandal; at best an indulgence, needing special penance or dispensation, and in the commoner view an offence to be forbidden altogether. In Eng-

land, in Germany, in Northern Italy, the stronger
traditions of domesticity prevailed, and many at least
of the humbler clergy were married, — though with
the stigma of " concubinage," and the nickname
" Nicolaïtan."

The Monk Hildebrand shared the general monastic notion.   The Pope Gregory saw the policy of
attaching the clergy solely and absolutely to the fortunes of the Church.   There must be no other interest, no other affection, no other human tie or duty,
but only that.   True, the policy met most formidable
resistance.   " Let the Pope find angels instead of
men!" some said.   But what should the Monk, who
held all austerities acceptable service, know of that?
True, wherever the experiment was tried, and as long
as it was tried, it led to horrible scandals, evasions,
and sins that might not be named.   What was that
to the Pope, strong in his conviction that he could
put down all irregularity, at any rate pardon it; and
who saw the absolute need of making his clergy a
body of partisans, — immoral if you will, fanatic or
sceptic, worldly or devout, cunning or mystic, as the
case might be; but at any rate thoroughgoing partisans, the more unscrupulous the better, — mere limbs
of the one organization, tools to be handled by the
central executive will?

He saw that family ties, like feudal ties, would
diminish so much from blind allegiance.   Therefore
there must be no property to be turned to a family
estate : the Church alone should possess anything.
There must be no wife or children : or, if affection
owned such ties, policy must disown them.   If they

could not be denied, they should be at any rate dishonored.   Under a ban of ignominy, they should not stand in the way of that perfect service the Church required.

Through violent struggle, through frightful scandal and cruelty, through shocking corruption and levity, caused by this remorseless policy throughout the entire Middle Age, there was no yielding, and is none to this day.   The grossest immoralities have been openly connived at.   Wars have been fought and fortunes squandered by some of the Popes themselves for their own offspring.   Yet, of the innumerable army of the Church's servants, not the humblest parish priest, not the loneliest missionary, may let one thought cross his mind of dispensation from that vow, in which the Church, these many ages, has found the secret of her strength.

The next great struggle of Gregory is known as the Controversy of Investitures : that is, respecting the right of temporal princes to appoint to sacred offices in the Church.

In itself, nothing could be more natural, nay, inevitable, than Lay Investiture.   The same man was both an ecclesiastic and a civil magistrate.   The holding of great estates, — whole townships or counties, perhaps, — and the civil duties, or political, that went with the holding of these estates, made it necessary, made it right, that the Bishop or the Abbot should own service to the Sovereign, and be in some sense under his authority.   The bishop's allegiance was signified by the symbolic act in which the feudal lord bestowed the crosier, ring, and staff or sceptre.* This allegiance was intolerable and unpardonable in the sight of the Pope; it was indispensable and not to be yielded on the part of the Sovereign.

Gregory threw down his challenge frankly, declaring the clergy wholly free from feudal obligation, and responsible to the Pope alone. No bishop might be appointed but by him; and, at his summons, a prelate of England or Germany, of France or Spain, must come to receive the symbols of authority in Rome. If any should disobey, "their blessing should turn to cursing, and their prayers to sin."

On the feudal model, Saint Peter was declared lord paramount, holding of his own right the kingdoms of the earth in fee. This was simply translating the doctrine of the Decretals into the political dialect of the day. It was likely to be accepted by none so promptly as by the Church's newest converts and allies. As lord paramount, in Peter's name Leo had bestowed the whole of South Italy on the Norman Robert Guiscard. To William the Norman, Conqueror of England, Hildebrand had given Peter's own commission, with a consecrated banner for his crusade, and a ring containing a hair of the Apostle himself. The royal power is to the ecclesiastical, he writes to him, as moon to sun: it shines only by the reflected light of that. "For if the Chair of Peter resolves and determines heavenly and spiritual things, how much more earthly and secular things!" †

His manifesto of supremacy speedily brought Greg-

* The crosier is the shepherd's crook ; the ring, symbol of marriage with his spiritual bride the Church ; the staff or sceptre, token of secular authority.

† Epist. vii. 23.

ory into collision with the Empire. For, by the theory of Church and State alike, the Emperor inherited the name and authority of Cæsar. In claiming that to Cæsar should be rendered that which is Cæsar's, he asserted the Imperial right to nominate, or at least to confirm, all officers of the Church in his dominion, — above all the Pope, who was at the head of it.

In this particular form, the question had been met by the monk Hildebrand twenty-five years before as counsellor of Leo. An occasion was not long wanting to the pope Gregory to assert the higher claim of authority over the Emperor himself, on a point of political administration.

Henry IV. of Germany was a mere child six years old, when left sovereign by his father's death. He had been indulged by a foolish mother. He was kidnapped at twelve, and put in charge of ambitious prelates, who alternately soured him by harshness and spoiled him by license. Now, at Gregory's accession, he was a young man of twenty-three. His violence had already driven a whole district into rebellion. Saxon peasants, raging that something was still left of his military defences, had torn his favorite castle to the ground. A mob in Cologne had driven its insolent bishop away in terror of his life ; and Henry swore (it was said) that he would yet ride his rebellious subjects with boot and spur.

The Pope sided with the insurgents. He summoned the young king * to his judgment-seat at Rome ; threatened at his refusal to " cut him off as a rotten

* King of Germany, until his coronation as Emperor at Rome.

limb;" and passed on him the awful sentence of excommunication.

The double terror of rebellion at home and the Church's curse at length broke down the passionate pride of Henry. Humbled and helpless, he crossed the Alps in midwinter, groping among the bleak precipices and ice-fields, — the peasants passing him in a rude sledge of hide down those dreadful slopes, — and went to beg absolution of Gregory at the mountain castle of Canossa.

History has few scenes more dramatic than that which shows the proud, irascible, crest-fallen young sovereign confronted with the fiery, little, indomitable old man. To quote Gregory's own words : —

" Here he came with few attendants, and for three days before the gate — his royal apparel laid aside, barefoot, clad in wool, and weeping abundantly — he never ceased to implore the aid and comfort of apostolic mercy, till all there present were moved with pity and compassion ; insomuch that, interceding for him with many prayers and tears, they all wondered at my strange severity, and some even cried out that it was not so much the severe dignity of an apostle as the cruel wrath of a tyrant. Overcome at length by the urgency of his appeal and the entreaties of all present, I relaxed the bond of anathema, and received him to the favor of communion and the bosom of our holy Mother the Church."

It was a truce which one party did not mean nor the other hope to keep. It was policy, not real terror or conviction, that had led Henry to humble himself before the Pope. It was policy, not contrition or compassion, that had led Gregory (against his better judgment, it is said) to accept his Sovereign's penance. In the war of policy, the man of the world prevailed. Freed of the Church's curse, he quickly won back the strength he had lost. He overthrew in battle the rival whom Gregory upheld.* He swept his rebellious lands with sword and flame. He carried his victorious army to Rome, and was there crowned Emperor by a rival Pope. Gregory himself was only saved by his ferocious allies, Norman and Saracen, at cost of the devastation of half the capital, — that broad belt of ruin which still covers the half-mile between the Coliseum and the Lateran gate. Then, hardly rescued from the popular wrath, he went away to die, defeated and heart-broken, at Salerno, with the almost despairing words on his lips: " I have loved righteousness and hated iniquity, and therefore I die in exile !"

But " a spirit hath not flesh or bones," as a body hath, and so it will not stay mangled and bruised. The victory lay, after all, with the combatant who could appeal to fanaticism as well as force. It was not the old man Gregory, — his form lean with fasting and vigil, bent under the weight of perpetual care, and scarred by a warfare of six-and-thirty years, — it was not him that Henry had undertaken to subdue; but that awful, unseen, omnipresent Power, — that matchless, sleepless, hundred-eyed, hundred-handed Organization. The spell of the curse he had defied, the shadow of the abasement he had undergone, never left him. More than all, he was betrayed by his vin-

* Rodolph, who was slain by the hand of Godfrey, chief of the First Crusade.

dictive, hot, and haughty temper. Twenty years later — vainly seeking mercy from his own son, the unnatural champion of the Church; vainly asking shelter in a monastery, claiming the humblest " benefit of clergy," as one who could read and sing — he died in want and forsaken, deprived even of the empty honor of a royal tomb.

"So let all thine enemies perish !" the victorious Church might say. For in that victory were security and triumph, almost unbroken, for more than two hundred years. And, as the first fruit of it, within fifteen years from the death of Gregory, Italy, Germany, France, and England had united in the enthusiastic and brilliant league which displayed the greatness and strength of Europe on the fields of Asia. The great Crusade which he announced in the first year of his pontificate had been triumphantly fought. The banner of the Cross floated over the battlements of the Holy City. The dream and prophecy were fulfilled in the new Kingdom of Jerusalem.

And so the work of Hildebrand might seem to be completed. But it is necessary to trace its results a little farther on. For the long conflict of Church and Empire, which makes the great drama of the Middle Age, was only begun. For its issue, centuries were still to wait.

The question so at stake between Pope and Emperor — that of Lay Investiture — was compromised, some forty years later, in a conference at Worms (1122). The prince might bestow the sceptre; crosier and ring must be given from the hand of the spiritual chief.

But this was compromise, not agreement. It was truce, not peace. There were two divine rights, not one. It was like the old metaphysical problem of an irresistible force striking an insuperable barrier. By the terms of the problem, neither could give way till they should both be spent. And so we have before us a struggle of which I can only hint, briefly, at the chief later crises and the final issue.

The pontificate of Alexander III. (1159–1181) was one long war with Frederick Barbarossa, most powerful of the German emperors. The incidents of this war we shall meet again, and we look at it now only as they touch this particular issue. Barbarossa upheld successively four rival popes against Alexander; forced him for years into exile; besieged him in Rome till his own army was two-thirds destroyed by fever; twice destroyed the Pope's most steadfast ally, the heroic city of Milan, in his terrible campaigns against the Lombard league. Yet even so, the fortune of the Church prevailed. The Emperor was forced to yield. At the famous scene in Venice (1177) — where three porphyry slabs in the pavement still show the spot— he prostrated himself before the Pope in the portico of St. Mark's, held the stirrup for him to mount, and led his mule by the bridle-rein. The story even went that Alexander set his foot on Frederick's neck as he mounted, saying, "Thus I tread the lion and the adder under foot." "*Non tibi sed Petro*," muttered the Emperor. "*Et mihi et Petro*," replied the Pope.

Thirty years later, in the pontificate of Innocent III. (1198–1216), the wildest dream of Catholic Christianity might seem to have been fulfilled. A Fourth

Crusade had made the Latin forces, under Baldwin, masters of all the East. For once, the Pope was recognized as Head of all Christendom. Constantinople, Antioch, Jerusalem, Alexandria, the regions of Armenia and Bulgaria, the Patriarch of Greece, owned him for their spiritual head. He gave and took away with his own hand the crowns of the Empire, of Italy, of England, and of Spain. At the moment of his death he was literally commander-in-chief of the armies and navies of all Europe, in expectation of the new Crusade, which was to sail the following year. We cannot forget, indeed, that the power was already undermined by heresy, deep and wide. A black background mocks that splendor, in the horror of the Albigensian crusade. And this reminds us that while as a political power the Papacy is now at its highest point of splendor, yet as a spiritual power, as a symbol of religious unity, its glory has already waned.

The next epoch, or moment, of this conflict is found in the long war of extermination waged by the successors of Innocent III. against the emperor Frederick II., grandson of Barbarossa, — the most enlightened, the most cultivated, the most modern mind, perhaps, of the entire Middle Age. All Italy lay at the mercy of this struggle, alike unrelenting on both sides. The events of it, continued through six pontificates, we have not to consider now. Its result was the literal extinction of the house of Hohenstaufen, proudest and ablest of the imperial dynasties. The crime against Italy was retaliated upon the Pope's allies in the terrible revenge of the Sicilian Vespers (1282). But a new Emperor, Rodolph of Hapsburg (1273–

1291), was a fast friend of the Pope, whom the close of the century found in victorious, complete, and assured dominion.

And so, at Christmas of the year 1299, Boniface VIII., most arrogant of the long line of pontiffs, sent out his summons to all Christendom to attend the festival of Jubilee, at Rome. In the stately pomp that conducted him to the high altar, two swords were borne before him, emblems of the temporal and spiritual power, wielded at once by that one hand, supreme over all earthly princes and lords. For had not the disciples said to Jesus, "Behold, here are two swords"? and had he not answered them, "It is enough"?

Here are the words of the Pope's declaration, made a little later,* as his challenge to Philip the Fair, King of France:—

"There is One Holy Church, Catholic and Apostolic; one Body, one Head; in its keeping two swords, temporal and spiritual, one to be wielded *by* the Church, the other *for* the Church, — by the hand of kings and soldiers, but at the beck and sufferance † of the priesthood, and the temporal to be subject to the spiritual : as it is written, — 'I have this day set thee over the nations and over the kingdoms, to root out and to pull down, and to destroy and to throw down, to build, and to plant.' Whoever resists this power resists the ordinance of God, — unless he shall pretend, like a Manichæan, that there are two First Principles (*principia*). Therefore we proclaim, declare, assert, and announce to every human creature, that he be subject to the Roman Pontiff, as wholly necessary to his salvation."

* In the Bull *Unam Sanctam*, November 18, 1302.
† *Nutu et patientiâ.*

The States General of France, summoned for this emergency — nay, the clergy themselves — protested against this enormous assumption. Boniface was unyielding, and passed upon the King sentence of excommunication. The edict was already drawn which should declare Philip of France deposed, uncrowned, disthroned. But it was one day too late.* The royal envoy at Rome, — William of Nogaret, whose grandfather had perished in the horrid crusade against the Albigenses — a lawyer, cold, stern, resolute, gained to his support the implacable enemies of the Pope among the Roman nobles. Boniface was driven from Rome; attacked and seized in the castle at Anagni, his birthplace and chosen retreat; buffeted in the face so that he bled by the iron gauntlet of Sciarra Colonna, "king of brigands;" kept three days famishing in terror of his life; and, when rescued at length from his enemies, the proud-hearted old man of eighty-two was utterly broken, and in a few months died insane, refusing with his last breath the holy offices of the Church.† So, said his enemies, was fulfilled the prediction of Pope Celestine V., whom Boniface had supplanted: —

> "Vulpes intravit; tamquam leo pontificavit;
> Exiit utque canis, de divite factus inanis."

* The Bull of Excommunication was to be published on the eighth of September, 1303. The attack upon the Pope was made on the seventh.

† I have followed the more striking and dramatic account which seems to have prevailed at the time, — more especially, perhaps, among the French, — and which will be found in detail in Michelet (*Histoire de France*, liv. v. ch. 2). That more generally received by Catholics asserts, on the contrary, that Boniface received his

The Church as a temporal never recovered from the blow struck on the cheek of her proudest sovereign. King, nobles, and commons had joined to brave its power, and the sword of the Law was stronger than the word of the Priest. In the confusions that followed, Law must decide what authority could not. The long "Captivity" at Avignon (1309–1378) had quite destroyed the moral dignity of the Papacy, which was, or seemed, a mere tool of French ambition and craft. The "Golden Bull" (1356), that charter of German liberties, had made the crown of Empire * finally and completely independent. The Great Schism (1378–1417) had divided Catholic Christendom for forty years between the rival "Obediences," of two Popes mutually excommunicating and denouncing each other.

The Universities became first arbiters of the dispute, then gradually gained an authority above either party to it. Compromises were offered: one, that each nation should have a pope of its own. A Council at Pisa (1409) meanwhile tried its ineffectual hand to heal the breach between the rival pontiffs,—which it bridged at length by disowning both and inaugurating a third.

Thus dependent on a new order of choice, the despotic Hierarchy became more and more a limited

enemies in his pontifical robes, and with such dignity that no man durst lift his hand against him (*Raynaldus*, vol. iv. p. 287).

* One ought perhaps to say " crowns," of which there were four, — the silver crown of Germany, conferred at Aachen (Aix-la-Chapelle); the iron crown of Italy, at Monza; the bronze, of Burgundy; and the golden crown of Empire, bestowed by the Pope in person, at Rome.

monarchy, and by the larger part of Christendom the Council was held to be a power superior to the Pope himself. The same inordinate pretension was maintained; but it was by sufferance, not in defiance, of the powers of the world. It was the bad faith of Sigismund, not any whole-hearted courage of the Council, which carried out at Constance that evil act of ecclesiastical authority, the martyrdom of Huss. And within another century the austere, magnificent, invincible dominion of Hildebrand or Innocent has declined to the unspeakable moral corruption of Alexander Borgia, the secular splendor and ambition of Julius II., the worldly infidelity of Leo X., the spiritual impotence and contempt, which led to the Reformation under Martin Luther.

IV.

THE CRUSADES.

THE term "Crusades" is generally given to a series of military adventures by which the Western Christians attempted to conquer and hold Palestine from the Mahometans; or, in the language of that day, to deliver the Holy Sepulchre from the hands of Infidels.

In this sense, the period of the Crusades lasted almost exactly two hundred years, — from the despairing appeal of the Eastern Emperor, and the preaching of Peter the Hermit, which kindled the great flame of crusading passion that blazed out suddenly in 1095, to the forlorn retreat of the seven surviving Knights of the Hospital from the garrison of Acre, in 1291.

Taken in a broader way, we have a considerable margin, before and after. The Norman Conquest of England, in 1066, was undertaken as a holy war, and was fought — like the crusade against the married clergy of Milan five years earlier — under a consecrated banner sent by Hildebrand, with the Pope's commission under the great round seal, and a ring inclosing a hair of the apostle Peter. To repel the Saracen by an armed league of Christian powers had been one of the dreams of Sylvester II., about the year 1000. The wars of Charlemagne against the Moors of Cordova, and his treaty with Haroun al Raschid, had been magnified into a vast crusading adventure and complete conquest of the Holy Land.

Again, Henry V. of England, as late as 1420, still felt it the duty of a Christian king to take up the unfinished enterprise, as his father had felt before him; and the Teutonic Knights, along the Baltic and on the plains of Poland, held sovereign power long after, over lands won by conquest under the banner of the Black Cross. Nor was the Holy War all outside the boundaries of Christian States; for, of all crusading adventure, none was more obstinate and bloody than that under Innocent III. against the Count of Toulouse and the heretics of Languedoc.

In short, the Crusade — that is, the "holy war" against all enemies of the Church — was the passion and the dream of the entire Middle Age. We may even say that it was the necessary outgrowth of the theory of the Empire-Church. The same assertion of supremacy over kings and emperors, the same claim of universal sovereignty resting on divine right, which involved the Church in armed struggle against a Christian Frederick or Henry, would necessarily commit it to an endless war against Saracen or Turk. The same religious frenzy that swept Syria with flame and drowned Jerusalem in blood would turn with equal fury to hunt out misbelief in France, or to kindle the fires of the Spanish Inquisition. Nothing shows so thoroughly the remorseless consist-

ency of that theory as this enormous license of crime
and violence, to attain the professed ends of righteousness and peace.

This — the working out of the scheme of Church
sovereignty by armed conquest — is the only point
of view from which we have, just now, to regard
that wonderful chapter of human annals. Still, it
may help clear the view, to give a brief outline, or
recapitulation, of the events generally included under the name Crusades.

In 1095, great multitudes gathered about a Church
Council held at Piacenza, in North Italy, and a few
months later at Clermont, in southern France, where
they were addressed in fervent eloquence by Pope
Urban II. The popular enthusiasm already roused
by Peter the Hermit, fresh from a pilgrimage to Jerusalem, was here organized and pledged to the great
adventure. The next year a disorderly vanguard of
some three hundred thousand men, women, and children
made their way in several detachments overland,
subsisting as they could by charity or plunder, with
horrible riot, especially in Hungary, as far as Constantinople; where such of them as survived were
ferried across to Asia, and soon perished in one great
slaughter under the walls of Nicæa. Meanwhile, a
well-appointed army, mostly French and Norman,
gathered under Godfrey of Flanders and other famous chiefs; which, after untold losses, sufferings, and
fatigues, took Jerusalem by assault in July, 1099,
and established a Christian kingdom there that lasted
a little under ninety years.

In less than fifty years, however, the tide turned

strong against this feeble monarchy. Edessa, one of its most important outposts, had already fallen, when the eloquent monk Bernard devoted himself with passionate fervor to preaching a new Crusade. This set out in 1147, under Louis VII. of France and Conrad of Germany, first of the House of Hohenstaufen; was soon crippled by jealousies and disorders; nearly perished in three great slaughters in Asia Minor; lingered awhile about the gay and luxurious court of Antioch; attempted the siege of Damascus; and returned, utterly defeated and hopeless, the following year.

The fall of Jerusalem, in 1187, raised a fresh passion of grief and fury; and the Third Crusade was led by the three greatest kings in Christendom. But Frederick Barbarossa, the only competent chief, perished at the river Cydnus, in Asia Minor; while Richard of England and Philip of France wasted their strength in useless sieges or miserable jealousies. The enterprise was foiled by Saladin, who made peace on generous terms. A pilgrimage as far as the walls of the holy city he might not enter, was all the lion-hearted king could win by his reckless valor in the field. His own vindictive temper, and the baseness of both his allies, — Leopold (of Austria) and Philip, — were more fatal to him than his disastrous campaigning in the East.

The dream of universal monarchy was never so near fulfilment as under Innocent III. A crusading force, under convoy of the Venetians, had taken Constantinople in 1204, by a treacherous assault, and established in a riot of blood and plunder a

Latin kingdom there, owning the spiritual dominion of Rome, which lasted till 1261, near sixty years. Meantime came the terrible and ghastly scenes of the crusade against the Albigenses (1208–1229). The Church had gained its first bloody victory over heresy at home; and Innocent was passionately eager to reclaim the lost conquest of Palestine. But he died in the vigor of his years, in 1216, at the age of fifty-six, — died literally of the fever of that passion, chafing at the long delays, while recognized Commander-in-Chief of the armies and navies of all Christendom.

The day had already been appointed for the embarkation, which he was to oversee in person and direct by his lieutenant. The expedition sailed, and captured Damietta, in Egypt; and ten years later (1227) Frederick II., grandson of Barbarossa, was king of Jerusalem by treaty with the Mussulman. But this show of victory was repudiated with rage by the hot-headed old man, Gregory IX., then (1227–1241) in the papal chair. Baffled by the Pope's curse, and divided by the cares of government in Sicily, Germany, and Jerusalem, Frederick returned to Italy in 1229; and Palestine lapsed back helplessly to the Turkish hands that have held it ever since.

Of the futile enterprises which followed, only two are deserving to be mentioned here: and these not for their successes, but for the remarkable character of their leader. Louis IX. of France (Saint Louis) was as sincerely devout, and as purely religious in his motive, as any who had been moved by the first tide of generous enthusiasm. He was also a good man, and merciful; a lover of justice, too, so that many a bitter quarrel was left to his decision; a king earnestly wishing the peace and good order of his people, whom, in his long and calamitous absence, he left to the wise regency of his mother, Blanche of Castile. In 1249 he sailed for Egypt, and gained some slight successes there. But his loved brother was killed in battle. His army was cut off by a horrible pestilence, in which Louis sustained his soldiers' courage by tending the sick in the hospital and helping to bear out the dead for burial. The very water they drank and the fish they ate were poisoned by the bodies cast into the Nile. Louis himself was taken prisoner; and, for reward of his valor and hardship, won the poor privilege of a pilgrimage to Nazareth.

Twenty years later, in 1270, the pious fervor still glowing in him, he set forth again, — this time to die on the voyage, on the Barbary coast. And two years after, Prince Edward of England — already wounded almost fatally by a poisoned arrow in the siege of Acre — heard of his father's death, and returned home to reign; the first whom, in the full meaning of that word, we call an English king. Within twenty years (in 1291) Acre was taken by the Mamelukes, and the Christian kingdom of Palestine was no more.*

* The following summary of the Seven Crusades may be convenient for reference : —

1. The First Crusade, under Godfrey, establishes the kingdom of Jerusalem in 1099.

Such, in brief outline, is the story of those two hundred disastrous years. History and romance have done their best to fill in that outline with groups of pictures, perhaps more vivid and impressive to the imagination than any other scenes of military adventure; so that the name brings to our mind not the misery, carnage, and horror that make up most of the dreary tale, but the splendors of knighthood, the glittering armor, the pomp of gorgeous squadrons, the brilliant crests, the waving banners, the red cross blazoned on the shield or on snow-white mantle, the tumult and eager hope, the passionate fervors of devotion, and all the glamour that is woven about the memories of Chivalry.

It is no part of my plan, even if I were able, to reproduce those scenes by way of description. A few sober historical lessons, at best, are all I can hope to find in that wide and gorgeous canvas.

An enterprise so long sustained; pursued with such fanatic eagerness, through so many horrible disasters and hopeless defeats, for an object so purely visionary and ideal (as at first sight it seems to us);

2. The disastrous Crusade preached by St. Bernard, led by Conrad and Louis VII., sets forth in 1147.

3. The Third Crusade, under Barbarossa, Philip of France, and Richard of England, is defeated by Saladin in 1190.

4. The Latin Fleet, under Baldwin, achieves the conquest of Constantinople in 1204.

5. Frederick II., having first sailed ineffectually (1218), becomes king of Jerusalem by treaty in 1227.

6. Louis IX. of France makes his disastrous campaign in Egypt, becoming master of Damietta in 1249.

7. He renews the attempt, lands, and dies in Tunis, in 1270.

so doomed from the start by follies and animosities
among its chiefs; showing so often a mere frenzy
and carnival of crime, as the means of reaching an
end assumed to be holy above all others, and as the
atonement and expiation of all other guilt,—has
absolutely no parallel in human history. There is
nothing else, not even the first great outburst of
Moslem fanaticism, with which it can fairly be
compared.

Again, the story shows, at first sight, hardly anything but a record of ferocity, disaster, and defeat.
The Church had undertaken a prodigious task, and
did her best to carry it out with such tools as were
at her command. The fundamental contrasts already
shown in the relation of the Church to Feudal Society could not have been more glaringly forced to
the surface. The Church, with obstinate and fatal
persistency, pressed through all these two hundred
years her theory of universal and absolute dominion.
The agents she had to enforce that theory were the
passions, violences, and petty independencies veiled
under the name of Feudalism. Hence the doom of
failure that was upon the enterprise from the start.

It is not merely that crime and violence, pillage
and murder, were set on foot upon an enormous scale,
as the expiation of crime, and as the means of founding Christ's kingdom upon earth. That lay in the
diseased conscience of the Church herself, drunk with
her dream of universal conquest. But more. There
was absolutely no other force that could be enrolled
to that vast enterprise; none but the rude, lawless,
jealous, vindictive, mutually destructive forces of feu-

dal society, and of the monarchies which had grown out of Feudalism.

The First Crusade had a really able and heroic leader in Godfrey. The Third lost the one man fit to direct it, in the death of Barbarossa. The last found all the virtues of the age combined in its pure-hearted chief, Saint Louis. Saving these, there was not even the chance of sincere alliance. The effort to reconcile those jealousies, in an aggressive league under one sacred banner, failed miserably. The wretched detail of scandal and feud among the leaders, the charges of treachery, greedy avarice, and personal ambition which disfigure the account from first to last, there is no need to dwell on now. They were the inevitable working-out of the spirit of Feudalism, when its heterogeneous forces were gathered in one huge camp, trained under a score of independent chiefs. The grossest vices of military life were never more grossly displayed than by these Soldiers of the Cross.

And so we find here again the incurable mischief of the double theory of sovereignty asserted by the Church. It was not enough to be a spiritual power, disciplined, patient, brave, gentle, — such as she had been, to a good degree, at an earlier day, — to confront and to subdue the shocking disorders, violences, and cruelties of the secular State. The Church must claim the powers, and grasp the weapons, and maintain herself by the methods, of political empire. She must be spiritual at once and secular, ecclesiastical and political.

And so, in her greatest enterprise, nearest to her

heart and pushed with her most persistent will, she must admit that whole flood of evil and violence. She must condone that monstrous riot of vice and crime. She must even triumph in the frightful license of military conquest, which her very mission was to check and rebuke. "To kill or to be killed for Christ's sake," preached St. Bernard to the Templar Knights, "is alike righteous and alike safe."

The divided life of the Church is reflected, again, in the armies of the Church. Religious fervor, passionate enthusiasm, military valor, alternating with bursts of penitence and contrition, rage of battle melting into tears of tender and devout emotion; and, on the other side, unbridled ferocity, brutal license, treachery, revenge,—every vice and every crime engendered in the life of camps. The streets of that same Jerusalem which the Crusaders had gazed at with tender and passionate emotion,—to whose assault they had been fired by what they took for the celestial vision of an armed Knight on the Mount of Olives,—ran blood (say the accounts) up to the horses' knees and bridles, in the vast massacre which followed the assault; and that hideous stream swept down on its surface the bodies or severed limbs of helpless captives,—men, women, and children,—slaughtered in cold blood without pity. Again a few hours, and the streets and squares were cleansed, to make space for the pious prayers and grateful thanksgivings of the weeping, kneeling, awe-struck conquerors.

The victors in the first assault of the Albigensian Crusade report officially a massacre of twenty thousand. "Shall we spare those, if we find any, of the true faith?" asked the soldiery. "Kill all," was the immortal reply of the priest; "the Lord will know his own!" *   And — for one more illustration of that temper — when a party of ruffians in Languedoc had scoured the country for murder and pillage, they came at length upon a group of seven helpless fugitives, whom with pious joy they instantly seized and burned alive; so, by one horrible sacrifice, expiating the deadly sins they had committed in the heat of passion. That "act of faith" insured their pardon for it all. After a century familiar to such horrors, these were the deeds to which Innocent III., deliberately and with open eyes, gave official license and encouragement.

I have no mind to follow up the strange and sanguinary story. It has instruction for us, only as the following-out of the ecclesiastical policy I have before described. For the Crusades are the one great enterprise in arms of the spiritual empire of Rome. All its pretensions of universal dominion are stated upon that effort. The series begins, continues, and declines with the greatness and splendor of that Empire. The crusading achievements run parallel — or rather alternate, stage after stage — with the efforts to meet in arms, or to subdue by curse and interdict, the secular power, the constant rival of the Church. They make part of the same long tale of ecclesiastical ambition.

* Arnauld, the Pope's legate, at the taking of Béziers, July, 1209 As to the authenticity of these words, see *Histoire des Cathares ou Albigeois*, by Carl Schmidt, vol. i. p. 229.

The purpose of an armed Crusade was very near to the heart of Hildebrand.* The Holy War was proclaimed by his immediate followers and disciples. The flame of its enthusiasm was diligently fanned by the whole line of his ambitious and able successors — by none more eagerly than by Innocent III., who literally died of its consuming fever. Its fires faded out only just before that sharp decline in the fortunes of the Papacy marked by the life of Boniface VIII. For near a century it succeeded in maintaining a Christian Kingdom of Jerusalem in close affiliation with the court of Rome. For near sixty years it reduced Constantinople under the dominion of the West, and made the Christian world nominally one empire of the faith. So that it serves very completely as a gauge or test of the aggressive power of the Papacy, and as a measure of the greatest height and breadth of spiritual dominion it ever attained.

In the view now taken, it is hard to see in the Crusades anything else than a horrible crime and a ghastly failure, incurred by the guilty ambition of the Church, — the translating into fact of the great Lie on which the pretensions of the Church were built.

Still, taken by itself, this is not the view we should be content to take. And it would not be a true view. We are dealing with human actors and human motives. As a Divine institution it is true, and on the ground of her superhuman claim, the Church is effectually condemned by these gigantic consecrated horrors. At the bar of history she can henceforth at

* See Epistles, book i., ep. 49.

best plead as a penitent; or, if unrepentant, abide the deep and unforgetting curse of outraged Humanity.

But that is when we judge the Church by its own pretensions, as man's infallible and heaven-appointed guide. Its unholy ambition, its prodigality of crime, simply reduce it to the level of its secular rivals in empire. Its crimes and violences are no worse in themselves than those of Feudalism. Its far-reaching policy compares even favorably with that of other builders and holders of imperial power. Its attack on Palestine in the eleventh century was no more wanton or wicked than England's attacks on Afghanistan and Egypt in the nineteenth. If these can be justified by any imperial theory or ethics of defence, to the same code the Mediæval spiritual empire may appeal, at least as fairly.

But there are two views of this matter not yet noticed, of which one seems to be plainly evaded and the other overlooked by the average historian. Indeed, to feel the force of either, one must go to first-hand evidence, in the documents of the time. The first is, the great real terror felt at the Mahometan inroad, which made the first plainly avowed motive of the Crusade; the other is, the great real success, in shifting the battle-ground from Europe to Asia, and so, in all human probability, delaying the European conquests of the Turks for three hundred and fifty years. If the latter view is correct, then the Crusades had a far higher success than any conquest they sought; for, without any exaggeration, it might be said that they saved the civilization of Europe from the storm which blasted that of Asia.

As to the morals of conquest and invasion, I do not think they need to enter into the account. Certainly, the Turks did not appeal to any code of international right to justify them in their steady and desolating advance. Certainly, they could appeal to no such code against the arms of Godfrey. The only thing that might possibly raise a doubt, is whether the terror was real enough or great enough to serve as the true motive — or rather, as a justifying reason — of the Crusade. Such a doubt cannot be met absolutely. The best answer we can give it is to listen to the words spoken at the time.

As to the appeals of Peter the Hermit, which raised the tempest of popular enthusiasm essential to any great enterprise, they, no doubt, were addressed not to statesmanship, but to pure passion or else pure superstition. The insults suffered by pilgrims, the abomination of desolation in holy places, the horror of infidel worship in sight of Calvary and where the temple of Solomon once stood, — these, and things like these, were the theme of his eloquence, as he rode from village to village, in pilgrim's garb, wild and lean, mounted on an ass, winning repute among the multitude as a miracle-worker and a saint. He was the inspired guide and the sufficient defence to the disorderly troop that went out as pioneers under Walter the Penniless; and, when he escaped the wholesale destruction of that forlorn company, he accompanied the host of Godfrey, to receive their homage under the walls of conquered Jerusalem.

It was a deeper and more intelligent motive, mistaken or not, that raised the armed force of the First

Crusade. The Saracens, we must remember, still held the fairest part of Spain and all North Africa, showing a hostile front to Europe. They had occupied Sicily and Southern Italy, disputing them against the Greek Empire and the invading Normans. The strength of Mahometanism was reinforced by a Turkish or Tartar horde, fanatic fighters and brutes in ferocity, who for more than a century had pushed steadily towards the West, and were now almost under the walls of Constantinople. The appeal of the Emperor Alexis, after recounting their hideous brutalities, goes on to say:—

"Almost the entire mainland, from Jerusalem as far as Greece, with many other lands and islands which we cannot enumerate, even to Thrace, is already invaded by them. Scarce anything remains to us but the Capital itself; and this they threaten to take from us at once, unless the help of God and the faithful Latins come to our relief. The Marmora they have occupied with two hundred ships, built for them by kidnapped Greeks whom they force to man them; and thus Constantinople is menaced at once by sea and land."

It was three hundred and sixty years from the date of this appeal that Constantinople was taken at length by the Ottoman force, which holds it to this day. Three centuries' respite, it is fair to say, was due to the powerful diversion effected by the crusading force.

Again, it is fair to listen to the motive set forth by Pope Urban before the great Council at Clermont, in 1095. I copy from the three reports of his address, or from the three several addresses, made on that occasion : —

"Turn," he says, "turn those arms which you have unlawfully stained with mutual slaughter, against the enemies of the faith and of the Christian name! By this act, well pleasing to God, redeem the robberies, burnings, plunders, murders, and other such like things, which they that do shall not inherit the kingdom of God. . . .

" Fear not enemies who fight cowardly with arrows from a distance, — men thin and weak from their dry and parched lands ; you, vigorous and strong, from a temperate climate. Even if you die of their poisoned shafts, it is glorious martyrdom. . . .

" Let those be now soldiers, who before were robbers. Now let them fight justly against barbarians, who before fought against kindred and brothers. Now let them gain eternal reward, who served before for petty hire. Let them toil for double honor, who wore themselves out for the ruin of body and soul. . . .

" Do you not know, — you Germans, Saxons, Poles, Bohemians, Hungarians, — though you do not yet feel the Turk and Saracen raging in your vitals, by what little space they are parted from you, by strait or river? Half Italy has long been held by the Saracens. They have come so far as to invade and besiege Rome itself, the See of Peter, still wet with martyrs' blood. Till now the Empire was our barrier on the north ; but to-day the Emperor barely keeps his hold on Constantinople. Soon you will see the same ruin falling on your own heads ; your wives torn from your embrace ; your daughters dragged from your arms ; children and young men hurried along with you into slavery. The great Charles expelled the Saracens from Italy, the Holy Land, and Jerusalem. Are the

Franks the only Christian nation? Almighty God will be with you. He will send his angel from heaven before your face, to direct your steps. Take arms, then, Christians! to rescue the sepulchre of the Lord. Eternal glory will be your reward, and inestimable worldly wealth besides."

We need not cross-question too sharply the grounds of this appeal. It is at least as good as the majority of the manifestoes by which generals and statesmen claim aid from the God of battles. The language I have quoted is no doubt genuine in substance, whether spoken in the formal Latin of the transcript, or in Urban's native French; and it answers well to the best political and moral sentiment of the day. How deep and genuine was the passion to which it made appeal, we may judge from the reckoning which has been made, that not less than two millions of Christian lives were sacrificed in the several crusading adventures. First and last not less than six millions enlisted for the adventure. For a century or more, it may be fairly said that sovereign, noble, or man-at-arms was dishonored who did not hold himself ready at call to embark in the holy war.

Even little children, in 1213, were drafted into an army by some fanatic, persuaded that innocence and not arms would win the victories of faith, and went famishing and crying over that hopeless march, pitifully asking, at each town they came in sight of, *Is that Jerusalem?* until they all perished of hardship, or were swept up into foreign slavery. A swarm of beggars and peasants, under the name of *Pastourcaux*, swelling at length to a ferocious horde of a hundred thousand, swept France from north to south, in 1251, in the fanatical hope of rescuing their holy king held captive in Egypt; and kept the country in terror, till they happily dispersed in three detachments and obscurely perished.

A proud, strong Barbarossa, a crafty Philip, a turbulent and headstrong Richard are lifted at once and alike on the tide of that great passion. A sceptic, self-indulgent, passionate Frederic II.—brilliant man-of-the-world that he is, and far too intimate with Saracen culture to feel any fanatic hate of it — must turn from his real enemies, and waste the best vigor of his life in the hopeless enterprise. Many a feudal lord sold or pawned at ruinous rates the landed estate which was his dearest pride as well as his real wealth, and beggared his family to enrich some church or monastery. Many a prince or noble took a vow never to return; or perhaps, safe at home once more, was scourged back by reproaches of wife or friend, to die in the next campaign. The passion was as genuine, and to us it seems as childlike, as that of boys. The disorders and feuds which made the enterprise hopeless from the start seem like children's quarrels, fought out with the fury and strength of men. The helpless way in which the heroes of the Crusade drifted into them, is of itself an evidence how frank and transparent the original passion was.

In other words, the Crusade was possible, because it just fell in with the temper of the time. The Church took advantage of that temper to promote its own policy, its power over men's conscience and soul, and its worldly wealth. It is but fair to say, besides, that the Church improved the time for some of its own nobler and better work. It proclaimed anew the Truce of God, the duty of peace among all Christians, soldiers in one army, pledged to one cause. It extended the term of truce, — from four days in the week to four months employed in preparation; to four years allowed for the campaign, to be sacred from private war. It proclaimed itself the special guardian and protector of those who must be left behind, — the serf to till the field, the wife to keep the home, the child whose father served in the army of the Lord. In this way, true to its better calling, the Church was able to enforce many a lesson of justice and mercy, too often defied in those days of strife.

Thus far, I have spoken of what we may conceive as the real motive of the Crusade, in the mind of its leaders, — in particular, the church policy that prompted and guided the enterprise. Other points, however, come into view when we look at it as an event in history. The unacknowledged motives and the unintended consequences must go to the making of our historical judgment.

The unacknowledged motives make the ground of our moral verdict on the act, which has been sufficiently implied already. The unintended consequences enter more or less into our notion of a general Providence — that is, the working out of impersonal Law — in the course of human events : not the wilful forcing of good out of things evil, but the series of compensations and adjustments, without which any historical evolution at all would be impossible. It seems best to suggest them not in detail, but in two broad views : first, as they affected society and the State; second, as they affected general culture and the Church.

As the first of these unintended consequences may be set down the check given to the enormous evils and disorders of feudal society. It does not appear that Feudalism carried in itself any principle likely to correct those terrible disorders. So far as we can see, its forces were committed to a war of mutual extermination. The sullen despotism of an Asiatic monarchy, or else a dead level of petty strifes hardly above that of marauding tribes, seems the natural goal of such a state of things. From this it was saved by two powerful influences, — the discipline of the Church, working from within in the direction of an ideal unity; and the turning of its energies outwardly, in the direction of crusading enterprise.

What we may call a common consciousness of Christendom would most likely never have existed, at least in any developed form, but for this or some equivalent. The sentiment of unity, as a check to feudal disintegration, was assiduously nurtured all along, through the symbols, creed, and instructions of the Church. The mere sight of the Cross, gilded or carved, at the peak of every pinnacle, or embroidered on every sacred robe, in all Christian countries, was a daily reminder of that unity below the discord. But not till the cross was worn upon the breast, or glowed on waving banners, or flashed from the emblazoned shield of great hosts gathered from all those lands, and marching to one end, could the thought of it enter those rude hearts as a moving force.

It may be said, then, that the public sentiment of Christendom, the consciousness of a common civilization and common law, was in large part the creation of these two centuries of crusading adventure. This effect was even strengthened by the vast misery and destruction which that adventure brought about. Not merely the humanizing sense of a common sacrifice and a common sorrow. But, it must be remembered, the genius of Feudalism itself was a spirit of uncontrolled independence, — which, in the progress of society, means a vast growth of crimes of violence. At first view, it would seem as if half the population of feudal countries were naturally what we should call a criminal class, — owning no lord, ever ready for any act of violence, any deed of blood. At a word from Pope Innocent, France swarms with vagrant adventurers, eager to slake their fury in the licensed horrors of the Albigensian Crusade. Half a century later, another word of another Pope brings upon southern Italy the unspeakable outrage of French invasion, to be expiated in the great revenge of the "Sicilian Vespers."

No doubt the Church was guilty of creating a part of the lawless passion which she stood ready to consecrate and condone. But the enormous slaughter of those two hundred years must have carried away as with a flood an unknown mass of latent criminality waiting vent, and secured to Europe, so far, better and safer conditions of peaceful progress. The murderers and plunderers of half Christendom found their booty and their grave in the devouring East.

Still plainer is the effect of the Crusades on the

higher civilization, which of right should be in keeping of the Church. A larger horizon was opened suddenly before the cramped intelligence and rude imagination of the Western nations. To the dainty view of the courtiers of Alexis, and of his lively and learned daughter, the historian-princess Anna Comnena, the knights and nobles of the Crusade were at best splendid barbarians.* The Eastern populations were in dismay at the allies they had invoked,—who, indeed, often showed themselves the most remorseless of their plunderers. Their most cordial wish would have been, that Latin and Turk should exterminate each the other.

The Crusaders not only found in Constantinople a luxury, splendor, art, learning, quite new and strange to them, — an irresistible bait to their lust of booty, — but they found these things, too, in the very enemies they went out to fight as infidel and heathen.

---

* Here is the picture of a Feudal Knight as he looked to those courtly eyes, taken from the description given by Anna Comnena of Robert Guiscard : "This Robert was Norman by birth, of obscure fortune, of lordly temper ($\tau\upsilon\rho\alpha\nu\nu\iota\kappa\delta$s), most crafty in spirit, mighty of hand, most formidable to lay hands on the wealth and treasure of the great, invincible in deed, effecting his aim against all contradiction. In size of body so great as to surpass the tallest ; of ruddy complexion and yellow hair ; broad-shouldered ; his eyes almost literally flashing fire ; where the form should be broad, well-shaped, and where slender, well-proportioned : thus was all in keeping from head to foot, as I have often heard from many. As to his voice, — Homer says of Achilles that when he shouted, the hearers had the idea of a noisy multitude ; and so this man's shout, they say, would put to flight many myriads. Being such as I have said in fortune, frame, and temper, he was, it would seem, invincible, and under obedience to no man. For such are mighty natures, even if they be of meaner fortune." — *Alexiad*, book i. p. 23.

More grace of courtesy, equal valor in the field, a better understanding and keeping of terms of truce, unsuspected wonders of mechanical skill and elegance in the arts of life, humanity and mercy contrasting too often with their own rude ferocity, were a revelation to them of something outside of Christendom better of its kind than anything that Christendom could show. Insensibly they learned to envy and admire what they came prepared to hate. Something like remorse at the destruction and waste they had wrought upon this gorgeous Eastern life, softened the temper of the invaders. Glimpses of a larger humanity brought about a reaction against their cruel and narrow prejudice. As Christendom became conscious of its own life in a new sense of unity beneath its discords, so it became capable and willing to receive an influence from abroad, greatly needed to enlarge the horizon and purify the atmosphere of that life.

This influence was seen first and most in the new freedom of thought and the quick germinating of a new poetic culture, in the populations nearest and openest to receive it. The heavy mist of monastic austerity began to lift from man's imagination. The early literature of Romance was due in great part to that new light shining from the East. Those heresies which stirred the Church's wrath were quickened into life by the breath that blew over from Saracen shores. The sunny south of France was the home, at one and the same time, of the lay of Troubadours and of the Albigensian doctrine, — which found shelter together in the gay court of Raymond of Provence, and were blotted out together in the horrible Crusade.

The Church might conquer for the hour, by sword and torch; but the new thought had life, and was sure to bloom again. The stern will of the Pope scourged Frederick II. into a war from which his policy and his intelligence recoiled;* but at home, in his beloved Sicily, the fairest flowers of Saracen fancy were cherished, and wrought into that wreath of poetic culture which he was first to weave about the brow of Italy.

And so, as the war-cloud dissolved and passed away, new and vigorous forms of life were found emerging from its shadow. The Crusade, which the Church had stimulated so eagerly and forced on so obstinately, is found to have undermined the very foundation of faith, on which the Church reposed. Her doctrine of austere morality, her teaching of a tender humanity, were contrasted against the avalanche of crime she had set loose, the appalling cruelty she had invoked. Her system of doctrine, which looked to the eye like a granite foundation of her spiritual claim, was honeycombed by a thousand speculations set adrift in that sea of adventure. Her rigid theory of no salvation outside her own bounds was contradicted, to conscience and common-sense, by the spectacle of a life more fair and desirable, a morality that seemed fully as good, in the lands of the Infidel.

A commercial civilization began to take the place of ecclesiastical discipline. The era of the Crusades was also the era of the birth and splendor of the Free Cities. A scientific spirit began to undermine old

* I would add, his humanity and conscience, if it appeared that he ever had any.

reverence for the one Creed. A warm breath of poetry and luxury began to melt away the sharp boundaries that had stood so long to divide sacred and profane. The Church by her own act had thrown down the barrier which guarded her domain from invasion of foreign influences; and her undivided spiritual Empire was the price she had to pay. The crisis was long in passing. It represents the struggle and agony of two hundred years. But it *was* a crisis. And when the long fever of the crusading period was past, Europe had already been borne into the consciousness of a new, a richer, and a larger life.

V.

CHIVALRY.

I HAVE already alluded to the Romantic literature that sprang up in southern France, as one fruit of the state of society growing out of the Crusades. It has a special interest for us as students of the period ; both because it is the earliest literary growth of Modern Europe, and as the voice of a civilization prematurely crushed in the horrors of the Albigensian War.

It is also the first exhibition of the Romantic spirit : that is, of a sentiment which we associate peculiarly with the manners of Chivalry, and with the homage paid to women by the social code of modern times. The phase of society it shows suggests to us the question : What was it, which gave that tone to barbarian and feudal manners, and has made the modern position of women so thoroughly different not only from that in the primitive barbarism, but from anything we find in the highest refinement of Pagan antiquity ?

This difference of position may be stated under three distinct heads : intellectual culture, which suggests such representative names as Mrs. Somerville, Harriet Martineau, and George Eliot; a certain moral dignity and authority, giving to women a lead and virtual sovereignty in modern society, — as in the examples of Mme. Récamier and Lady Holland, or as shown in the moral heroism of Elizabeth Fry and Florence Nightingale; and the defence thrown round those who are physically weaker by a strict code of Etiquette, or minor morals, insuring to them the necessary forms of dignity and respect. It is with the last two of these that the subject in hand has especially to do. And I may here say, provisionally, that they both point to an aristocratic state of society, as distinct from despotic on the one side or democratic on the other. Of this, more presently.

I have just mentioned a few representative names of women in modern society. It is not too much to say, that an ancient Greek or Roman — Aristophanes or Plato, Cicero or Horace — could not possibly have made the position of either of these women intelligible to his thought. Let us glance at a few of the names best known, of classical antiquity.

Perhaps Helen in the Odyssey comes nearest of anything in antiquity to the modern woman of society, — as Penelope is the purest Greek type of the queen of home. Both belong, it will be noticed, to the most intensely aristocratic state of society that ancient history has recorded. It may even be doubted whether the social rank accorded to the modern *lady* might not have been interpreted to the Greek mind through these noble Homeric types; but it could never have entered into the spirit of Greek society. The women of Greek tragedy — Clytæmnestra, Antigone, Electra — are not characters, but *dramatis personæ.* They are grand but sombre silhouettes, cast by a later imagination upon the curtain of a legendary past.

In historical Greece I recall only the single example of Gorgo, wife of Leonidas, who, as child or woman, has left a conspicuous memory of honor. And she, it will also be noticed, belongs to the most rigidly aristocratic state of Greece; to a time earlier by a generation or two than that "fierce democratie" which has left the deepest mark on history. Mahaffy, in his "Social Life of Greece," tells very instructively of the change that came about with the fall of the "tyrants" and their petty courts, where poets and women were held in honor; and of the hard, rude life of the city home in the age of Pericles, — the time of manhood suffrage among the free population, and of pushing to the wall those who had not the protection of the vote.

The Greeks themselves accounted for the disappearance of women from their public life by the following legend.* When Neptune strove with Pallas which should give a name to the new city, Athens, he struck the earth with his trident, and there sprang forth a horse armed for battle; but at the stroke of the goddess there came up an olive, sign of prosperity and peace. The votes of the men, we are told, would have given the award to Neptune, but Pallas called the women to her aid, and was victorious. Jealous at this, the city thenceforth abolished female suffrage, which seems to have existed in the mythic time; and, whatever the political aspirations of Athenian women, we hear no more of them, except it be in the

* Found in Saint Augustine's *De Civitate Dei*, xviii. 9.

broad farce of Aristophanes, travestying the debates and tricks of the male Agora. A foreign woman, like Aspasia, is no real exception. Pericles made her his wife, but could not make her a citizen; and her brilliant career boded no good to the state or homes of Athens. The pleasantest picture we have of Greek home-life is in Xenophon, where a young husband tells Socrates how, in a tender and fatherly way, he tamed his "wild bird," his shy girl-bride of fifteen, and taught her the simple skill by which she might become the trusted manager and mistress of his estate.

In Rome the historic names are more familiar, and stand out more distinctly, each with some strong mark of pathetic interest. The chaste and thrifty Lucretia, amidst her maids; the mother of Coriolanus, supplicating her son to spare his native city; the school-girl Virginia, rescued from slavery by the sudden, sharp blow of her father's knife; Cornelia, with her "jewels,"—her brave, high-born boys,—or in her austere widowhood, when they had died, first martyrs of the century of civil war; Cicero's daughter Tullia, a memory of pure human sorrow in the brutal and selfish struggles of the time; Portia, Cato's daughter, the noble wife of Brutus;" Agrippina, the courageous and devoted wife of Germanicus,—these are nearly all the names that history delights to honor.

Of all States of antiquity, no other paid so genuine honor to matron or maid. But, take them at their best, the comparative poverty of the associations they suggest contrasts strongly with the wealth of feminine influence to be found in all periods of modern society.

A different ideal began to be formed when the memory of Christian female martyrs was first held in honor. But many centuries had yet to pass, before these became the glorified Saints of the Roman calendar and of Christian Art.

The two causes commonly given of the difference which came about in these centuries, and which separates the modern woman so widely from the ancient, are these: The influence of Christianity, creating a moral ideal of womanhood, which, through the teaching of the Church and the impressions of Art, has penetrated the modern mind and gives the key to modern manners; and the old German reverence for women, described with such emphasis by Tacitus,* which entered as one element into the constitution of feudal society, and established the wife's or daughter's rank in the feudal household.

Both these influences, Christian and Pagan, may count for much. Examples here and there of Christian martyr, queen, or lady, hint what that ideal may have been, as it entered into the life of the high-born and powerful, softening the harsh temper of Feudalism. As to the women of pagan Germany,† I do not know that we have anywhere a true picture of them, unless it be that type of fierce pride and passionate devotion in Chriemhild of the Nibelungen, and in the full-length portraits by Gregory of Tours of the

---

* The words of Tacitus are: "They hold that in them [women] is something divine and prophetic; and neither scorn their counsels nor neglect their warning" (literally, `responses, as of an oracle).

† The famous picture given by Ammianus Marcellinus describes to us the women of Ancient Gaul.

barbaric queens Fredegond and Brunehild. These, if they prove anything, prove that the ladies of that rude time were quite as violent, treacherous, and cruel as their lords. The barbaric type of woman is even farther from the modern than that of pagan antiquity.

The change, accordingly, of which I speak seems due to something more precise than either of those influences, and different alike from both. The spirit of Christianity in the early Middle Age, as touching the relations of men and women, was purely ascetic, anti-social, guided by monks and priests, — whose notions on the subject have that strange mixture of austerity and grossness which we are apt to think of as the fruit of the confessional.* The Church ideal is contrasted, point by point, against the Feudal. In fact, the contrast was too sharp to admit of much influence either way, from one to the other.

We must bear in mind, too, the essential haughtiness and ferocity of Feudalism, and its horrible brutality of temper. Now pride and cruelty, inherited from the old barbaric life, show nowhere more brutally than in the relations between the armed knight or noble and the defenceless woman — though she might be wife or daughter, maid or mistress — delivered to his grasp.† To take a case of nothing grosser than

---

* The political marriage of Countess Matilda at forty-four with a boy of nineteen, Guelf of Bavaria, is set down by the monkish annalist to "incontinency."

† As historical examples, preserved at full length, however distorted, we have the queens of Lothair II. in the ninth century, and of Henry IV. in the eleventh. Barbarities so gross as those here charged would most likely have been impossible, in the highest social class, when Chivalry was in vogue.

mere cruelty: An English Knight, giving fatherly counsel to his daughters, warns them against exasperating the hot temper of their future lords, by this "little story." A certain lady had persisted in nagging her husband in some dispute at table; when — at a loss for better argument — he settled the point by knocking her down with his fist, and then kicking her in the face, which so bruised and disfigured her that for shame she never showed herself again before any guest.

This, we observe, is told not as an exceptional case of barbarity (which perhaps it is), but as a sample of what women had to fear if they were like-minded with that poor lady. Cruelty, in short, such as one hears of among the most brutal of the very lowest orders in England, or in the savagery of the frontier, was distinctly a feature of feudal times. And that cruelty was perfectly impartial to man, woman, or child.*

The influence which partly corrected it — at least, in the case of women — is known to us in a general way by the name of Chivalry. This, it is held, softened the manners of that rude time, and tempered the Knight's fierce courage with the spirit of knightly courtesy. It is worth while to inquire how and how far this is true.

There are different ways of tracing the effect, and of accounting for it. Some regard Chivalry as having

---

* I speak here only of the treatment of social equals. What it was towards the humbler unprotected classes, we may see in that most pitiful and tragic account given by Michelet in *La Sorcière*, before referred to.

had no real existence, apart from military Knighthood; at best as being the moral ideal conceived in a feudal aristocracy, — the soul, so to speak, of which Feudalism was the form. Others, again, speak of it as if it were an institution precise and formal as a monastic Order, or modern Free-masonry. The French historian, Martin, says that the word means, properly, the act of consecration, or inauguration, by which — following an old Celtic custom mentioned by Julius Cæsar — the young warrior devoted himself to the service of his lord, and entered formally on his military career; in particular, *mounting the horse*, which was the final act of the ceremony.

The initiation of the young Knight has often been described. It came, like everything else of a formal nature in that time, to take a religious character. It supposed a threefold novitiate, as varlet, youth, and squire; a vigil, — watching by night in arms, with set prayers; a preparatory bath, which was a sort of baptism. After all these, the candidate was clad in symbolic robes of white, red, and black,—white, to recall the vow of purity; red, to show that the Knight's blood must be freely shed for the right; black, as symbol of the death he is ever ready to face: and lastly, he was solemnly invested with arms, to be used only in honorable conflict. The whole ceremony is an appeal to that mingled religious and martial enthusiasm (*joie*) so intensely characteristic of the time, which made possible the stupendous enterprise of the Crusades.

But the name Chivalry implies one thing more, to explain the associations of the word, and to show its effect on modern manners. It implies that unwritten but imperative Code, curiously elaborate, by which it prescribed the relations of knight and lady. This belongs especially to the period of the Crusades. Several things worked together at this time to bring women to the front, and to give them a social rank unattainable before. The mere fact that for generation after generation armed men left Europe literally by the hundred thousand (for years at any rate, and oftenest never to return); that during a whole century any man of rank would have been dishonored if he had held back from this vast adventure, — this one thing carried with it an immense effect on the position of their mothers, wives, and sisters who were left behind.

In many a case, women of that time fully shared the crusading ardor. Thus Adela, Countess of Blois, whose husband came home before the campaign was over, compelled him to return to Palestine, where he "fought gloriously and found a glorious death." We are surprised at finding something like a Court of noble ladies amid the horrors of battle or siege, — as that of Queen Eleanor at Antioch. Saint Louis is accompanied by his wife Margaret to Damietta; and, when prisoner, he will make no terms with his captors without consent of "the Queen, who is his lady."

Blanche of Castile, his mother, was of another mind. "When she saw her son wearing the cross, she was struck as fearfully as if she had looked upon him dead." His duty was to his people; there was grave danger in his absence. But he said: "Have we not still her who was the support of my childhood and guide of my youth?—her, whose wisdom has saved the State in so many perils, who in my absence will want neither courage nor strength to suppress disorders?"

Again, to this authority the Lady of the feudal household was already long trained. In the picture we get of Mediæval society, the ladies of the castle must have had a weary and monotonous life at best: almost perpetual imprisonment; gaunt stone walls; neither chimney nor glass window; screened from the bleak wind, at best, by hanging draperies; no books; next to no furnishing or household art; with raiment often of the scantiest;* tied up helplessly as dolls, one would think, in the stiffly gorgeous fashions of the day. Yet it is clear that great authority devolved on them in those frequent seasons when their lords were away, in battle or at the chase,—generally for a few days only, but still leaving them a very responsible conduct of affairs. The name "Lady" itself, in its derivation and traditions, hints at such authority. And it is hardly possible to exaggerate the effect in the spirit and all the forms of feudal society, when this authority was so greatly extended, through near two centuries of crusading adventure.

The effect was none the less powerful for having

---

* Apparently (poor things) without any night-clothes at all. "Quant la royne se esveilla, elle vit la chambre toute embrasée de feu, et sailli sus toute nue, et prist la touaille, et la jeta toute ardent en la mer."—Joinville, *Histoire de Saint Louis*, ch. 128. See also *Morte d'Arthur*, book xii. ch. 1.

been diffused and somewhat obscure; none the less
real, that few historians appear to have recognized it
save in the most general terms, or in special famous
cases, — as in that of the queen-mother just referred
to. In the administration of local laws, where each
baron was a petty sovereign; in the defence of castles
from attack, of which Sir Walter Scott gives some
examples; even, as in the case of Joanna Countess
of Toulouse, actual command of forces in the field, —
we see how power was held and used by women.

Froissart has left a striking picture of Philippa of
Hainault, queen of Edward III., at the battle of New-
castle against the Scotch: "The Queen of England
came to the place where her army was, and remained
until it was drawn out in four battalions. . . . She
now advanced among them, and entreated them to do
their duty well in defending the honor of their lord
and king, and urged them for the love of God to fight
manfully." * To which they pledged themselves to
their best service, — better, perhaps, than if the King
had been there in person. Her intercession, a little
later, to save the lives of the six burghers of Calais,
makes one of the most familiar and touching of all
historical scenes. Like everything else in history
especially dramatic, it is doubted by certain critics;
but, like everything else in history especially dramatic, it is likely to remain an article of accepted faith.
The generation that told it was very likely to have
seen it.

* This was a century later than the Crusades; but a time when
foreign war had the same effect, to throw power into the hands of
women in the absence of men of rank.

Here is another picture from Froissart of the Countess of Montfort besieged in Hennebon : —

"The Countess, clad in armor, mounted a war-horse, and galloped up and down the streets, calling on the inhabitants to defend themselves honorably. She caused damosells and other women to cut short their kirtles [another text says, "tear up the pavements"], carry stones to the ramparts, and hurl them on their enemies. She mounted a high tower, to see how her men behaved ; and seeing the enemies' camp forsaken by the men-at-arms who had come to the assault, she came down instantly, mounted her horse armed as she was, collected three hundred knights, sallied out at their head by another gate, galloped up to the enemies' tents, cut them down and set them on fire ; then, finding her retreat cut off, made speed with part of her company to the castle of Brest, where they were received with great joy."

So the Countess of Salisbury, esteemed one of the most beautiful and virtuous women in England, when besieged in the castle of Wark, " comforted much those within the castle ; and from the sweetness of her looks, and the charm of being encouraged by so beautiful a lady, one man in time of need [says Froissart] ought to be worth two." King Edward's coming relieved the castle. And now, —

" As soon as the Lady knew of the King's coming, she set open the gates, and came out so richly beseen that every man marvelled of her beauty, and could not cease to regard her nobleness, with her great beauty and the gracious words and countenance that she made. When she came to the King, she knelt down to the earth, thanking him of his succor, and so led him into the castle to make him cheer and honor, as she that could right well do it. Every man regarded her marvellously; the King himself could not withhold his regarding of her; for he thought that he never saw before so noble nor so fair a lady: he was stricken therewith to the heart with a sparkle of fine love; he thought no lady in the world so worthy to be beloved as she. Thus they entered the castle hand in hand."

The deference and loyal obedience to women shown in these examples, in a time of rudeness, cruelty, and incessant war, was part both of the gallantry and of the intensely aristocratic temper of the time. The feeling of family honor, the feudal pride of rank, made it fit that the "lady of the land" should rule in person, rather than give authority to any lieutenant of meaner birth.

Two very celebrated names are brought together in Shakspeare's "King John," which may serve as two types of the feudal Queen,—Eleanor of Guienne, and Blanche of Castile. Queen Eleanor had accompanied Louis VII. on the Second Crusade, where he had to take her away by main force from the coquetries and intrigues she persisted in at the gay court of Antioch. After her divorce from Louis, she married Henry Plantagenet, transferring near half of France to the English crown, and was at the heart of the long family quarrels which divided that unhappy house,—the mother of Richard, Geoffrey, and John; an ambitious, high-tempered, cruel, and unprincipled woman, whose early training had been amid the gayeties of southern France, who herself had presided in Parliaments of Love, and been sung in tender strains by troubadours.

Blanche, the queen-mother of Louis IX., was typical in another way, — austere, pure, vigilant, faithful to the utmost as guardian of the people and protector of law amidst the unspeakable miseries inflicted on France by the ill-advised Crusade. Too jealous of her maternal authority, she constantly humbled and grieved her daughter-in-law, the gentler Margaret, but never lost the reverence of her son, who at news of her death showed "so great dole, that for two days one could never speak to him."

So came about that *homage of woman* which is in great part the soul of Chivalry. It is symbolized in the ceremony of investiture of the young knight. Each successive piece of armor, from helm to spur, is delivered by some lady, who fastens it with her own hands, while she recites the special service it betokens, — the mailed hand, strong to strike for justice; the mailed feet, swift to the undoing of a wrong. It was confirmed by the custom which put the boy of noble birth into the tutelage of a lady, whose will he was bound to obey, and whom he must regard as the sovereign of his life. Come to manhood, the romantic code of the time required him to pledge his personal service to some one lady, — who might be in rank far above him, to whom he might perhaps never venture to speak a word in his life, — who was invested with a claim to all the extravagance of homage, and all the exaggerated expression of it, that he could pay.*

* One famous and very romantic case was that of a knight who devoted himself to the service of the Countess of Tripoli, having heard from afar of her transcendent beauty, and for all his life did not so much as aspire to lift his eyes to her, or even that she should

We understand at once the peril that lay in this worship, — often fantastic, sometimes grotesque in its fashion of speech or act, sometimes capricious, presumptuous, immoral. But we see, too, that it built up a strong fence of custom and dignified ceremonial, which might and did powerfully protect women in the exposures of an age essentially violent and lawless.

In connection with this, there is reason to think that the singular institution of Courts or Parliaments of Love was a more important agency than has generally been represented. As they may be said to have presided at the birth of modern romantic literature, and to have promoted the first movement of thought outside the enchanted circle of theology, they deserve a brief mention here. Besides, these Courts seem in all likelihood to have been the real creators of that code of modern manners by which the social predominance of women has been asserted for about seven hundred years.

We gather that it was in no spirit of mere levity or travesty or fun that this singular tribunal was organized, or merely to divert the long monotony of an idle life by the parody of Court and Parliament, but because women found something of the protection they needed in its organized and formal rule. How formally it was in fact organized is not clear. The name appears to be given very loosely,— perhaps to a single referee as to some point of social or sentimental etiquette ; sometimes to what seems to have been a council of ladies of rank, in full robes of ceremony.

One gets a very pretty picture of these stately groups of noble ladies, clad in green, with necklace of gold, gathered under the broad elm-shadows in the sunny May-time of the South, with their gay retinue of minstrel knights and squires, in grave debate on the points of manners and morals brought before them. These debates are represented as being strictly formal and logical, conducted in set stanzas pro and con, every conceivable dilemma being argued out with a subtilty and intricacy not excelled in the regular Courts of Law. The questions discussed were mostly, no doubt, matters of sentiment and gallantry, — of which many amusing cases have been recorded, and many more invented. But they were also questions of morals and decorum. The decrees — technically, *Arrêts d'Amour* — distinctly claimed authority over conduct; and were confirmed, we are told, by the precedents of Roman Law, the decisions of Church Fathers, and the testimony of Greek and Roman Poets. The name " Court of Manners " might seem to have as good title for this tribunal as " Court of Love." *

* In Chaucer's curious poem ''The Court of Love '' — which represents the God of Love as holding his Court in person, and ends with a quaint litany sung in his praise by a choir of birds with little texts of Latin scripture — the Lover's Code is formally set down in twenty Articles. These are an expansion of the earlier and simpler code, the frank sentimentalism of which may be thus rudely disguised in rhyme : —

> Virtue alone of love can worthy make ;
> More than one love may no true lover take ;
> Nor true love be of joy insatiate :
> True love is love's reward, and claims no other ;
> None but a felon tells the love-tale of a brother.

This curious tribunal came up early in the time of the Crusades, and continued for more than two hundred and fifty years, — that is, from 1120 to 1382. Its origin takes us back to the sentimental rhapsodies of the Troubadours, — the echo in verse of the same romantic temper that delighted in tales of gallantry and the pomp of arms, — and to the court of Toulouse, then the most brilliant in Europe, most famous for the splendors of tournament and the "gay science" of minstrelsy, brightest at the very eve of the horrible twenty years' Crusade which turned that fair land to a smoking ruin.

The contest of wit followed the display of arms. After three days of Tournament, — in which boys, youths, and knights had respectively shown their skill, — a fourth day followed, devoted to the contests of Verse (*tensons*). In these, the lady-judges, quick of wit and apt in rhyme, would often take part, with improvisation or retort; while their verdict conferred the glory of victory, or imposed the shame of defeat : —

> "Ladies, whose bright eyes
> Rain influence, and judge the prize
> Of wit or arms, while all contend
> To win her grace, whom all commend."

It belongs rather to the history of Literature to speak of these poetic contentions, the first pallid flower of modern verse. We here learn how the light, easy, loose-flowing Provençal rhyme came to have its conventional rules, and to be developed into a "science" as formal and as artificial as that of heraldry; and how it had its legitimate successor in the Italian tales and the French allegorical romances, imitated by Chaucer, Spenser, and Shakspeare. And from these, again, we come by lineal descent to the most popular, characteristic, and voluminous — I was going to say, most elaborate — form of literature in our own day. The maxims and ethics of the modern Sentimental Novel have come straight down to us from the Mediæval Romance, — expanded and (we may hope) improved by time, but without much change of substance.

There is one difference, which shows the change of date. What the Court of Love debated as abstract principle, or laid down as formal precedent, the Sentimental Novel assumes for its starting-place, and illustrates in the infinite play of incident, amidst the infinite diversities of modern manners. The early romances attempt something of the same thing, — as in "Amadis of Gaul" and "Morte d'Arthur," — with no end of vague, aimless adventure, with quaint childlikeness, and with rare passages of great tenderness and beauty. Thus, from "Amadis of Gaul":—

"The Child of the Sea was now twelve years old, and he served the Queen. But now that Oriana was there, the Queen gave her the Child of the Sea, that he should serve her. And Oriana said that *it pleased her;* and that word which she said the Child kept in his heart, so that he never lost it from his memory. And in all his life he was never weary of serving her; and his heart was surrendered to her. And this love lasted so long as they lasted; for as well as he loved her did she also love him.

"But the Child of the Sea, who knew nothing of her love, thought himself presumptuous to have placed thoughts on her, and durst not speak to her; and she, who loved him in her heart, was careful not to speak more with him than with another; but their eyes delighted to reveal to the heart what was the thing on earth that they loved best. And now the time came, that he thought he could take arms if he were knighted; and this he greatly desired, thinking that he would do such things that, if he lived, his mistress should esteem him."

In all romantic literature it would be hard to find anything prettier than this spirit of perfect chivalry mirrored in the noble children. That this tender, respectful homage should have been conceived as one of the possible phases for a man's affection to take, shows the immense departure from the pagan and classic time, — shows how far the way was prepared for the modern, nobler play of sentiment. The ancient hero might, like Hector, be all that was tender and true; but he had no *upward* look to his beloved. Religion might and did create a certain celestial, passionless ideal of womanhood. But it was for Chivalry to feel, and for Romance to tell, "the divinity that doth hedge" the object of a worthy love, which is the creed of the best modern novelists.

Here I will quote from Miss Preston's ingenious and delicate exposition : —

"Chivalry, the *motif* of all Mediæval romance, was the youngest dream concerning the social relations of the modern world, after its conversion to Christianity, — a part of the general ecstasy of its recent regeneration. It was the bright, audacious ideal of a love between mortal man and woman, as wholly supersensual as the allegorical love of the Redeemer for his bride the Church. The knight assumed, under the formal sanction of the Church, a triple vow, which constituted his practical religion,—to serve his master Christ, to succor the defenceless, to love one woman, and her supremely. It seems not naturally to have occurred to the Latinized mind of southern Europe to inquire, *What woman?* If, as indeed usually happened, she chanced to be the wife of another man, it was equal. The love of Chivalry was a something which transcended all accidental relations and prudential arrangements. And the love which is so melodiously celebrated by the more refined of the southern Troubadours is, in very truth, just such a sublimated sentiment. It is incapable of coarse offence. Natural jealousy cannot attain unto it. We may listen for hours to the echoes of these rapturous lyrics, and find them always the same, — sweet, ardent, innocent because unmoral, breathing an air of sunny license, awakening not the faintest vibration of the sense of right and wrong." *

It is an extenuation of the sentimental laxity of this code that it was a sort of protest, in the name of natural feeling, against the hard secular ambition that generally made the feudal marriage, — of which that of Eleanor † of Guienne with Henry of England, ten years her junior, was a signal and fatal example. A second marriage of sentiment — possibly Platonic — to a second mate was not only distinctly allowed by the lay code, but is even said to have been sanctioned or dissolved by the offices of a priest. It came to be

* "Troubadours and Trouvères."

† To this Eleanor is ascribed the following apocryphal and notorious addition to the Code : —

  " More loves than one may knight or lady take ;
   Nor nought can love deny for true love's sake."

a saying, that the formal marriage is incompatible with love. "Madam," said Sir Launcelot of the Lake (it was by the funeral barge of the maid of Astolat), "I love not to be constrained to love; for love must arise of the heart, and not by no constraint." "That is truth," said the King and many noble knights. "Love is free in himself, and never will be bounden; for where he is bounden he loseth himself." The code itself is sometimes ascribed to the knights and ladies of Arthur's court; and with all its highflown sentiment, its deadly jealousies, its rudeness, and its fatal mischiefs, it is nowhere illustrated so well as in that marvel of adventure, the "Morte d'Arthur," from which these words are taken.

Launcelot was no saint, as we know. We find quite another ideal of Knighthood in this passionate lament :—

"Then went Sir Bors unto Sir Ector and told him how there lay his brother Sir Launcelot dead. And then Sir Ector threw his shield, sword, and helm from him; and when he beheld Sir Launcelot's visage, he fell down in a swoon. And when he awaked, it were hard any tongue to tell the doleful complaints that he made for his brother. 'Ah, Launcelot,' he said, 'thou wert head of all Christian knights; and now I dare say,' said Sir Ector, 'thou Sir Launcelot, there thou liest, that thou wert never matched of earthly knight's hand; and thou wert the courtiest knight that ever bare shield; and thou wert the truest friend to thy lover that ever bestrode horse; and thou wert the truest lover of a sinful man that ever loved woman; and thou wert the kindest man that ever strake with sword; and thou wert the goodliest person that ever

came among press of knights; and thou wert the meekest
man and the gentlest that ever ate in hall among ladies;
and thou wert the sternest knight to thy mortal foe that
ever put spear in the rest!' Then there was weeping and
dolour out of measure. Thus they kept Sir Launcelot's
corpse on loft fifteen days, and then they buried it with
great devotion."

The sentiment so assiduously trained has had its
share in creating that larger world of thought and
imagination in which we live. What lay at the heart
of Chivalry — the homage paid to Woman — was in
reality the first and most essential condition of the
comparative security and elevation of modern manners. Nothing is frivolous or absurd, in the view of
history, which leads plainly to an important result.
Chivalry, says a French historian, "is one of the great
phases of the development of the human soul. Love
of Woman is the ideal of Chivalry of the Middle
Age, as love of Country is the ideal of classical antiquity, and as exclusive Divine love is the ideal of
the first Christian centuries."

That invisible shield of homage and respect, slight
and often deceptive as it may have been, made the
comparative purity and dignity of women possible in
an age of incredible license and ferocity. The code
of social ethics was imperfect, extravagant, romantic,
impossible, perilously immoral, looked at from some
directions; yet in one sense it did save society for
something better. It became an organized public
opinion, — the first of all, the strongest of all, the
public opinion of a privileged class: imperative, formidable, irresistible, because its judgments must be

enforced through the imagination alone. What the
terrors of the Church were to the multitude, that the
terrors of the Code were to the proud noble.

What, it has been asked, insured obedience to its
decree? The same, it has been answered, that forbade the Knight to stay at home in peace, while his
companions-in-arms were in the toils of chase or the
perils of war; the same that obliges the Gamester,
who owns no claim of justice, yet to pay his debts
of honor; the same that compels the Duellist, in defiance of public law, and hating the code, yet to stand
up (like Alexander Hamilton) to be the victim of his
antagonist's sword or bullet. The one all-sufficient
penalty is Dishonor.

One other curious testimony witnesses to the
strength, at this age, of the sentiment that lay at the
root of Chivalry. That homage of woman, which
was its inspiration and ideal, was in spirit utterly
hostile to the ascetic teachings of the Church; yet it
succeeded in making the Church its best ally. As
long as they could, churchmen argued against it, but
in vain. What they could not prevent, they did their
best — as their fashion was and is — to appropriate.
A tender pietist of the ninth century had maintained
the mystical doctrine of the Real Presence; and had
coupled with it declarations that seemed to claim for
the Mother of Jesus a sanctity more than human.
The Real Presence had in the course of three centuries become the established creed; and along with it,
in the age of Chivalry, men were not far from paying
worship to a feminine Divinity.

It was during the period of the Crusades that the

doctrine of the Immaculate Conception of the Virgin Mary first took strong hold upon the imagination of Christendom. In the very middle of the twelfth century, half way between Godfrey and Richard, when the crusading fervor was at its height, Saint Bernard, the devout and impassioned orator, who stirred half Europe to frenzy for the imperilled kingdom of Jerusalem, set himself in vain to plead and preach against the new doctrine, — in particular, against the "Festival of the Immaculate Conception" held at Lyons in 1140. The doctrine waited till our own day (1854) to be formally registered in the Roman Creed. But the sentiment and the fervent belief of it were anticipated by more than seven centuries, as the true religion of Chivalry. It needed hardly a change of phrase for the Knight to turn the loyal homage he paid his liege-lady to the worship of "Our Lady," the only being his heart was moved really to adore.

I shall take occasion here to add a few words of moral. Whatever has been gained for women socially, so far, has been gained under the forms and privileges of Aristocracy. It is a much more interesting thing to us to remark, that what has been so gained we have to keep, if we can, under the levelling conditions of Democracy. What was the privilege of the few is to be made, if possible, the right of all. How this may be done, it is for the best wisdom and temper to trace out. The time to women of most absolute and conspicuous social supremacy was the time of the French Monarchy of the last century: not a good but an evil time, — the time of Madame Parabère and Madame de Pompadour; the time of

Marie Antoinette and the Princess de Lamballe,—
when, as M. Taine reminds us, the throne was still
held up by the fading memory of what Feudalism
had done for an earlier age.

The Revolution, in avenging mankind on the insolent luxury of the class, introduced a time of coarser
manners. "The age of Chivalry is gone," said Burke.
And with it, he thought, had disappeared forever
"that generous loyalty to rank and sex; that subordination of the heart which kept alive, even in ser-
vitude itself, the spirit of an exalted freedom; the
unbought grace of life, the cheap defence of nations,
the nurse of manly sentiment and heroic enterprise;
that sensibility of principle, that chastity of honor,
which felt a stain like a wound; which inspired
courage while it mitigated ferocity, which ennobled
whatever it touched, and under which vice itself lost
half its evil by losing all its grossness."

There may be some difference of opinion what the
Chivalry of the eighteenth century was worth, which
(as has been said) permitted every vice, and recognized only a single virtue,—readiness to fight a duel.
Burke's eloquent lamentation finds no echo in the
conscience of our day. Still, there is danger lest
something may have perished with it which the world
should not willingly let die. The great wars of this
century, the rude conflicts of opinion, the democratic
drift, all tend to make men impatient of the formal
courtesies of an earlier time. This cannot be helped;
it need not, perhaps, be regretted. But in the change
it may be feared that women have lost more than
they are aware. It is a sad descent, after all, from

"Waverley" to "Vanity Fair." The spirit of anti-chivalry which shines in brilliant satires on "the woman of the period" is an ill exchange for the romance it threatens to displace.

Observers have warned us of an increasing rudeness of manners in these last few years, both in Europe and America. I do not say that it is so; but I do say that it rests very much with women whether it shall be so. They can, in self-defence, insist more on those rules of courtesy and ceremony which a careless good-humor so easily forgets to enforce. Laws of justice are to protect the weak; rules of debate, to protect the minority; customs of society and etiquette, to protect those who cannot make good their rights by brute force. If we remember what was the rude and barbarous origin of society, and then think what it is to-day, we are fairly amazed at the miracle which has been wrought to make the strong and haughty submissive, and to put the weak in the place of authority and power.

It is Chivalry that has wrought this fine miracle for us; and what is left us of the formal courtesies which are the defences of that authority, is our inheritance from the days of Chivalry. It is our recognition of a sphere within which women can still be, as they were then, sovereign and paramount. That sphere, it is true, is conventional and strictly limited; but no possible or imaginary widening-out of the political horizon could compensate the loss of it. I can imagine that an intelligent woman should not understand (as, indeed, how can she?) or believe in the knightly homage which every generous-minded man is eager to pay her, in what we may call the chivalrous period of his life, — say from eighteen to eighty. But, understanding that such a sentiment is possible, I cannot imagine that she would consent to break the secret charm, the invisible spell, which still gives her power to claim it.

Once again. The great widening in our day of the recognized field of women's culture and activity points to a time when a riper civilization will make them sharers with men on more equal terms in all the largest aims and noblest work of life. It is quite time, already, that the small jealousies of superior and inferior, as between the two halves of humanity, should cease. They are in bad taste, they are irritating, they work harm chiefly to the weaker, they only widen the gulf they are meant to bridge. On what terms the equal alliance is to be had, it is quite too soon to predict. Experiment and mistake, defeat and disappointment, are so far the conditions under which each forward step must be taken. Our glance upon a part of the painful road travelled in the past leaves us two thoughts in closing,—one to encourage, one to warn. To encourage : for, since that miracle has once been wrought, which bound the strong in a certain devout homage to the weak, nothing need be despaired of in the moral future of humanity. To warn : lest the invisible spell woven about our ideal of womanhood should be dispelled — its charm read backward, its magic word revoked, its delicate thread unspun, the law of its hold forgotten — by those who owe to it the reflected glory of what has been, and the fairer hope of what may hereafter be.

VI.

THE RELIGIOUS ORDERS.

WHAT was, at bottom, the source of Ecclesiastical power? How did the Church get and keep her fast hold on men's imagination, which is the deepest source of power? How was she able to work on the conscience and conviction of men (having nothing but these to appeal to in the last resort), so as for centuries to defy all other authority, and to come off victorious in every passage of arms she had with the powers of the world?

In one sense, these questions cannot be fully answered. The atmosphere of our earth is invisible and impalpable; but it presses with many tons' weight upon every one of us, and is in fact the greatest mechanical force we have to allow for in our engineering; while it is not likely that, standing outside, we could form the least notion of what it really is. The Mediæval Church moved and had its being in an atmosphere (so to speak) of its own creating, which we can very imperfectly estimate, standing as we do outside. Still, there are some symptoms and conditions of it very instructive, on ever so imperfect understanding of them.

I have said something already of the system of its doctrine and ceremony and discipline, and of the powerful appeal through them to the imagination. I have myself, standing in the old Cathedral at Avignon, — amid the thunder of cannon, the deep pealing of the great cathedral bell, the loud strains of martial music, the powerful harmonies of the organ, the intoxicating fumes of incense, and the gorgeous ecclesiastical pomp that heralded the festival of "Christ's Body," — felt for one hour of my life, with a sense almost of terror, the mightiness of that spell by which the Church for so many ages held captive the souls of men. These things count for much. But they were, after all, only the outside show of what rested on a deep moral foundation, and made the spiritual atmosphere in which men breathed and lived.

In particular, the Catholic Church has had this source of strength,— that its moral ideal, its theory of what makes the perfect life, has been from the beginning incorporated in Institutions, and exhibited in organized forms before the world ; that it could always appeal to this ideal, and to this visible witness ; that any crisis could be met, or any movement of reform begun, by drawing from the inexhaustible reservoir of moral force stored up in its Religious Orders. We have now to see the value of this resource at the most critical and momentous period of its existence.

In order to bring the topic within convenient limits, it will be well to say that I have in mind three groups of Religious or Monastic Orders, — the Resident Monks (or "regular clergy"), of which the best known are the Benedictine and Cistercian ; the Military Orders of Knights of the Temple and of the

Hospital; and the Mendicant Orders of Dominicans and Franciscans.* The last two groups, military and mendicant, belong especially to the time of the Crusades. The Military Orders were founded early in the twelfth century, for war against the Saracen; the Mendicant Orders early in the thirteenth, to help in the war against heresy and unbelief.

It is to be understood, further, that these Orders simply represent an enormous reserve force, or volunteer militia, which the Church has always had at command, gathered under many names, and subject to many different forms of discipline. Those names and forms amount to several score at least,—I think, to hundreds,—some of men, some of women, enlisted for a great variety of services, and known by a corresponding variety of costume and discipline. A sketch of some of them fills eight thick quarto volumes of the standard authority.† Those I have mentioned are to be taken merely as types. The easiest course will be to speak first of the features common to them all; then of some points that belong specially to each.

First of all, to find the source of the moral power embodied in these institutions, we must conceive as distinctly as we can the ideal pattern professed in the moral doctrine of the Church. It is in some ways fundamentally different from our own moral ideal, or what we are accustomed to consider as the Christian ideal. We are apt to do it injustice,—both by failing to see it as it is, and by judging it too much by certain

* They include also the Augustinians and Carmelites.
† Helyot: Paris, 1714–19.

consequences it inevitably led to. Of these I shall have a word to say presently. Our first aim must be to get if we can into the attitude of those who honestly held it, and see how it appeared to them.

We may sum up very broadly by saying that Poverty and Celibacy are the two features which most distinctly mark the Catholic idea of the higher religious life. I have already had occasion several times to bring these into notice, — first, as shown in the austerities and ascetic practice of the Eastern Monks; then, as the essential conditions of the great work done by the Missionaries of the Church, in converting and civilizing the barbarous tribes; then, as the basis of canon rule in the discipline of the Priesthood; and lastly, as contrasting the Church theory of life most sharply against the spirit of Feudalism.

It is well to keep these points in mind. But it is also needful, now, to look at the matter more attentively. In particular, we should understand that what I have called the Catholic ideal, which was at the root of monastic life, was held in perfectly good faith to have been the true teaching of Jesus and his disciples. Of Jesus himself, as our example, it was incessantly cited, that "though he was rich yet for our sakes he became poor;" that he kept himself free from all domestic ties; that he voluntarily took upon him the condition and service of a slave, and voluntarily died a slave's death upon the cross.

Poverty was taught by such texts as these: "Take no thought for the morrow;" "Blessed are the poor;" "Give to him that asketh thee;" "Let him that hath two coats give to him that hath none;" "If thou wilt be perfect, sell all that thou hast and give to the poor;" "No man that warreth entangleth himself with the affairs of this life;" "God hath chosen the poor of this world rich in faith;" "It is easier for a camel to go through the eye of a needle than for a rich man to inherit the kingdom of God."

The moral merit of Celibacy was harder to make out from Scripture, doubtless, since family life is both at the foundation of civil society and the source of all the common virtues. But at least the higher estate was thought to be signified in the birth of Jesus from a virgin, and in his own unmarried life; in his saying, "If a man hate not father, mother, wife, and children, he cannot be my disciple;" and in such texts as where — speaking of those who "have made themselves celibates [as the phrase is generally unstood] for the kingdom of heaven's sake" — he says, "He that is able to receive it, let him receive it;" or where Paul says, "Let them that have wives be as they that have none;" or where the Apocalypse speaks of the "one hundred and forty-four thousand which were not defiled with women, for they are virgins, which follow the Lamb whithersoever he goeth."

It is not necessary to follow out these hints of New Testament asceticism to the deductions which monastic writers are fond of drawing from them; or to copy from those writers the humiliating and often brutal terms in which they speak — not simply of sins of indulgence, or of marriage in itself, but of the very nature of women, as to be thought of only with abhorrence and contempt. I have shown before how this monastic extravagance was met by the counter extravagance of Chivalry, which found in women the objects of a fantastic but very serviceable worship.

It is a curious symptom of this double perversity of sentiment that we do not find anywhere in these times a single hint—at least, I cannot remember any —of fatherly tenderness to a daughter, or brotherly love to a sister. Of high-flown sexual or anti-sexual sentiment we have abundance ; and, if that is all, we could not have a livelier proof of the distortion of natural and wholesome feeling under those two false ideals.

It is however necessary, and perhaps it is enough, to remember that absolute Poverty and absolute separation of the sexes under the name Virginity were the two *essential* features of the religious life, as conceived by the Mediæval Church, and realized, as well as might be, in the Religious Orders.

Now it is no answer to the Catholic theory, to say that Poverty is hostile to the natural order of human society, or that Celibacy is hostile to the natural order of human virtue. Such notions belong to the modern mind, but not to the mediæval mind. The very theory and claim the Church was built on, is that Christ introduced a supernatural order of society and a supernatural order of virtue. Argument from the ordinary conditions of life or the natural moralities is irrelevant. " My kingdom is not of this world," says Jesus. The more it could be shown to be alien and abhorrent to the principles on which this world is governed, the clearer the proof of its superhuman origin. Reason is mere rebellion. The infidel may deny ; the believer has only to submit.

Nothing, accordingly, is more marked than the audacious and uncompromising tone in which the Monastic ideal is assumed throughout as the Christian ideal of life.

Again, it is easy to point to the victories of that faith as a proof that it is indeed the truth of God. Saint Margaret, standing in pure maidenhood, helpless and unharmed, beside the great dragon disabled under that invisible spell, is the type in Art not of a sublime theory merely, but of a long record of fact, — disguised often in fable and legend, yet fruitful in historical results. How closely the martyr spirit was allied in its source with what we know afterwards as Monasticism, I have illustrated before.* And of the later phases of monasticism it may be said, without any exaggeration, that Poverty and Celibacy were the armor with which the Church had overcome the world.

Nay, they were the weapons with which the Church struck, in its great battle with the Empire, for the sovereignty of the world. The reforms of Hildebrand were a revolt of Monasticism against the secular temper of Feudalism in the Church. The long war waged by Gregory VII. and his successors against the State was the attempt, all but successful in appearance, to bring all civil and political society under monastic control. The great Military Orders of the twelfth century were the armed alliance of Monkhood with the Church. The great Mendicant Orders of the thirteenth century were a vast monastic body of reserve, strengthening the Church in the

* Early Christianity, pp. 172-175.

long crisis of its struggle, fighting bravely but vainly against its decline. The astonishing creation of the Jesuit Order in the sixteenth century was a revival of the intensest monastic spirit, as a foil and counterpoise to the reforming enthusiasm evoked by Martin Luther. So that, for many a century, Poverty and Celibacy were in truth the power that gave its victories to the Church, and all but overcame the world.

Nor will this seem wonderful, if we think of the immense strength of *absolute* devotion to any service; and add to it the immense increase of strength which comes from taking away what might hinder that absolute devotion. The Church well understood the power and victory that lay in the monastic vow, and steadily taught her doctrine and pressed her discipline so as to keep the monastic ideal constantly in view as the true consummation of the Christian life. " If thou wilt be perfect, sell all that thou hast and give to the poor." " He that is able to receive it, let him receive it."

Other things were added to these two,—the vow of Obedience, insuring that the vast army would act at need as one man, and all its resources of individual genius and energy would be used as tools of a single will. And, besides this, special demands were made of the several Orders :—of the earlier Monks, to live in a common dwelling, with strict community of goods, under the rule of Abbot or Prior; of the Knights of St. John, to tend the wounded and sick in hospitals, and, in common with the Templars, to be ready at call to fight the Saracen; of the Mendicant Orders, to own absolutely no possessions, but to lead a wandering life and subsist on alms; of the Jesuits, to hold themselves at the Pope's order for missionary service, wherever they might be sent. Each of these is an immense increase of the store of moral force at the service of the Church. But the essential conditions of monastic life are those two, — Poverty and Celibacy : " Sell all that thou hast and give to the poor ; " " He that is able to receive it, let him receive it."

Again, it is beside the purpose to say that these cannot make a rule of conduct for men in general. The very theory of them is that they are a rule, or way of life, for those only who make religion a special vocation. Whether religion, in its professed higher form, ought thus to be taken out from common life and made a separate vocation, is a very serious question, into which I do not propose to enter now. Taking the view of it held at the time we are trying to understand, there is no obvious reason why a man who feels drawn that way should not make a " vocation " of religion, as well (for example) as of sculpture, or law, or scientific discovery. We do not blame men for devoting their lives to such walks as these. Nay, if they undertake such tasks at all, the more exclusively they follow them up, the more we honor such men in their calling.

There is one point of difference, — that the " religious " life assumes itself to be the standard by which all other lives are to be judged; and this is a standing affront to the common pride of men. An astronomer, a chemist, or an engineer makes no such claim, and so he invites no such jealousy. But even this prejudice did not lie against the religious profession at a time when the only confessed rule of morals was the teaching of the Church. That the monastic ideal is extravagant and false to us is not to the point. The age that created it honored its full claim.

We see, then, what an appeal to religious ardor lay in the very sternness of that ascetic ideal: " He that is able to receive it, let him receive it !" What man thinks himself unable ? What man of average moral courage does not feel himself stirred by that appeal ? I have spoken before of what we may call "the ascetic passion," and of the powerful hold it has on minds of a certain class.* I have shown the striking evidence of it in the crowds that were drawn to emulate the strange austerities of the East; or were eager to en- roll themselves under the severe rule of Saint Bene- dict; or thronged to the rude hills and woods where Saint Columban drew the reins of that rule more sharply; or with Saint Boniface took on them the hardship and hazard of missionary life in barbarian forests.

The enthusiasm caught and spread like a conta- gion. Benedict from the beginning found it necessary to set up the rigid fence of a four years' discipline, before granting the privilege of the vow that made it a lifelong yoke. The dreary austerities of Columban seem only to have stirred a livelier emulation among the candidates for that profession.

And, in a very real sense, it was a privilege. As Count Montalembert will tell you, the monastic life, instead of the gloom and austerity we might think,

* Early Christianity, p. 173.

was one of proverbial friendliness, hilarity, and good cheer. A single night spent in the hospitality of the monks of St. Bernard, on one of the passes of the Alps, does not count for much by way of testimony; but it helps me very much to understand the testimony from other sources, to the cheerful, calm, contented spirit claimed always to be characteristic of monastic life, — at least, as we find it in conditions fairly favorable.

And why should it not be so? If we will think of it, the life of a monastery is only a carrying out and carrying on of the friendly, kindly, cheery life we enjoy together in our youth, at college, and, more cordially yet, in a professional school together. Just those features of college life which endear it most to students are what we sometimes call its "monastic" features, — survivals from a former period, in a time that begins already to murmur and protest against them. Yet, out of our own experience of life, what can we remember in its way so captivating?

It is not worth while here to go into the routine and the daily round of duties of monastic life. To most of us the very thought of them would be weary and intolerable. Of our own student life the brevity makes half the charm. Forty years of it instead of four would be apt to make an average man a sluggard, an imbecile, or a sot. So it was with the monastic orders, — to believe one half the outcries against them in their most flourishing days, or to watch the periodical efforts at reform. Popular as that path of life had come to be, it was of necessity mostly filled with average men. The baser side of it fills whole volumes of vain protest, and rings in many a popular song and satire,—long before Chaucer's vigorous picture, and long after.

The better side of it makes whole volumes, again, of some of the sweetest and noblest biographies ever written. The heroes of monasticism are not the heroes of modern life. All put together, they would not furnish out one such soul as William of Orange, or Gustavus, or Milton. Independence of thought, liberty of conscience, they renounced once for all in taking upon them the monastic vow. All the larger enterprises, all the broad humanities, which to our mind make a great career, were rigidly shut off by a barrier that could not be crossed. All the warmth and wealth of social and domestic life was a field of forbidden fruit, to be entered only through the gateway of unpardonable sin. Things — as we understand and handle them—they might not see or know, but only the shadows and forms of things. The ideal life of the monk is a life of pure contemplation. His active service is to defend the tradition of other men's thought, to urge upon the popular conscience the ghostly hopes and fears that assail the popular imagination, at best to drive out devils by prayer and fasting.

To us it is a life pallid, artificial, unwholesome,— even if not, as I fear it often was, squalid, comfortless, slovenly. But the half of human nature which it allowed to grow was developed often into a singular sweetness, serenity, and moral beauty. I will mention only, as types, the bright examples of the Dominican and Franciscan Orders, Saint Thomas

Aquinas and Saint Bonaventura, — the serenity of temper and immense mental activity of the one, the devout and exalted mystic fervor of the other, and the warm, generous, lifelong friendship between the two; * and, besides these, the exceeding moral purity and beauty that rays out from the pictures of the artist-monk Fra Angelico, who never painted those celestial faces but on his knees.

The monastic ideal of human character does not come very near our notion of the greatest and best a man can be. As it recedes in time, its features become unreal and dim to us. Yet it is a type which we could not spare from that vast picture-gallery in which History shows us the possibilities of our common humanity, without losing something of the very noblest and best she has treasured there.

Such examples, however, are far enough from showing us the average of monastic life. This was, I suppose, in moral quality about like the average life outside, allowing for its special narrownesses, bigotries, and exemptions.

We have, to begin with, the deadly jealousies which often broke out between the monastic orders, — as they will sometimes between allied forces in the same campaign. Thus, for one pitiful example, on the 7th of May, 1318, four of the seceders from the Franciscans, professing to return to the more rigid discipline

* "That (pointing to the Crucifix) is the book I learn from," said Bonaventura to Thomas, who wondered at his depth of spiritual knowledge; and visiting him afterwards, he saw an angel beside him, dictating, as he composed his treatise on the Trinity. So each knew that the other was inspired, and a saint. (See Vaughan's "St. Thomas of Aquin.")

of their founder, and contumaciously refusing to accept the laxer rule, were burned alive as heretics at Marseilles. More than two thousand were so burned, in the next fifty years, before that austere heresy was rooted out. The long story of wrangling and calumnies that preceded this shocking tragedy need not be rehearsed.* It is enough to see that the very fervor of the motive, the heat of the religious life, begot of itself the intensity of jealousy and hate in a vulgar mind.

And then, from Damian (Hildebrand's coadjutor) down, there is a succession of charges and protests against gross and infamous vices, which seem the characteristic vices of monastic life, — gluttony being the most universal and the mildest. Discipline labored incessantly against these abuses ; but the task always had to be done afresh. The natural resort was to fall back on the original rule, and reinforce the first motive. This could often be best done by building again upon a new foundation. The effective remedy (for a time) was not reform but secession, and a severer rule in some new place. Hence, in part, the great multiplicity of the religious orders. I will give only one example.

Saint Bernard (1091–1153) is the most eminent example of monastic life at the time of its greatest authority and splendor. He was for years the chief counsellor of the Pope, the trusted adviser of sovereigns and people, the moral dictator (it has been said) of half Europe, the eloquent preacher of the Second Crusade, the champion of Church orthodoxy against

* See, in particular, Hauréau : *Bernard Délicieux.*

the swarming heresies of the day, and in chief against
the brilliant free-thinker Abelard.   As an instance
of his power, it is said of him that, "charged by the
Pope to excite the religious zeal of the people of
France and Germany [in the Crusade], he accomplished his mission with fatally memorable success.
Fields, towns, cities, and castles were in many places
almost depopulated; and innumerable legions, fired
by his prophetic eloquence, hurried to the East, nine
tenths of whom never saw their homes again."

From early youth he had been a zealot for monastic life.   Five brothers and a sister he had urged
into that way of salvation.   The lax Cistercian rule
did not content him; and he withdrew with a few
enthusiasts into the rude valley of Clairvaux, which
his name has made famous, — then so bare and bleak
as to chill their very heart by the sight, and from its
terrors of brigandage known by the name Wormwood.
But he was a fiery disciplinarian, and made them
share his rough diet of beach-leaf broth and bread
made of barley, beans, and cockle.   He had no patience with those who complained of hardship, ill fare,
or fever.   "It no way befits religion," he writes,* "to
seek remedies for the body, nor is it good for health
either.   You may now and then take some cheap
herb, such as poor men may,—and this is done sometimes.   But to buy drugs,† to hunt up doctors, to
take doses, is unbecoming to religion, and hostile to
purity."   So wilfully harsh and rough he made that
seat of authority, from which, like a king in the wil-
derness, he ruled the conscience of his time.   In all

* Epistle 345.   † Species, "spices."

10

these toils, which he underwent with lean and wasted frame, in a life which was one long malady, he seems to his biographer "like a lamb that is forced to drag a plough."

Louis VII. of France, in remorse at burning alive some thirteen hundred inhabitants of a revolted town, was won by him, against the persuasion of his counsellors, to embark in the disastrous enterprise of the Second Crusade (1147). Conrad of Germany, more discreetly, long hung aloof; but Bernard so moved his conscience in advance, and so charged personally home upon him in public discourse, that in contrition and deep emotion he hastened to take the fatal vow. Bernard had already displayed his eager zeal in the suppression of heresy in the South of France. In the great assembly at Sens — where Abelard had been summoned to meet the charge of heresy, while king and nobles, prelates, and a great throng of students waited breathless for the dispute between the chief religious authority and the most daring and brilliant disputer of the time — the manhood of Abelard suddenly gave way; he stood dumb before the expecting crowd; he submitted dumbly to the arrogant charges of his opponent; he appealed to Rome, professed submission, craved pardon of the Church, and went to die in the convent at Cluny, an humbled, contrite, and heart-broken man.

Under the insidious temptation of such triumphs, Bernard carried his austere authority too far. He claimed, perhaps believed, that he was inspired to predict a glorious success to the Crusade; and when the miserable remnant returned to reproach him with the deceit, he could only fall back on the poor equivocation of saying it was their own sins that lost the victory. As if he did not know the iniquities of war beforehand! as if the very host which his own word had hardly kept from the great crime of a massacre of innocent Jews could possibly be holy and stainless warriors of the Lord! With him the authority of monkhood reached its height of splendor, and after him it slowly waned.*

We see two powerful causes at work to contribute to this decline. The first is the steady and inevitable departure from the monastic ideal, in the increasing wealth and luxury of the Religious Orders. Their ostentatious sanctity was an irresistible appeal to the corrupting bounty of a credulous time. Modern luxury had not been invented, it is true; and there was no such thing as Art, except for the glory of the Church. If there had been, it is hard to imagine that those generous rills would have flowed so steadily to that centre; that even in a far wealthier age the Religious Houses would have grown rich so fast. One is tempted to think that the very climate and soil were more generous then than now.†

The richest estates, the noblest architecture, the

* The deaths of the three great Abbots — Suger (1152), Bernard (1153), and Peter the Venerable (1156) — mark the date when the Church had clearly degenerated from being a power mainly spiritual to one whose aims were at least as much political. The dynasty represented by these three names, with that of Norbert († 1134), has had no successor of equal eminence since.

† There is some astronomical and some geographical ground for this. The summer season was perceptibly longer in the thirteenth century than now; and the primitive forest had not been so thoroughly cleared away.

most sumptuous hospitality, had come to hide, decorate, or corrupt the primitive austerity. A few rugged ascetics, like Bernard, strove vainly against the tide. The Soldiers of the Cross had come, from the miseries and hardships of the East, to outdo all the splendors of their brethren in repose at home. Their appeal to the imagination was still more irresistible. Their life had trained them to a more vigorous self-assertion and a larger capacity of indulgence.

The Order of the Templars had begun in the league of a few Crusaders in Jerusalem, more devout, loyal, and resolute than the rest, to devote themselves absolutely to the service of the Temple. It had grown to inordinate wealth, — still testified by the names Temple Bar and Temple Garden in London, their old estate, and the Boulevard of the Temple in Paris, marking where their castle-palace used to be, — and to infamous forms of luxurious vice, it was said, and insolent impieties, charged against them in the ferocious prosecution that at length exterminated the Order in 1312.

The Order of the Hospital, dedicated to John the Baptist, had begun with a group of charitable pilgrims in Palestine, who devoted themselves to the care of the sick, bruised, plundered, dying, of their fellow-pilgrims; and for that sacred service sent out their brethren, never singly but two and two, to solicit alms,—which so flowed in upon them, and their numbers so increased, that in a few years they enrolled a special military service of Knights of St. John, rivals and peers in arms of the haughty Templars. Then, last to leave the Holy Land, they held Cyprus till driven out by the Turk, when for a season they became lords of Rhodes. Forced to an honorable surrender, they next occupied Malta, which they held victoriously in one of the most astonishing sieges on record,* and have been known as Knights of Malta almost to our day. As a piece of secular history, nothing can be more splendid than the record of that heroic Order. But the glory of this world was carrying them farther away from the stern simplicity of their foundation. Military discipline held them up longer than mere monastic discipline could have done. Still, the day of their greatest splendor was also the decline of the genuine ascetic life.

The other cause was the great moral shock from the failure of the Crusades. It is hard to say whether the disastrous result of arms abroad or the ghastly success of fagot and sword at home did most to undermine the spiritual strength of Rome. Some symptoms of the intellectual chaos it will be more convenient to consider at another time. The moral disorder is what concerns us now.

The great Crusade had been begun under the absolute conviction that it was the will of God, and must certainly prevail. More than a century of costly, heroic, often desperate enterprise had been spent upon it, — to result in ignominious and hopeless defeat. Where was the strength of the Lord's arm? Where was the promised help of God?

Meanwhile, the Infidel was triumphant in the East; nay, pressing and threatening close upon Christian

* Making the most brilliant chapter in Prescott's "Philip the Second."

Europe. The Church was bloated with the wealth of slain and impoverished men, who had staked all and lost all at the call and assurance of the Church. Was Mahomet, then, better able or more faithful to defend his own than Christ? Let us worship him, then, men said, instead of Christ! So came on a terrible invasion of despair and unbelief. How genuine and deep the terror must have been, we may see in the desperate endeavors put forth by Innocent III. to crush the rising heresy in Languedoc; in the long and obstinate contention waged by Gregory IX., vainly, to force the emperor Frederick II. as champion of Christendom to a war of hate and extermination against the Saracen.

To the appalled conviction of Christendom, the Emperor himself, its official champion, the most brilliant and powerful sovereign of the time, was at heart an infidel! His name is given, among fifteen or twenty others, as supposed author of an imaginary book, which shows the depth of unbelief that had taken hold on the heart of the age, — "The Three Impostors." No man ever saw a copy of that book.* It was most likely never written, except in the appalled consciousness and imagination of the time. But the rumor went, that minds trained in Christian faith, taught from infancy the mysteries of Christian truth, had come to believe that Moses, Christ, and

* There is a little tract with the title *De Tribus Impostoribus* (Milan, 1864), apparently written some time during the period of the Reformation, most likely near the end of the sixteenth century. The bibliographical notes appended make it probable that no such book appeared at the earlier date.

Mahomet were the three great Deceivers of Mankind. The Jew, the Christian, the Saracen, had been equally deluded. Let them join now in a common unbelief! This charge was specifically made against Frederick in 1239, by Gregory IX.* The infidelity it betokens was something deeper than the mere decay of morals. It was the sapping of the very foundations on which the possibilities of church piety or morality, as then conceived, could rest.

Luxury and unbelief, — these two : and to meet them, as before, a new outburst of monastic fervor; a new organization of religious zeal; a falling back, once more, on the primitive passion and austerities of monasticism. The two symptoms are encountered respectively by the two reformers, Saint Francis and Saint Dominic. The first is the founder of the Franciscans, called also the Gray Friars, the Minorites, or the Cordeliers.† The other is the founder of the Dominicans, called also the Black Friars, the Preachers, or the Jacobins.‡ Together they are called the Mendicant Orders,—signifying that they had no fixed habitation and were bound to hold no property at all, but to subsist absolutely on alms, which they solicited day by day. Both are also sometimes called Preaching Orders : though preaching by way of dogmatic instruction was the special charge of the Dominicans,

* See the letter in Mansi, vol. xxiii. p. 87.

† Friars, that is *fratres*, "brothers ;" Gray, from the color of their tunic ; Minorites, as being least of all in their own esteem ; Cordeliers, from the knotted cord which took the place of belt.

‡ From the street *St. Jacques* ("*Sancti Jacobi*") in Paris, where was one of their famous Houses.

while the Franciscans rather appealed to the conscience by way of rhapsody and passionate fervor.

Saint Dominic (1170–1221), when we first know him, is a young Spanish monk, with the immense capacity of devout fanaticism that runs in Spanish blood. He had been deeply stirred on a journey through Southern France, with his superior, at the radical heresies of that worldly and gay population, so afflictive to the stern monastic temper. In particular, he was distressed and indignant to see that poverty and austerity were on the side of the heretic teachers as against the enormous tyranny and self-indulgence of the servants of the Church. They convert men, he said, "by zealous preaching, by apostolic humility, by austerity, by the show of holiness,— which is after all only a show. We must meet zeal by zeal, humility by humility, the show of holiness by the reality, false preaching by true."

Whatever his own sweet and heavenly spirit according to his Catholic eulogists, his name is a synonym of bleak and intolerant fanaticism. It is fatally associated with the blackest horrors of the crusade against the Albigenses, as well as with the infernal skill and deadly machinery of the Inquisition.* The Order, however, which he founded can justly claim something else besides these horrors ; since it in-

---

* Special Courts for the hunting out and extirpation of heretics were established during that crusade under Dominic and his followers, and made independent of the local authorities. The Inquisition as a permanent tribunal was established in 1233, the same year that Dominic was canonized, and put, in 1244, in charge of the Dominican Order.

cluded, with many other illustrious names, the two greatest intellectual teachers of the Middle Age, — Albert the Great and Saint Thomas of Aquinum. Their intellectual work will concern us a little later.

It belongs more properly to our subject now, to give a brief notice of the other Founder. In Saint Francis (1182–1226) the monastic spirit culminates in a pious fervor, a simplicity of self-renunciation, a certain poetry and passion of the religious life, with which we do not quite find any parallel, at least any in so gracious and winning shape.

This of the inner spirit, however. The outward form is often grotesque, repellent, even if not contempt-ible.* Recovering from a fever that interrupted the gayety of his youth, he conceived an ardent passion for a religious life; and with eager fervor professed that he espoused a Bride of divine and ravishing charms, with whom no earthly beauty could compare, — Poverty. When his father sought to restrain him by process of law, he renounced his authority; stripped himself stark naked before the Court, thus baring himself visibly of all worldly goods; accepted only the mantle which the bishop threw over him in charity, and tied it round him with a knotted cord; chose a damp pit for his sleeping-place; fervently kissed the very ulcers of the patients he waited on in hospitals; and went out to lead a life of absolute

* There is, for example, his strange Christmas tableau, in which he introduced a stable, with ox and ass standing beside the manger, — when he bleated like a sheep as he uttered the word *Bethle-h-e-m*, and licked his lips as if he tasted honey when he pronounced the name of Jesus.

beggary, preaching to wild creatures and the birds, singing on the way his hymns of rapturous praise and joy, — to our brother the flaming Sun, our sister the beaming Moon, our brothers the winds and clouds, our sisters the little singing birds, our brother the Spirit of Life, our sister the Death of the body, who gently releases us from the pains of life.*

Of his rhapsodies, the following do not submit to be abridged : —

" Praised be my Lord for our Brother the Fire, through whom thou givest us light in darkness : he is bright and pleasant, and very mighty and strong!

" Praised be my Lord for our Sister the Water, who is very serviceable unto us, and humble, and precious, and clean !

" Praised be my Lord for our Mother the Earth, which doth sustain us and keep us, and bringeth forth divers fruits, and flowers of many colors, and grass ! "

It is not, perhaps, difficult to understand this fervor and tumult of joy in the simple act of casting off all claim to earthly possessions of any sort. Even a vulgar mind, I should think, a vagrant and a tramp, must feel sometimes a certain wonder and luxury at finding himself floated, without any exertion of his own, on this great sea of Humanity that laps us all about, and is so ready to hold us up if we begin to sink.

Happily, not all or most of us can be tramps, and so put Humanity to too severe a test. But think of

* Very literal pains ; for when he died, his skin, from self-flagellation, was one sore from head to foot.

the same thing as it comes to a religious man, who
has felt vaguely a half-belief in a Providence that
will feed him as it does the ravens, and clothe him
as it does the lilies! He has in his destitution a
new sense of nearness to the mighty Hand and the
everlasting Arms. The dole of charity that comes to
him at his need is, as it were, the immediate gift of
the Infinite. He learns, too easily perhaps, to trust
the Bounty to which he has made his confident appeal. Anxieties come with possession. Anxieties —
bitter anxieties — come also with loss; and yet the
first sense of loss is sometimes the sense, if only mo-
mentary, of a great relief. Voluntary renunciation, I
should think, would always bring with it an experience of great joy. This deep lesson of the religious
life we are apt to forget, and it is perhaps just as well
that we should. But it is brought home to us very
vividly in the strange and yet perfectly intelligible
raptures of the ascetic saint.

I cannot follow out the biography of Saint Francis,
however briefly. His protest in the name of absolute
poverty against growing laxity bore the usual fruit.
The ideal of monastic life can only be held in its in-
tegrity by those who are "able to receive it," and
they are always few. The home of the Founder's
poverty was glorified, in time, by one of the most
costly· and sumptuous of religious edifices. The
"Brothers Minorite," as they called themselves for
humility, became grasping and importunate in their
beggary, till it was complained that the wealth of the
State would all run to their hands. To prevent disputes, cities were partitioned into districts for the four

Mendicant Orders, each being "quartered" on its own district. The monks proved formidable rivals to the established clergy, threatening to monopolize all the fees from holy offices. The "Minor Brethren," as Saint Francis had called them in genuine humility ("Fraticelli," as they came to be nicknamed afterwards), were at least not inferior in their latent capacity of wealth. Their gray gown and knotted cord wrapped a spiritual pride and capacity of bigotry, fully equal to the rest.

The wild fanaticism which came to be known as "the Poverty of Christ," forbidding them to claim property over the very food in their mouths, or clothes on their backs, was a logical travesty of their Founder's doctrine. Men should literally neither toil nor spin, they said; the earth would spontaneously yield them everything. The deadly heresy of "the Eternal Gospel," — declaring that Jesus laid down only an imperfect law, to be completed in their new dispensation of the Holy Ghost,— was born from the bosom of this Order, to be hastily disowned and suppressed.* "The kingdom of the Father was past," they held; "the kingdom of the Son was passing; the kingdom of the Spirit was to be."

Puritan seceders, who thought to restore the austere rule of the Founder, and wore a longer and more pointed hood, were forced back to the regular discipline, on pain of being burnt as heretics. The horrible fate of the Templars was taken by many as a

* Exhibited especially by the followers of Joachim, and in the shocking tragedy of Fra Dolcino, vividly told by Milman (" Latin Christianity," vol. vii. pp. 41-51).

beginning and omen of the destruction that would soon pass upon all the hated Religious Orders. And so this final burst of enthusiasm and splendor in the religious life was among the prognostics of a state of things in which Monasticism must fade quite away. A torrent of odium, in the fifteenth century, beat impartially upon all its forms. The revival of it under Francis and Dominic led to a more sweeping Reformation, which struck first and hardest in the sarcasms of Erasmus, or through the biting satires of Ulrich von Hutten, at the abuses of the Religious Orders. The Dominican Savonarola and the Augustinian Martin Luther became the harbingers of a new order of thought, compelling other ideals, and a different embodiment of the religious life.

VII.

HERETICS.

ERESY is "free-thought;" hardly ever "free-thinking" in the modern sense. It is oftener simply "dissent." It implies a body of established opinion, against which it maintains its own independence. It follows the main course of the stream of thought in a separate channel of its own, sometimes underground. In proportion as the dominant belief shapes itself to a Creed claiming authority, heresy becomes more sharply defined against it. Free-thought then bears an ill name. It invites controversy; it provokes persecution. It is often crushed and silent; it is never quite killed. It disappears, like water spilt on the ground, but only to bubble out in some new place.

In the era of its greatest pride, and at the moment of its proudest triumph, the Church found itself confronted all afresh by this sleepless, tireless, deathless enemy. The era was the golden era of the Papacy, which as a spiritual power among men culminated about the middle of the twelfth century. The moment was the victory of the First Crusade, and the visible founding (as men thought) of the Kingdom of the New Jerusalem under Godfrey; and again, the enthusiasm of the Second, when it might seem as if monk and priest held the popular heart in the hollow of their hand.

The heretics of the twelfth century make a chapter of themselves, obscure but of great significance, in the history of this period. Their story is but an episode. It begins in a passionate fervor of homely piety ; it goes out, a century later, in the awful tragedy of the Albigensian War. The Church easily triumphed over this untimely birth of a religion more free than she dared to tolerate. But there was a moment of great terror, when it might seem as if the foundations of her power were shaken; and the conflict she entered into was felt to be a conflict for her very life.

To us the chief interest is not the ecclesiastical, it is the moral, issue. With what arms should the Church, believing herself the Divine Protector of truth, contend against heretical error ? How should she meet a spiritual adversary, who only attacked her in the field of thought and faith ? Would the weapons of her logic, the mystery and miracle of her sacraments, her supernatural authority and spells, — would these be enough ? So Hildebrand had thought, when he fearlessly faced the Emperor with excommunication, but gave his safe-conduct to Berengar, saying that error must be fought only by arms of charity and truth.* So Saint Bernard had thought that " heretics are to be caught, not shunned ; caught (I say) not by weapons, but by proofs to convict their errors ; to be charitably reconciled, if it may be, and called back to the true faith." " I approve the faith,"

* See Epistle vii. 28.

said he, "but not the act [of the persecutor]; since faith is of persuasion and not of force." *

But the battle might prove too obstinate and formidable. The alternative of failure and ruin might come too near. The whole fabric of Christianity itself, as men understood it then, was at stake. Not only civil order and justice, the interests of human society upon earth, but the existence of that Divine Society which began with the Creation, and would subsist after the Judgment, and was then in keeping of the Church, might seem involved. At least it was so, if the theory of the Church was sincerely held. And we must give men in responsible places the credit of holding their own theory sincerely, if we will understand, I do not say the merit, but at least the logic, of their acts.

The form of heresy which we meet at this period is very radical. It deals not with surface opinions, or with points of detail. It strikes — knowingly and boldly — at the very root of the sacerdotal theory itself, to which the Church was so thoroughly committed by its Decretals. Its five points touch with fatal logic the very essentials of ecclesiastical faith: the Baptism of infants; the Lord's body in the Eucharist; sanctity of the priestly Order; worship of the Cross; and invocation for the Dead. No mystic rite, said these daring heretics, could do away the original curse, unless there were penitence, conversion, and faith. No priest not of holy life could give the sacrament effect, to the saving of the soul. The Font was but a bowl of water; the Bread nothing

* Sermons 64, 66.

but a baker's loaf; the Mass a form of idle words; the Temple a convenient enclosure; the Cross an idolatrous sign, a memorial only of torment and horror; the Priesthood a class of sinful men, more arrogant and corrupt (probably) than other men, with no miraculous virtue in their word or touch.

To us these are, very likely, quite harmless propositions. It hardly occurs to us, even, that they may give offence. But that is because of five centuries of rationalism behind us, preceded by two centuries of battle, which separate us from the passion and terror of the controversy they stirred. It is only by a distinct effort that we can — not reproduce the passion and terror now, but — so much as conceive that they were possible, nay, real, then.

To see this a little plainer, we must attend for a moment to the dark side of the Catholic theology, which begins to be more prominent a little before this time, though it did not come into full relief till after the time of persecution which followed. I have had occasion to speak before of the mild tone we find in the appeals of the Early Church to its converts, as contrasted with the grimness of its theory.* But the logic of the theory would have its way. Hell, as the absolute and unescapable doom of the vast majority of mankind, must be taken for granted, perhaps, and appealed to now and then, to magnify that salvation of which the Church had the only key.

It is, in fact, just at this time that the vivid conception of the horrors of Hell finds its way into religious expression, so as to awe and oppress the

* See Early Christianity, p. 257.

11

imagination.* But it seems to have been too vast
and terrifying a thing, in that day, for the familiar
uses of daily exhortation, — in fact, until the tremen-
dous conflicts following the Reformation, — and some
mitigation of its horror must be had. So, at least as
far back as Augustine, it began to be surmised that
the pains of the eternal world must be for healing
and purification, where any room is left for a possible
penitence hereafter.† And there had grown up —
just by what steps it is not easy to trace — the developed theory of Purgatory, "that little ecclesiastical hell," in keeping of the Priesthood, familiar to
us in the later Catholic theology. The pains of this
mitigated hell are not absolutely hopeless; but they
are held (as explained by Thomas Aquinas) to be far
more searching and terrible than any torment that
can possibly be endured in this life.

But, what is more to the point, this doctrine
brought, or seemed to bring, the penalties of the fu-

---

* The first distinct expression of this sort that I have noticed is
in the lines of Hildebert : —

Tu intrare me non sinas	Ubi rei confunduntur,
Infernales officinas,	Ubi tortor semper cædens,
Ubi mæror, ubi metus,	Ubi vermis semper edens,
Ubi fetor, ubi fletus,	Ubi totum hoc perenne,
Ubi probra deteguntur,	Quia perpes mors Gehennæ.

What follows is more familiar : —

   " Me receptet Sion illa " (" Mine be Zion's habitation ").

The " Dies Iræ " is about a century later.

† The general doctrine of the Eastern Church respecting the
judgments of the Future Life would appear to be that they consist
in *purification by fire*. (See the testimonies in McClintock &
Strong's "Cyclopædia," vol. vii. p. 797.)

ture world within the compass of men's imagination, and make them more real to their fear. It was possible, then, to draw some comparison between them and the torment of hunger, fire, sickness, wounds, and torture in the dungeon, which were but too terribly familiar in men's experience. Above all, it brought the future world, so to speak, in direct contact with this. It lighted a dim ray of hope to relieve its horror. It made the Priest an immediate minister of help; it gave inestimable value to his prayers and spells. It deepened and made more vivid the feeling of the penitent, that only in the offices of the Church could he find hope or mercy.

The doctrine of Purgatory could accordingly be appealed to and turned to daily use, where threats of Hell might invite only defiance, despair, or a deadlier unbelief. In its practical effect, therefore, it rather darkened than softened the tone of religious appeal. It made Church authority more despotic and harsh. It disposed the Priesthood rather to enhance and exact the terms of the salvation in its keeping, than to make itself simply the ministry of mercy and help. These, I say, are the consequences that seem actually to have followed; not those we might at first expect.

I do not say, either, that the terrors of Judgment are much more prominent than before in the religious writings of that day. We are much more struck by the amplifying and speculation which appear in the treatment of theological matters, than by anything threatening in its tone. We detect the effect in other ways:— in the more frequent use of the Church's curses; in the harsher tone and sharper measures of its Councils; in the darkening temper of its conflict with the powers of the world; in the superstitious tales which abound in the writings of Peter the Venerable, towards the middle of this century, and the austere gloom of that view of life which appears in Pope Innocent's " Contempt of the World," at its close; most of all in the bitterness, degenerating to malignity, shown by a superior and noble mind like Saint Bernard, when he deals with the rising heresies that assail his creed.

Again, the Devil is, as it were, visibly nearer to men, and Sorcery is more the terror of their daily life.* The rude but vivid symbolism of religious Art brings its wealth of decoration to illustrate the darker superstitions of the Church mythology. All these things are more or less characteristic of the time, — which, we must remember, is that just before the systematic persecution for heresy on a great scale, and the horror of religious wars within the confines of Catholic States. In these things we cannot draw the line very sharply. But we shall not be far out of the way, if we take the latter part of the twelfth century as the date when the terrors of the Church begin to predominate in its appeals; when fear, instead of reverence or conviction, becomes the real foundation of its authority; when from spiritual it has recourse to carnal weapons ; when the great monastic age is past, and the motive of the conflict is more palpably political.

* The first tale of the popular diabolism that I have found in ecclesiastical literature is of date 1148 (Mansi, xxi. 722).

Thus we find a certain degeneracy of moral tone —
along with the most heroic courage, the severest self-
denial, and the most fervent devotion — in the later
exponents of that monastic piety which now rules the
Church. It is no injustice to associate that degeneracy of moral tone with the exaggerated ambition of
the Church on the one hand, and with this special
development of its doctrine on the other. Both are
characteristic of the time I speak of.

A truce had come in the conflict with the Empire,
— with a sharper struggle impending on that side,
and not far off. For the moment, the Church was
victorious in the Crusade, and might seem safe at
home. But, even then, came the challenge of a new
Protest against the very theory on which its power
was built; a challenge the more formidable, because
it was not an attack on any outwork, but the proclamation of a positive, a fearless, a zealous, a radically
hostile order of religious faith.

Moreover, it was the revival of an old, we may say
a quite forgotten, Gospel. It claimed to be simple,
primitive Christianity, — pure religion and undefiled,
without priest, without ritual, — such as we find it
in the New Testament. A legend has come down
which tells how it was transmitted, like a watercourse
running underground, from the primitive and apostolic time.

According to this story, when Constantine became
Emperor of Rome, and made that evil gift to Pope
Sylvester of temporal sovereignty in the West, —
whence came the tradition of a carnal, worldly, and
domineering Church, — a holy man named Leo with-

drew in voluntary exile into a secluded valley of the
Alps, where, for more than four centuries, had sub-
sisted a fragment of one of those German tribes routed
and driven back by Marius in the great Cimbrian
invasion. They had received the Gospel in its purest
form from Saint Paul himself; * and they now received Leo to dwell among them as a sort of patriarch
and apostle of the true faith.

That faith did not want its witnesses. The names
of Vigilantius and of Jovinian — violently assailed
by that "surly mastiff" Saint Jerome for their attack
on relic-worship, pilgrimage, and priestly celibacy —
meet us in some dim connection with the Alpine
legend; and we are reminded that the southeast of
France, where the streams of that secluded valley ran
towards the Rhone, has been from time to time the
home, or school, of a faith comparatively independent
of Rome, and often hostile to its hierarchy.

This primitive Gospel of Leonism † (so-called) was
strengthened by certain sympathies, or affiliations,
which it found among the converted German tribes,
especially the "Arian" Burgundians and Goths, persecuted by the "Orthodox" Franks, and taking flight,
some of them, to the safe refuges of the Alps. Here,

---

* That is, probably, the Gospel of Paul as opposed to the Romish
Gospel according to Peter. See Peyrat : *Les Réformateurs au Douzième Siècle.*

† This name, in the legend cited, is derived from the probably
mythical Leo, of the age of Constantine. De Thou says that, by a
manifest error, it was commonly referred to the Iconoclastic Emperor
Leo (726). Another derivation takes it from the city of Lyons,
long the home of this Gospel, and of Waldo, its real or imaginary
propagandist, founder of the *Waldenses.*

at any rate, lived a secluded and pious population of
the Valley,* — the same essentially, no doubt, with
those of whom the French Protestant De Thou gives
a very striking picture some centuries later, when
they were victims of a still crueller persecution : —
their retreat, dens and caves of the earth ; their
wealth, cattle ; their food, such hazardous and scanty
harvests as they could add to their milk and flesh ;
their raiment, sheepskins with the wool on, the fore-
feet tied about the throat and the hind-feet about the
loins, eked out by undergarments of coarse hempen
cloth ; of rude but genuine fervor in their devotion ;
their children taught with pious fidelity to read, sing,
and pray ; their way of life poor, pitiful, and unsav-
ory to the last degree, yet filled with a certain quiet
and religious content. Such is the earliest picture,
drawn from the life, which we find of the Waldenses,
those steadfast and long-enduring Protestants of the
Alps.†

Now it came to pass in the first years of the new
century, when the echo of the victory at Jerusalem
may be supposed to have reached the deep recesses
of their retreat, that one Peter of Bruys ‡ (*Petrobru-
sius*, as he is known to us in the polemics of the day)
went forth like another John the Baptist, full of the
Spirit and of power, and lived for twenty years as an
evangelist in the South of France, which he seems to
have filled completely with his doctrine, till he was
overtaken by the wrath of the Priesthood he had

---

* *Vallenses*, or *Vaudois*.   † See De Thou, vol. ii. p. 87.

‡ The name of a cold and sombre gorge on the west slope of the
Savoyard Alps.

challenged, and burned alive by a mob of monastics somewhere about 1120.

But, meanwhile, he had had one day of popular triumph at Toulouse, where at a great bonfire of blazing crosses — the great wooden crosses torn from church and cloister — he prepared the feast for a religious holiday, and proclaimed the new Resurrection of Christ in the Spirit, the sanctification of men's common life, the abolition of monks and clergy. " He roams among you," says Saint Bernard, "a ravening wolf in sheep's clothing. The churches are without people, the people without priests, priests without their due reverence, — in fine, Christians without Christ."

Thus the seed was planted of what widened afterwards into the famous and greatly dreaded heresy of the Waldenses and Albigenses. Distinctly, at its start, it was the proclamation of a new gospel. " The end of all things is at hand," it proclaimed. " Repent, watch, pray. Confess — but not to the priest; he is greedy and impure ; he seeks not pasture for the sheep, but their fleece. A priest who is a sinner cannot pardon. Forgiveness of sin is with God alone." * A gospel very simple and very old, — as old at least as the prophet Ezekiel, — but always vivid and fresh in its appeal to the hate and terror of the sacerdotal Order.

* These phrases are taken from *La Nobla Leyczon*, a poem ascribed to the Waldenses of this period, and possibly composed (it has been suggested) by the fiery preacher and bard himself. It will be found, with an English translation, in Gilly's " Narration of an Excursion to the Mountains of Piemont and Researches among the Vaudois and Waldenses." (London, 1824.)

So far it is simply a moral revolt, a protest of the conscience, such as always makes the motive and the strength of a genuine reformation. But for its symbol it needs a specific doctrine, one which emphasizes sharply the contrast of the new and old in their essential principle.

Now, ever since the middle of the third century, the Church had been committed more and more to the theory of Sacerdotalism. Its Priesthood was a consecrated body. Its Offices were miracles and spells. Its rite of Baptism had the mysterious and awful power of removing the birth-curse of inherited guilt. The elements of its Eucharist were literally the Lord's body, the physical germ of the immortal life. Its Excommunication banished the unfaithful and unbelieving to the horror of outer darkness forever.

And ever since that time, reappearing in various forms of heresy and schism, there had been a Puritan protest. The exciting cause had always been some laxity of morals, some corruption of life, covered up under the claim of official sanctity. The symbol of it had always been the one point of the sacramental efficacy of Baptism. Is that the efficient cause of regeneration, and of itself a passport to eternal life ? And shall we say it is just as valid, no matter how impious and unclean the hands that perform the rite ? Can an unholy man do a holy thing like that ?

Or, on the other hand, is Baptism a sign of faith and a mark of regeneration ? Then how can it be received by an infant, which knows nothing of guilt and cannot possibly repent ? To this the ritualist

must reply — as Bernard replies, in the gloomiest
of imagery — by speaking of the organic life of humanity : not, as we understand it, developed from a
wholesome germ, and working towards a higher and
broader life ; but, like a diseased tree, corrupt at the
core, capable of yielding only the fruit of death,
under a curse from which the mystic rite is the only
rescue. To withhold it from the new-born babe is a
horrible thing. It is to risk for the young life an
eternity of desolation and horror.* The Reformer
may or may not hold that Sin is a birth-curse, doom-
ing every human creature to eternal death unless
miraculously rescued. At any rate he will insist
that personal penitence and faith are the only way of
salvation, and that baptism is but the sign of these,
— a mockery and blasphemy unless it is their sign.

Again, admitting, as the established dogma teaches,
that Sacrifice is the appointed way of ransom, the
Reformer knows but the one offering made once for
all. If sacrifice is not only the method of salvation
but the law of life, at least he will say, with Paul,
that the daily offering required is the "living sacrifice" of right conduct and self-denial.

Now the Church, with fatal persistency of logic,
had changed all ethics into ritual and symbol. That
gracious figure of the "living sacrifice" it had turned
into the hardest literalism. An Altar must be set up
everywhere, and a priest's hand must lay upon it
every day the flesh and blood of the living God, or

* Among the theological speculations of the time occur discussions of the duty or possibility, in certain cases, of baptizing the
infant *before* its birth.

else the very way to heaven would be closed. I have
said enough before of the dogma, and of its essential
part in the sacerdotal theory.*　　Its philosophical
basis, expressed by the term "Transubstantiation," †
we shall have to consider when we come to the theology of the great Schoolmen. What strikes us at this
period is the crude and childlike stories of miracle,—
such as the broken bread being shown in the form of
bleeding flesh, or of an infant whom an angel is seen
to divide into fragments with a sharp knife,—which
we find in writers so eminent as Peter the Venerable,
Abbot of Cluny, friend and host of the sceptic Abelard. All these we may regard as the blind struggle
of Sacerdotalism to stamp itself in images which
startle and appall the popular mind.

Side by side with the Creed which has worked
itself out into such shapes as these has come down
the primitive, obstinate, heroic, anti-sacerdotal tradition, which has made the starting-place of many
a radical protest, from the Puritan Novatians of the
third century down to the English Independents of
the seventeenth.

That tradition, in its most logical form, is not only
Protestant but Baptist. The early reformers of the
twelfth century were both a Protestant and a Baptist
sect, appearing at a point of time when the Church
had staked its existence and its dominion more thor-

* See above, pp. 19–21.

† This philosophical basis of the doctrine — the change of the
metaphysical " substance " — is first found clearly stated by Hildebert of Mans (*De Sacramento Altaris*) about this time, but, as yet
(so far as I can find), without the technical term " transubstantiation."

oughly than ever on the divine authority of its Priesthood; when that theory seemed most completely triumphant in its conflict with the Empire at home and the Infidel abroad. To the Church's claim that heresy was fatal. The one function of the Church was to rescue human life from the universal curse by its perpetual sacrifice, — that is, by physical acts which none other than she could do.• All else turned on that. And her very ability to do that rested on men's absolute, distinct, unquestioning faith that she had both the authority and the power.

And again, it was not a conflict which raged in the abstract region of ideas alone. It had to do with every act, with every rank, with every situation of human life. The Church was not merely the teacher of a system of belief, however essential to salvation. Her empire took in every thought of men's hearts, and every action of their lives. Her theory could not tolerate a divided empire, any more than a nation can tolerate a divided sovereignty. Heresy was treason. The conversion of a province was organized rebellion. The heresy of Peter de Bruys had spread throughout the South of France. Theoretically, that was a province in insurrection. The weapons to subdue it, by the same theory, must be not carnal but spiritual. How to find them and how to apply them was the very difficult question the Church had now to meet.

The death of the Reformer, at the hands of an irresponsible mob, did not settle this question; it only made the question imminent and palpable. The flame of heresy had spread through a whole broad

region, from the Alps to the Pyrenees. It was not
only that the new gospel touched those who were
naturally eager and quick to welcome some new
thing; not only that the buoyant and restless temper
of that population responded to the passionate appeal
against priestly arrogance and corruption. The South
of France, where Greek, Gaul, Goth, and Saracen had,
one after the other, fought against the stronger force
of Roman or Frank, was the natural home of revolt
against spiritual authority.

The South of France was ruled by the most brilliant sovereigns of the time, the Counts of Toulouse;
just now by Alphonso, surnamed Jordan, the very
mirror of chivalry. The flowering-out of romantic
verse, the tournament and song and adventure which
gave a brief lustre to that Court, do not exactly belong to our present subject; but they must be thought
of as the bright background in a landscape that was
presently to be dark with the storm of religious war.
Nothing could be more alien to the temper of Monk
or the pride of Priest than the easy tolerance which
heresy found in that sunny and indulgent atmosphere.
The influence of the Crusades, too, in stimulating intellectual revolt, both by what they did and by what
they failed to do, we have already seen. For the
present, we have only to follow out a line or two,
bearing on the point we have already reached.

Towards the end of his reforming career, Peter de
Bruys had been joined by an ardent younger disciple
of the same faith, known to us only by the name of
"Henry the Deacon," or "Henry of Lausanne," and
as giving the name to a sect, or popular religious

party, of "Henricians." He appears to have come from the Italian side of the Alps, a passionate pilgrim, into the North of France, and thence to Tours, where the famous heretic Berengar had left a memory curiously mingled of horror and veneration. Saint Bernard speaks of him as a renegade monk, and tells shocking stories of the immoralities he was charged with, as he roamed at random, followed by an eager and admiring crowd. These scandals are told, in still greater detail, by the biographer of Hildebert,* the learned and kindly bishop of Mans, whose mild temper turned to gall at the rude effronteries he had to meet.

The same accounts, however, show us not exactly a fanatic or an impostor, but rather a religious enthusiast, a preacher of righteousness, a man abstemious and ascetic to the verge of maceration, an orator of marvellous power. Tall, of striking presence, his mass of hair and full beard contrasting strongly with the priest's tonsure, to the common people he seemed a prophet. "Go your ways!" they cried, when Hildebert approached with his benediction. "To the mud and mire with your blessing! We will none of you. We have our own priest and pope, holier than yours!" Money poured out freely, to be spent in gifts of charity. Men and women of loose life came forward, with passionate contrition, to be comforted, and united in holy matrimony. Such zeal reacted (so runs the account) in worse immoralities than before. It was short-lived, no doubt, and at any rate very offensive to the Priesthood, who called the new

* See Migne, clxxi. 94–98.

prophet "the Devil's own snare, and the right-hand man (*armiger*) of Antichrist."

Silenced here, he turned to the South, and joined Peter de Bruys in Languedoc (1117). After this reformer's death, Henry continued his career for some thirty years, once confined for a time in a monastery, but escaping. At length, condemned of heresy, he was imprisoned again, and soon after died (1147).

But the heresy which had been so formidable in the South of France that Bernard, in the infirmity of years, had been forced into a painful and laborious pilgrimage to confute it on the spot, now reappeared, more formidable than ever, in Italy, — in Rome itself, where for nine years Arnold of Brescia maintained a Republic in open defiance of Emperor and Pope.

The populace of Rome had broken out in rebellion against Pope Lucius II. (1145), who was stoned to death, and kept his successor Eugene II., a monk of Bernard's own training, in perpetual exile. Arnold had been a disciple of Abelard; and his defiance of authority took the same general turn with the other reformers of the time, — that is, a free gospel, anti-ritualistic, anti-sacerdotal, fervid and hot in its denunciation of priestly vice. But with him it became, besides, a political enthusiasm, which kindled town after town of his native Lombardy, and carried him, on a wave of popular triumph, to his brief rule in Rome.

Here the old forms of the Republic were revived, with Consuls and Senators, under the presiding genius and eloquence of Arnold; and here he ruled, in manifestation of spirit and power, for some nine years. Then a new force came to the papal throne, in the person of an Englishman, Nicholas Breakspear,—a peasant born, rude and bluff, who by sheer ability and pluck fought his way to that supreme eminence, where he sat for five years as Adrian IV. He straightway, to the amazement of Christendom, laid the rebellious city under an interdict. The spell broke the courage of the Romans. Under that "terror of the Lord" Arnold was forsaken, and forced to fly. The next year (1155) he was betrayed into the hands of Frederick Barbarossa, delivered over to the Pope as part of the new compact of alliance, and by him first strangled as a rebel, then burned as a heretic, and his ashes cast into the Tiber, lest anything that had been his should be kept as a sacred relic among the people.

We are now just past the middle of the century, and on the verge of that most vigorous assertion of papal claims by Alexander III. against Frederick Barbarossa, which makes the stormy and heroic history of the next twenty years. We have just seen how the Church, for the first time, had carried its theory of secular sovereignty so far as deliberately to put a man to death by its own hand as a rebel to its power. The death of Arnold of Brescia was the first blot of this kind on the Church's conscience. It gave a certain shock to men's minds and a sense of guilt, which the papal government softened, as best it might, by disclaiming its own direct agency in the act. The famous symbol of the "two swords" begins to demand explanation. The spiritual sword alone may be handled directly by the spiritual power; the sword temporal must be wielded only through the carnal hand of magistrate or ruler. The point in casuistry — as just seen in the case of Arnold — is sometimes a very fine one. And, just as things are now, it is quite imperative that the Church's policy, in the face of rising and extending heresy, shall be carefully determined.

A few years back (1139), it had seemed enough to decree respecting "rejectors of the sacraments" (the Petrobrusians and Henricians of the day) that "we condemn them, and enjoin that they be repressed by outside powers," — that is, by the State.* But it might happen that the State would do no such thing. The Count of Toulouse, an independent Prince and a good Crusader, had almost openly patronized and protected the arch-heretic. And again, it might happen that heresy would not down at the State's bidding; that something in the spirit of the time, in the very nature of free-thought, would prove too strong for that shadowy authority. And on that issue might depend the very existence of the spiritual power itself, — what its defenders would uphold as indeed the Kingdom of God on earth, and the only hope of perishing humanity.

All the more, because the whole sunny South of France, opening broadly on the bright Mediterranean,

---

* The same Council reinforces the "Truce of God" (Art. 12), denounces Tournaments, — *detestabiles illas nundinas vel ferias* (Art. 14), — and conflagrations, — *horrendam incendiorum malitiam* (Art. 18). It also forbids heredity of church benefices (Art. 16), and enjoins security of person to non-combatants, travellers, and others (Art. 11). These services to the higher civilization should not be overlooked in this connection.

— the highway of the Crusade; before all the rest of
Europe in enlightenment; alive all over with the
budding germs of a fresh civilization, — was infected
to the core with the poison of a deadlier heresy.

At least, it is plausible to connect the eager and
passionate fervor of the Albigensian faith with the
adventure of the Crusade, which laid that sunny coast
so easily open to the invasion of strange doctrines
and practices from the East. Something, it is likely,
in the young glow of Chivalry and Romance was well
disposed to receive anything that might seem a golden
dawn of free-thought. The more hostile to monastic
and ecclesiastical rule, the better welcome that new
life must find. Abundant seed of it came over from
the Levant in the same fleets which brought back
the baffled, doubting, despairing troop that had sailed
out for conquest of the Holy Land. Its rank growth
came thickest, at the very time the reaction set in
after the disastrous enterprise which had been urged
with fatal promises by Saint Bernard.

There is some obscurity about the origin and nature of this heresy. Its sacred books were destroyed;
its records were carefully blotted out. All but its
name would appear to have perished in that awful
devastation which befell, under Innocent III. and his
successors, on the soil of Languedoc.

It seems clear, however, that it was not merely the
growth of the seed planted by Peter de Bruys and his
disciples, and not merely a contagion, or importation,
brought in from the Levant by the returning fleets.
And instead of the easy-going " free-religion " which
we might have looked for in the land of chivalry and

romance, its tone appears to have been ascetic, even harsh. Its ritual was one of extreme, even gaunt simplicity. Its disciples were not voluptuous knights and ladies, but a grave, frugal, and temperate population, with a simplicity of life and a mutual devotion like the pious communism of the early Church at Jerusalem.

It is likely, indeed, that the new rites had to do with the Oriental notion of the corruption of matter; with ascetic practices, to get free from evils of the flesh, — whence the name *Cathari*, or " Purists," by which the sect was most broadly known; with forms of symbolism shocking and profane merely because they were unauthorized and new; with rejection of the Old Testament, also, and an urging of the contrasts of natural Good and Evil, which seemed a revival of the old Manichæan Dualism, — nay, the worship of Satan and Antichrist.

From the beginning down we meet at intervals that Dualism which — under the names Gnostic, Manichee, Paulician, Catharist — has made the incessantly recurring terror of the Church. To the Christian conscience it has always seemed a lapse towards the peril and mischief of Paganism. It did often include practices which were pagan in origin, and which savored (possibly) of pagan license.

What is Paganism, after all, but a worship of the blind mystery of Nature, and more often of the dark side than of the bright side in Nature? The forms of Natural Evil which constantly assail us, before which we are as utterly ignorant as we are utterly helpless in the last resort, — storm, violence, pain

death, — press closest on the imagination and terror
of men, and have their symbol in the names that
stand out strongest in popular mythologies — Typhon,
Moloch, and Apollyon.   Life itself seems not an orderly development, as the philosopher would persuade
us, or the work of a wise and kind Providence, as the
pious heart believes.   To the common eye it is rather
a conflict of good and evil, light and darkness, gladness and pain ; a conflict obstinate and unreconciled ;
a conflict in which the hero may hold his ground for
a while, but must fall at last, — in which the coward
is struck down at once, ignominiously.   Ignorant,
abject, and helpless, the natural man stands in awe
before a pitiless, blind Force, which seems to him
absolutely indifferent to our pain or gladness, right
or wrong.

We may say that this is at bottom the same conflict
which is seen and reconciled in Christianity ; the
same which the Church has always recognized in its
doctrine of salvation, and its symbol of Christ and
Antichrist.   But we have also seen how, in the better
Christian thought of Augustine, in his rejection of his
own early Manichæism, the ground of conflict is
shifted from the outward world to the Conscience,
from the realm of natural Fatalism to that of spiritual
Freedom.*   And to this solution, however illogical its
creed or unworthy its practice, the mind of Christendom has always given its assent.

Now the Catharist doctrine had in it a strong dose
of the old Nature-worship of Force and Fear.   It may
even be regarded as, in a sense, a race-religion, — a

* See Early Christianity, pp. 131–137.

Slavic rendering of Christianity, just as we have the
recognized Greek, Latin, Arian-Gothic, and Protest-
ant-Teutonic forms. For the Slavic Bulgarians had,
in their barbaric mythology, their Divinity of Evil,
their Black God (*Czernebog*), — suggested, naturally
enough, by their long northern winter of darkness
and cold ; and their Christianity was deeply colored
by their primitive Dualism from the start.*

Stimulated (it is said) by some Paulician exiles
from the East, their form of faith became aggressive
and propagandist, strongly organized, and very much
in earnest. It invaded Italy in the eleventh century,
after a steady advance through what is now Northern
Turkey. It established its headquarters in Bosnia,
which it held for several centuries, and whence it
may have done something to feed the flame of that
furious war of races which we know as the Hussite
War. In Southern France it fell in with the hostility to priesthood and sacrament which was already
a part of the popular religion. And here it proved
itself no mere speculative fancy, but a creed eagerly,
devoutly, passionately held, as was seen later in the
wild scenes of self-immolation so common in the
Albigensian Crusade.

A word of its interior nature and constitution.
The motive of its discipline, which was strict and
very severe, was to be free from the dominion of
Matter, the evil principle. Hence it demanded austerities of its professed holy men (the " Cathari," or

---

* This statement of the subject was read and approved by a
young Bulgarian theologian, — who, by the way, suggested the
spelling *Tsarneboy*.

Pure) * which, when emulated on the sick-bed by
those who aspired to be saints, were sometimes carried to the point of deliberate starvation. In particular, it forbade the taking of life or the eating of
flesh. Its most characteristic ritual consisted in the
gift of the Spirit by laying-on of hands, and a peculiar rite of absolution for the dying (*consolamentum*).
Its only devotional forms were the Lord's Prayer and
the Apostolic Benediction. Its subjects seem to have
been a people peace-loving, industrious, and frugal;
generous and devoted to one another, especially to
their religious chiefs; and, like those of all time
whose pietistic zeal is touched with communistic
fervor, capable of the intensest enthusiasm and self-
·devotion.

The strength and coherence of their organization,
and their profound repugnance to the Roman hierarchy, quite as much as their heresies of creed, were
what brought them into such deadly collision with
the powers of the day. Their fervor ran often, doubtless, to passion and excess; and it may possibly have
had (as religious passion so often has) a weak side
toward the plainer moralities, common enough when
men begin to fancy that the life of faith has emanci-
pated them from the law of righteousness.†

Albi, not far from Toulouse, became the religious
capital of the new heresy; and those who embraced
its crudities and protests, above all those who shared

* These made a recognized sacred class, in number about 4,000.

† In the account here given I have chiefly followed Schmidt,
Histoire et Doctrine de la Secte des Cathares ou Albigeois (2 vols.
Paris, 1849).

the enmity and hate it bore from Rome, were known by the common name of Albigenses. Their "damnable heresy," declares the Council of Tours (1163), "has crept like a serpent into the Lord's vineyard." True believers are summoned to watch and guard. As yet, however, the Church does not strike with carnal weapons. Anathema, excommunication, non-intercourse — arms taken from her spiritual arsenal — are still her methods. There must be no dealings of trade with the misbelievers: they must be fenced off like an infected district. Their conventicles are to be hunted out, their worship forbidden. And in the "Inquest" or search-warrant which this policy implies we have the germ of what grew afterwards into the gigantic tribunal of the Inquisition.

Along with the Albigenses, a kindred sect under another name comes upon the field. The Waldenses are held to be so called from Peter Waldo, a merchant of Lyons, who about 1160 gave all his wealth to religious uses, and became not so much the founder of a sect, as representative of the cause for which Henry had lived and Arnold died, — the austere, fervent, anti-priestly gospel of the Alpine valley. So that we have, in the first half of the century, a Reform known to us by the name of its three brave, eloquent, and ill-fated pioneers, — each a great religious enthusiast, proclaiming his gospel of free salvation; after the middle of the century, we have a broad, popular movement, in two great sects more or less allied, — the Albigenses and Waldenses, inseparable in destiny and fame as the earliest champions and martyrs of our modern liberty of thought.

Comparing them, the one would appear more speculative, vigorously organized, and intellectually bold ; the other more simple, genuine, and practically in earnest. Peter Waldo, so it is said, might easily have made his peace with Rome, and been recognized, perhaps, as Founder of a new religious Order of Poverty, like Saint Francis. But his method went deeper. He caused the Gospels to be translated and diffused in the popular tongue; and so started an independent religious culture, fundamentally hostile to the Church. The names by which the sect was known all denote a very simple and humble community. They are "Poor Men of Lyons," — for brevity, "Leonists ;" or *Sabotati*, from the wooden clogs they wore; or *Humilitati*, "the Downtrodden."

So the Waldenses appear in history as pioneers of the "Forerunners of the Reformation." Like the Wicliffites and Lollards of England, the Hussites of Bohemia, they represent a faith which had its home and temple in the hearts of the people. This faith cared nothing for sanctity of official priesthood, for splendor of altar and ritual. It was too direct and straightforward to pardon, too simple to understand, the compromises and policies inseparable from a vast Institution laden with a multitude of tasks and open to innumerable assaults. It was too humble-minded to comprehend the great sweep of events, which only begin to be intelligible to us at the end of seven hundred years. True prophets, as we see them now, of a better time and creed, it was not possible then but that they should be victims and martyrs of the hierarchy they defied.

The time came, when that Hierarchy must either surrender its ground as the one Divine institution among men, or determine on some more effectual method to maintain its power. Alexander III. (1159–1181) had been pope for twenty years. Partly by policy and craft, as in the case of Henry II. of England and his impracticable Primate Thomas Becket; partly by indomitable resolution, as in his hard-won victory over Barbarossa, — he had carried the Papacy through the stormiest crisis of its long struggle. He had guided the Council at Tours to the declaration of policy against the Albigenses, already described. And, for the last great act of his administration, he now (1179) summoned the Third Lateran Council, for more deliberate adoption of a course, to meet the peril in the proportions it had already grown to.

The Acts of this Council are deserving of special attention, because they first clearly announce the policy of persecution for opinion's sake, to which the Church has been slowly — and, as we may believe, with deep misgiving and reluctance — committed by its inexorable theory.

The initial measure is not essentially different from what we have found before, — non-intercourse with heretics, who are further to be deprived of Christian burial. But there is a certain deliberate malignity in what immediately follows. A long list is recited of bandits and marauders, probably the ruff-scuff of the returned Crusaders, who are craftily mixed up with heretics in faith. The allies of the Church are hounded on against them as enemies of society, —

with what justice, it is not hard to see. Their goods
are to be confiscated; their persons are to be reduced
to slavery. And, as if all the secular hates and
passions of the time were not enough, two years'
"indulgence" is promised to their assailants, and all
the privileges of Soldiers of the Cross.*

To these counsels of deep iniquity the Church has
at length been led. The process, we may well believe, was slow, and was followed reluctantly. Like
all the great crimes of history, it was extenuated —
perhaps sanctified — in the eyes of its perpetrators by
a seeming necessity. The logic of history is inexorable. To this pass had been brought at length that
which called itself the Church of Christ, indivisible
and one !

Those which I have recounted are the first definite
steps of persecution, deliberately initiated by church
authority. They are interesting, as showing the cau-
tious and hesitating steps, taken at long intervals,
before that policy ripened — as it did some thirty
years later, in the time of Innocent III. — into the
horrors of the Albigensian War, and the Office of
Inquisition, which we find fully adopted in the next
great Council (1215), the same at which the doctrine
of Transubstantiation was formally recognized as part
of the authoritative Creed. So the finest subtilties of
metaphysical theology go hand in hand with the final
act by which the Church exchanges the voice of appeal for the policy of terror and the hand of violence.
As Witness of the Truth and Defender of Righteousness, its history will not interest us any more.

* See Act 27 of the Third Lateran Council (1179).

The official report of the indiscriminate massacre at Béziers (in 1209) of twenty thousand men, women, and children, heretic and Catholic alike, and the reply of Innocent III., applauding and urging on the work, may be found in the standard Catholic authorities.* This horror was all in vain. In 1243, at the Council of Padua, the complaint is still that heresy is on the increase; and to the same place and date belongs the atrocious code of Frederick II., which enjoins that heretics "be burned alive in the sight of men."† How the Waldenses were hunted, literally like wild beasts, for a course of centuries, is told in Gilly's "Narration," before cited. Of this great horror the conscience of Humanity has spoken in Milton's noble sonnet "On the Late Massacre in Piedmont."

Yet there is an interest besides — special, tragic — in the acts which have been now described. In all this dreadful business the Church was not quite forgetful of *other* duties to humanity, besides the vindication of purity in belief. The same decrees include — along with assertions of her independent sovereignty and the stereotype manifesto of monastic reform — declarations against wanton conflagrations and the plundering of peasants, those two great curses of the feudal wars ; against tournaments also, "those detestable games and holidays ; " and in favor of the Truce of God. They contain merciful provision, too, for Lepers, who, we may suppose, had appeared in the wake of the returning Crusade ; and they enjoin that the Church shall provide "schools for the poor,

* See Migne, ccxvi. 139, 151.   † Mansi, xxiii. 586.

as a tender mother." Certainly, the Church's left hand did not know what her right hand did !

The illustrations of ecclesiastical policy which we have now seen are not open to the discreditable evasions by which modern defenders of Rome have attempted to cover up her guilt in the vaster horrors of St. Bartholomew and the Spanish Inquisition. They show that the policy of Persecution was adopted by that Church deliberately and with open eyes. But it was under pressure of a false theory honestly held, and of a real terror at imaginary danger. It was also with strong compunction and humane recoil. If, on the one hand, we make this admission of a more merciful spirit in the Church, then, on the other hand, there is nothing that so damages her claim of celestial wisdom or supernatural guidance. Nothing so completely disproves that Infallibility to which she asserts so many fantastic, sentimental, and rotten claims.

VIII.

SCHOLASTIC THEOLOGY.

BEFORE approaching a subject so vast in all its proportions as the Catholic Theology of the Middle Age, it is necessary to draw a few definitions and limitations.

The name Scholastic Philosophy, in its broader sense, is given to the whole intellectual movement of some five centuries, in which thought is dominated by the creed; that is, from the middle of the ninth century to the middle of the fourteenth. In the narrower sense in which I shall take it, we have to do only with the latter half of this period, dating from the time when the issue of Nominalism and Realism was sharply defined in the theological controversies of the day.

Again, if we take the great age of Scholasticism as reaching through the twelfth past the middle of the thirteenth century, we may say, in a general way, that the earlier was its controversial and the later its constructive period, while the bridge between them was the philosophy of Aristotle, introduced through the Arabian schools. The great familiar names of the twelfth century are Anselm, Abelard, and Saint Bernard, all of them hotly engaged in controversy. Those of the thirteenth are Albert the Great, chief encyclopædist of the Middle Age, and Thomas Aquinas, its most consummate theologian. Neither of them hints at conflict or doubt. In them both, faith is absolute, submissive, and serene.

To these two periods, again, we may add a third, to include the names of Raymond Lully, Duns Scotus, Occam, and their followers; and this we may call the period of criticism, analysis, or decline.

It may be necessary to say a word of the theological motive behind this great era of intellectual activity. The earlier movement of thought begun in the ninth century with Scotus Erigena was cut short, as everything else was, by the growth of Feudalism and the revolution in Church and State resulting from it, and was not resumed till after nearly two hundred years. It was during this interval that what we may call the *unreasoning* form of church dogma became so deeply rooted in the popular mind, and so powerful in shaping church policy.

This could not be without some protest of the understanding. In particular, the doctrine of the Lord's body and blood in the Eucharist, stated in such bald and offensive terms by Paschasius Radbert,* and embodied in many a legend and marvel, was sharply challenged (about 1050) by Berengar of Tours, and so became the initial point of the debate. " If it is the actual body of Christ you mean," said he, "and if it were larger than yonder tower, it would have been consumed long ago." The challenge, thus crudely put, was taken up by Lanfranc of Canterbury, and after him by Anselm. It forced them to restate their

---

* See Early Christianity, p. 271; also above, p. 20.

philosophy so as to accord with their faith; and it
led the way to those definitions and discussions which
mark the earlier period of Scholasticism. The later,
or great period of constructive dogma, beginning with
Peter Lombard, may in like manner be taken as the
protest of Theology against the heresies of the twelfth
century already described.

The term "scholastic" is taken, it is said, from the
Cloister-Schools, founded by Charlemagne; though, as
we saw before,* these Schools were a tradition from
a much earlier time; and, as we shall see, they were
developed into a vast university system, much more
closely identified with the great age of Scholasticism.
At any rate, not groups of independent thinkers, but
Schools, under the avowed patronage and direction of
the Church, were what gave the speculative development its name. The philosophers and theologians of
the Middle Age were "Schoolmen."

Within the limits already stated there is a certain unity in the philosophic development, which it
will be well to keep in view. The hundred Latin
folios, more or less, in which it is recorded, are in a
sense an enormous Dialogue, like one of Plato's; in
which, it is true, nothing is settled, while yet the argument has a certain completeness in itself as a work
of art.

The speakers, too, — as Plato often skilfully ar-
ranges them, — come generally in pairs. They represent one or the other tendency, analytic or dogmatic,
critical or constructive, sceptical or mystic, which the
history of speculative thought shows us from the be-

---

* Early Christianity: The Christian Schools.

ginning. Thus the theme of Anselm, the first name
of special interest to us, introduces to us at once, in
sharpest contrast, these two : William of Champeaux,
whose realism was so pronounced that his pupils
"thought they could see universals with their eye,
and touch them with their finger;" and Roscellin,
the nominalist, whom Anselm could never pardon for
declaring that color exists not in itself, but only in
the object.   Next we meet Abelard, the brilliant disputer, paired against the imperious dogmatist Bernard; then, as controversy wanes, the mystic school
of Saint Victor on one side with that rigid formalist
Peter Lombard, "master of sentences," on the other;
then the great encyclopædist Albert, with the dreamy,
ingenious, patient enthusiast, Roger Bacon; the prodigious industry and intellectual subtilty of Thomas
Aquinas, with the brooding piety of his dear friend
Bonaventura; the refined and intricate analysis of
Duns Scotus, with the speculative agnosticism, the
frank partisanship, the real religious fervor of William Occam; till we come to the downright pantheism of Master Eckhart, in whom the mystical "Son
of God" is every ransomed soul.*   And so, where
the movement begins, there too it ends, in a sweet

* "The soul having perfect vision of God beholds him not alone
in (*per*) that glory which is the divine essence, but is herself the
divine glory. . . . Then the soul ceases to be in that existence
which she had before in her own kind, and is changed, or rather
transformed and absorbed, into the Divine Being (*esse*); and that
ideal being flows on (*defluit*) which she had from eternity in the
divine essence, of which being John saith in his Gospel, 'That
which was made, in the same was life.'" — *Eckhart, as cited by
Gerson* (Raynaldus, vol. v. p. 451).

and fervent piety, which sublimates all dogma, so to speak, into a celestial, illuminated atmosphere.

The duality of this movement, so often to be noticed, lies partly in the nature itself of philosophic development. The mind is always endeavoring to find the exact point of stable equilibrium that represents pure truth, and as often misses it by a momentum (as it were) which carries it just beyond the mark. The development thus necessarily becomes a debate. Not till the pendulum is dead does the motion come to rest. It is never — that is, while vital and genuine — mere erudition or mere speculation. Each debater speaks to some one point that has been started on the other side. The ball is kept in motion by being passed from hand to hand.

Aside from its motive and its effect, the debate seems often, it is true, mere mental gymnastics on a gigantic scale, or at best a vast ball-match of the human intellect, in which the champions display the reach that can be made by thorough training and eager competition in their own line of skill. To use Taine's fine expression, "These men seem to be marching, but are merely marking time." The difference lies in the motive, which is the serious pursuit of that truth which seems highest and most important of all; and in the effect, which is in contributing some appreciable share to the higher life of humanity. At its very lowest value, Scholasticism is a unique chapter in the history of the human mind. Even the scientific thought of the nineteenth century is deeply in debt to those weary debates on Universals, those subtile analyses and patient theoretical constructions, which have fastened in the modern mind the general conceptions that are the types and forms of things.*

Again, the nature of the dualism spoken of will be seen as soon as we consider that side of the movement which is all that concerns us now. The scholastic theology is that part of scholastic philosophy which deals with the analysis, the development, or the defence of religious dogma. The vast encyclopædia of Albertus Magnus, or the scientific genius of Roger Bacon, interesting and curious as they are, do not come strictly under our view. We understand by Scholasticism a mode of thought which accepts the church creed as its platform; which assumes its dogma exactly as geometry assumes its axioms and postulates. Whatever its abstract speculations, by far its most important field will be theology. Its expounders are the representative voices of the Church. Of those I have named, Albert was a bishop, Anselm an archbishop, Bonaventura a cardinal; all of them were churchmen, and all of them but one were monks.

The scholastic period, again, exactly corresponds with the dominance and chief glory of the monastic orders. As these declined, ecclesiastical faith declined, and scholasticism faded out. From its very nature as religious thought, it shared from the first a double tendency, constructive or dogmatic on one side, critical or negative on the other.† This double tendency

---

* See a valuable little book entitled "The Secret of Christianity," by S. S. Hebbard (Boston: Lee & Shepherd).

† Compare Early Christianity, p. 102.

accompanies it all along. When the pressure of the controversial motive is taken off, it works out one way in the direction of a mystical pantheism; in the other, in the direction of rationalizing analysis. The hardened core of dogma is deserted by them both; while these two forms or tendencies, the analytic and the mystical, divide between them all the later movements of speculative thought, — one way materialism and science, the other way idealism and metaphysics.

Mysticism and Scepticism have been called opposite poles of the same thing. Mysticism claims to know divine truth by immediate intuition. Scepticism denies that such truth can be a matter of knowledge at all, properly speaking. Both agree in making it a subjective experience of the individual mind. Both these tendencies are found, more or less consciously, wherever religious belief is professed at all. But the period we deal with is fundamentally religious. It begins with the deeply fervent and mystic pietist, Anselm of Canterbury (1033–1109); it ends with Eckhart, father of German spiritual theology (1250–1329), the forerunner of Nicholas of Basel and of Tauler.

It is a happy turn of history which connects the first phase of the movement we are studying with the personal traits of Saint Anselm. Living as a child on the sunny southern slope of the Alps, his dreamy piety was fostered by his mother's tenderness; a certain austere love of solitude was stimulated by his father's harshness; and he used to see in the bright summits the celestial home of angels, just as the

Greek in the snowy peaks of Olympus saw the abode of gods. In manhood, this temper grew into a passionate love of the dreamy, contemplative life of the monastery; and he sought the most famous one of those days, in Bec of Normandy, under Lanfranc (then Abbot there), whom he succeeded in both his posts of honor, and in the good-will of the Norman kings.

But we have to do with the spirit of the man, not the incidents of his career: — his passion of meditation, such that he would sit dreamy and silent at the common table, and his companions had literally to slide the food into his hands lest he should starve outright; his perfect obedience, such that (it is told) he neither went to bed nor turned himself in bed without a hint from his superior; his capacity of original thought, such that he made the two only contributions of that long period which are still remembered in the history of speculative dogma; his temper, so unworldly that "he shuddered at the very name of property;" above all, his fervent piety, such that each point of dogmatic faith becomes in him a moment of profound personal experience, so that, to a remarkable degree, the intellectual movement which dates from him is the genuine outgrowth of his own religious nature.

Anselm is generally said to be the author of the modern governmental theory of the Atonement, or at least of the debt-and-credit view that led to it. This is doubtless true; although we find long afterward that his solution is not recognized. Peter Lombard, for example, still holds that man's ransom by Christ is from the power of the Devil; that is, as he explains, from the power of Sin.*

So far as one can judge, the theory of the Atonement does not seem to have been very prominent in the early times, which were mainly content with the practical side, particularly as shown in the literal sacrifice of the body of Christ in the Eucharist, and in the personal humiliation he voluntarily underwent. Still, that problem would naturally exercise many thoughtful minds. Anselm begins his dialogue on the subject by mentioning the comfort and relief his view has given to some inquirer, whereby he is encouraged to write it out.

Here is the point on which it turns. Man owes to God the absolute devotion of a perfect life. To fail of this by a single error of thought, or a single wandering of affection, or a single infirmity of will, is to forfeit all claim to divine mercy. But no man can pay that debt, even for himself, much less for another. Who, then, shall pay it? Anselm's words are these: "None can make the satisfaction except God; none owes it except Man; hence, it must be that a God-Man makes it." And, in order to make it, God becomes man in Christ.†

The logic seems to content him, whatever we may think of the fallacy that lurks in it. We have not to do, however, with the detail of his argument, only

---

* Thus, Peter Lombard says that we are redeemed *a servitute Diaboli, id est a peccato (servitus enim Diaboli peccatum est) et a pœnd.* I do not think that the view of Anselm reappears till we come to Duns Scotus (1274–1308), who says that Satan is overcome *justitiâ non potentiâ.*

† *Cur Deus homo?*

with the very remarkable appeal by which he fortifies
it, — an appeal purely to the very heart and core of
the conscience, not to any of our modern postulates
about the metaphysical infinites. " Suppose," he
says, " that you saw this perfectly just man, and
knew him to be absolutely free from guilt. Now,
weigh against that one life all the misery and all the
guilt of the whole human race; and suppose that by
one blow falling upon that head you could remove it
all, — would your conscience let you strike that
blow ? " " No," says the respondent. " Would it let
you even lay a hand on him for harm ? " " No, not
even that." " You are right," says Anselm. That is,
*it is morally impossible to punish the innocent for the
guilty.* Our moral judgment is of infinites, and not
of finites: there is no common measure in the comparison. It is by his pure service that Christ ransoms
us, not by his bloody sacrifice. I do not know anywhere an appeal so effective and so direct to the central point of personal experience as that which thus
suddenly brightens up the obscure path of scholastic
theology by the radiant axioms of the moral sense.

Still more characteristic of Anselm's style of thought
is his celebrated argument for the existence of God.
This argument is said to have dawned on him as a
divine illumination after hours of complete absorp-
tion in abstract thought; and he can write it out, to
his mind, only in the form of religious meditation or
direct prayer to the Almighty. This, and Augustine's
Confessions, contain the only extended logical argument I know of in the form of prayer.

I will give the point of it in his own words. " The

Divine Nature," he says, "so truly is, that it cannot even be thought not to be. For something can be supposed to exist which cannot even be thought of as not existing; and this is greater that what *can* be thought of as not existing. Wherefore, if the greatest conceivable can be supposed as not existing, then the greatest conceivable is not the greatest conceivable, — which is contradictory. So truly, then, there is something than which nothing greater can be conceived, that it cannot even be conceived as not existing. And that art thou, our Lord." And at this lucid demonstration he bursts into praise: "Thanks to thee, good Lord, thanks to thee! For what I believed before, through thy gift, I now so clearly understand, through thy light, that even if I would not believe thee, I could not fail of understanding thee."

I do not expect to make this curious verbal turn intelligible. I am not sure that any of us see it exactly as it looked to him. The argument is plain enough: that, as real existence is one of the attributes of the highest nature we can conceive, — and we can conceive of a nature absolutely perfect, namely, the Divine, — actual existence must be one of its attributes; and so, God really exists. Otherwise, "the greatest conceivable is not the greatest conceivable." To our mind, the fallacy is manifest. How could a clear and able mind, like Anselm's, thus stake the fact of existence on an act of thought?

In fact, he does see the fallacy just as we do, as soon as he puts himself in the position of a critic of his own argument. "It is one thing," he says, "for a given object to be in the understanding; quite another thing to understand that it really exists. For when a painter thinks out beforehand what he is going to make, he has it in his mind; but he does not know that as existing which he has not yet made. But when he has painted it, then he both has it in his mind, and knows that what he has now made, is." How, then, does he rest satisfied that at bottom his argument is sound ?

To this the answer must be partly from the system of thought·he held, and partly from the language in which he thought. For we have to think in words; and the Latin tongue is far weaker than ours in expressing the distinction between thoughts and things. Thus, the Latin phrase *Deus est bonus* means either "God is good," or, "There is a good God." In the former case, it states a mere attribute: in the latter case, it states a fact. Latin makes no difference, and a mind trained to think in Latin must find it harder to see the difference. It is not likely that Anselm was not keen enough to see the point so obvious to his critic. As we have seen, he states it frankly, and thinks he has fairly allowed for it. But his thought itself, the very habit of his mind, had been shaped by forms of speech which admitted at every turn just such ambiguities as I have cited. Such Realism as Anselm's I do not think could possibly have been invented in the English tongue.

The Realism I just spoke of consists in ascribing objective reality to the forms or conceptions of our thought. Its highest and most characteristic example is in that I have quoted, in Anselm's argument for the real existence of God. But the same thing runs through the whole texture of his thought. Nay, it runs through the entire structure of the scholastic theology, just as it belongs to the whole structure of the language in which that is written. In Latin, it is impossible to avoid that ambiguity. Here, we come upon the famous controversy of the Nominalists and Realists; and I must ask you to be at the pains of attending to a few easy illustrations.

Realism, in the sense here used, ascribes *real existence* to abstract and general terms. Nominalism regards them as only names, employed for convenience in classification. The controversy, it is true, is inconceivably subtile and perplexing, as it widens out or runs into details; and its plainer bearings are disguised under a cloudy atmosphere of quaint and technical phraseology, —

> " Where entity and quiddity,
>   The ghosts of defunct bodies, fly."

Still, the thought that lies behind it all is not so very difficult or obscure, I would think; while it is absolutely necessary to an understanding of the first principles of that philosophy by which Catholic writers have attempted to explain or defend their creed.[*]

In speaking of the Gnostics, I had occasion to illustrate their notion of Æons, or Emanations, by the grammatical gender of certain abstract terms in Greek.[†] The same thing meets us in a still plainer

---

[*] It is true that the Nominalists claimed to be, and doubtless believed themselves to be, as orthodox as their opponents ; but Anselm himself calls Nominalism (whose test phrase is *universalia post rem*) a " heresy in logic." See Gieseler, Part iii., § 73, note 7.

[†] Early Christianity, p. 59.

way in Latin. Thus, a crowd of names which to us are purely abstract — as honor, intellect, heat, cold, and the like — are masculine; virtue, and the names of all the cardinal virtues, prudence, fortitude, temperance, justice, are feminine. In Latin, we must speak of them respectively as *he* or *she*. Now have they any real existence apart from our feeling of them or our thought about them?

Is there any such thing, for instance, as heat? No, says Professor Tyndall; heat is only a "mode of motion." Yes, says the incorrigible realist, represented to this day in the popular mind, and by some physical speculators of the old school; and perhaps he will give it a hard name, and call it Caloric, and so persuade himself that it exists independent of bodies that we call hot or warm.

Is virtue anything? Yes, we promptly answer: it is a quality of all true souls. Then change the emphasis: Is virtue any *thing?* Half of us are perplexed what reply to make. The Epicureans were the nominalists of antiquity: to them, it was enough to say that the world is "a fortuitous concurrence of atoms," and that the agreeable is the highest good. The Stoics, on the other hand, were such vigorous idealists that they conceived virtue as residing in the very constitution of the universe itself, which was intrinsically divine. Hence, the pathos of that despairing cry of the Stoic Brutus: "Alas! I have found thee, Virtue, but an empty name." "'What is Truth?' said jesting Pilate, and stayed not for an answer." Is there, after all, no such thing as truth, except the accurate statement of a fact? To the mind of antiquity virtue was as real a thing as, for example, carbonic acid is to us. The virtuous man holds it in him as a quality, just as aërated water contains the gas; and the former notion was as natural and simple then as the latter is now.

We find the same spontaneous working of thought everywhere. To the popular mind Time and Death are very real beings: it is almost as if we could draw their very likeness. Time is devouring. Death is cruel. We imagine them in disposition and act as well as in name. Night and day, the seasons of the year, the ages of man's life, earth, sea, forest, and the Nature which includes them all, are examples equally familiar. In a mood of strong emotion we appeal to them, and almost listen for an answer. We call it personification, perhaps. But popular speech, and poetry — which is a melodious distillation, or fifth essence, of popular (not scientific) speech — cling to the form which science has emptied of its meaning. One is a survival of the old Realism, the other an invasion of the newer Nominalism.

Observe, too, that it is this unconscious realism which makes all the glory and heroism of life. Men die, not for a statement of fact, but for the Truth; not for a name, but for an ideal reality; not for a territory with its inhabitants, but for a country; not for a piece of colored cloth on a staff, but for a flag. "What is Honor?" says that incorrigible nominalist Falstaff. "A word. What is that word honor? Air, — a trim reckoning!" Yet, in the balance of the powers of this life, "that word Honor" will outweigh all appeal to interest, and to the common heart means something quite as tangible. It is not too much to say that all the larger capabilities of human nature have been evoked by what we may call men's unconscious Realism, as opposed to their analytic Nominalism. When the great teachers of the Church maintained the first as against the other, they knew that they were defending the very life of their faith.

Take now a step away from these ideals in the direction of more tangible realities. Let us consider the great and famous question of Universals, whether they have any actual existence. Now universals, says Albertus Magnus, are of these five sorts, — genus, species, variety, property, accident. Is there any reality in these, except as names of classes, which we distinguish artificially, and for our own convenience merely? The Realist says, "Yes: they are the most real of all existences." The Nominalist says, "No: the only real things are individuals, which we classify by their nearer or remoter likeness." Let us see.

An example of that popular Realism I have spoken of is found in such very common phrases as these: the Nature of Man, the Rights of Woman, and so on, spelling with a capital M or W. "The proper study of mankind is Man," says Pope. Is there any such thing as Man, apart from individual men? We hear much of the destiny and capabilities of Woman. Is there any such thing as Woman, apart from individual women? "Yes," answers the Realist, unhesitatingly; "Man exists as an archetypal idea in the Eternal Mind; Woman was the final thought of God in the creation." Here we have got back into pure

Platonism, and that conception of the Logos, or self-conscious reason of the Infinite Mind, familiar to the founders of Christian theology.

The modern critic demurs. What was once a grave, even solemn, conception of philosophy seems to him mere tawdry rhetoric, or looseness of phrase at best; and he insists on the duties of *men*, the rights of *women*, — unless he has so far lost his ideality as to deny them instead, and fall back (like the Epicureans) on tangible interests, mere pleasures and pains of sense.

But observe how the popular mind clings to the realistic conception, and finds it a truer as well as more sounding and stirring phrase, to speak of that august "universal" Man; to argue vaguely, perhaps, but broadly, in behalf of that gracious "entity" Woman, than of the "quiddity" or "hæcceity" of ever so many particular men and women, — just as the sublime impersonations, Truth, Right, Honor, or the sacred graces, Faith, Hope, Charity, are more impressive than any adjectives used in place of them to describe the corresponding types of character. There was some method in the madness of that wild idealist in the first French Revolution, who affirmed that the Rights of Man are so sacred as, for their vindication, to be well worth the sacrifice of every individual of the human race!

So far, it is likely, in strict analysis the Nominalist has the better of his opponent. But a step within the range of organic life brings us new difficulties and new solutions. In what does the *species* of living things consist? — merely in the properties of the individuals ? or is there any real existence, apart from those individuals, of the group of qualities, making them what we call a natural group ? *

If we cut a bud in winter, — say a horse-chestnut bud, — we may see with a powerful microscope, it is said, the very petals and stamens of the blossoms that are to grow upon it in spring. This involution and evolution may help us a little way. But no one would say that all future blossoms of all future seasons and generations are contained in the single germ of the first nut. That germ, Mr. Spencer tells us, has a property of assimilation and co-ordination, which we may liken to polarity in a crystal, that determines the successive evolutions, under the law " that homologous units of every order become differentiated in proportion as their relations to incident forces become different." And I am content to take his statement both of the law and of the fact.

But I am not sure that all these hard words, which Mr. Spencer is so fond of, help us much. I have, it may be, three different scions, which I wish to graft into a wild apple-stock. To the eye, touch, taste, or chemical analysis, they are absolutely undistinguishable; the stock that feeds them with its sap is the same to them all; every influence of soil and season is identical. One will produce apples hard, tart, and red; one, tender and sweet; one, streaked, russet, and slightly astringent in flavor. Where does the " spe-

* For a modern statement of the point, take the realism of Linnæus in the assertion "Characters do not make the genus, but the genus gives the characters ; " with Darwin's comments thereon in " The Origin of Species," chap. xiv.

cies " or " variety " exist, — the " potential " shape or flavor, which I am just as sure of before they are set as I shall be in harvest-time, five years hence ?   I make bold to say that no man knows anything about it, except the simple fact.   And this includes the further fact, that the properties of a " universal " — the " quiddity " and " quality " of the particular fruit — existed *somehow* before, at least five years before, the fruit had any being at all that made it possible to be classified, and so to have a name of its own.

When we say, again, that the superb plumage of the peacock or the mocking-bird's capacity of song is contained " potentially " in a few granules of the egg, what is it precisely that we mean ?   Is it not, after all, " a universal before the fact ? "

The mathematician can go one step farther, and conceive of the " potentiality " of the fruit or of the bird as expressed in a mathematical formula, — a vast equation (so to speak), of which it would fatigue us even to imagine what its constants and its variables must be, — which, in the case supposed, will contain at least two constants : the figures 5, and $\frac{5}{13}$ (nearly), one standing for the number of petals, the other for the arrangement of buds.   In the case of a pine-apple, the former symbol would be the figure 3 instead of 5.   We may even say that the change of a variable in the supposed equation would determine a new genus, and that the change of a constant would determine a new species or variety.   But where does this imagined formula exist ?   The only apparent answer is, In the Infinite Mind.   And, if we ask further how this is, we find that we have taken off, after all, only one film from the veil that hides our absolute ignorance — or, perhaps, put one more on.

Thus we have before us, in modern garb, the unsolvable question of Universals, interminably disputed among the Schoolmen. The question they attempted with more or less success to answer was: "Does the universal exist before the object, or in the object, or after the object" (*ante rem, in re, post rem*)? Those who said *before*, without demur or qualification, were Realists; those who said only *after* were Nominalists. And the debate between them was, in form, a debate on the right interpretation of the technical term.

But the question has a far wider reach than the mere classifications of our science or the generalizations of our common speech. It enters into the very sum and substance of the theological constructions of the Middle Age.

To begin with the very highest object of contemplation that can occupy the human mind. We have seen how Anselm identifies the very existence of the Deity himself with his own ability to state it logically in a form of words. Is God, then, according to the Nominalist, a mere generalized expression, or abstract Name? Does that Name mean only the synthesis of natural laws and forces, which makes to our thought the Order of the Universe?

Take the next step in the theological development. Nothing is more striking, or more perplexing to our habit of thought, than the easy assurance with which the old theologies argue from the position that the First Being, regarded as also a First Cause, must be endowed with Reason, or conscious intelligence, as manifest in the works of creation. Not only they proceed very simply to "hypostatize the Logos," as it is called, — that is, to ascribe to it an independent and (as it were) personal existence, making it thus a second Divinity, or Son of God by eternal generation, which the gender of the Greek word might suggest,* — but they find absolutely no difficulty in identifying it with the conscious personality of Christ. Indeed, they find a sufficient proof of that identification in the phrase of Paul: "Christ, the power of God and the wisdom of God." They naïvely turn Paul's statement end for end, and say that "the power of God and the wisdom of God is Christ."† Their mind sees absolutely no difference between subject and predicate, between an attribute and a person. Not only the Ontology of Anselm, but the Christology of the whole Mediæval Church is thus seen to be simply an illustration of the realistic philosophy, as unconsciously assumed by all the earlier theologians.

Now this philosophy is at least as old as the first development of Christian doctrine, — probably a good deal older. Even Aristotle, says Mr. Lewes, is unable to see the distinction of "objective" and "subjective" truth, so obvious to us. To the earlier religious thinkers the human mind is very literally a mirror, which throws back, when it is untarnished, veritable images of the eternal world. In their view, clear

* See Early Christianity, pp. 58, 102, 186.

† Thus, it is a common turn of argument to say that Christ is the Son of God in a like sense as human wisdom is "child of the heart of man." See, for example, Damian, in Migne, *Patrologia Latina*, cxiv. 28.

reflection is just as good testimony of fact as clear observation, — just as a fact in astronomy is equally good to us, whether reported through a reflecting telescope or a refracting one.

Their Realism was probably not reasoned out as a theory, till it was forced sharply into consciousness by the controversy with Nominalism. But it was assumed as a postulate in their philosophy: the contrary doctrine was a late after-thought. Thus, Origen asserts that "the only Son of God is his Wisdom *hypostatically existing*." * "This Word," he says again, "is *a living thing*." † "How," he asks, " could created things live, except by [the attribute of] Life? How could *that which is* truly exist, except as proceeding from Truth? Or how could there be substance to reasonable things, unless the Word or Reason existed previously? Or how should they be wise, if Wisdom were not?"

To us the question would have to be reversed. We know nothing of Life, apart from organic things; nothing of Wisdom, except as men are wise and true. The realism we find so hard to understand, Origen does not argue, does not even assert: he assumes it as something too obvious to be proved. It is the same doctrine that makes the transcendental "intuition," and the mystic's "inner light." If no other religious philosophy is possible, at least no other is

* *De Principiis*, ch. 2. The Latin is that of Rufinus : the Greek ὑποστατικῶς is the assumed original. Compare Paul : "I live no longer, but Christ liveth in me" (Gal. ii. 20) ; and, "I no longer do [it], but Sin ('Αμαρτία) that dwelleth in me" (Rom. vii. 17).

† *Animal vivens*.

so positive, so consoling, **so** sublime, as this which "sees all things in God."

Exactly the same habit of thought, equally difficult and strange to us, is seen in the daring realism that changed the gracious symbol of the Real Presence into the fixed, hard dogma of Transubstantiation. I have just referred to the gross and literal form this dogma took before that period of obscuration, during which it fixed its roots so firmly in the popular mind. It must not be supposed that this was without the strong protest of the more critical and rationalizing minds. The first real controversy of the Middle Age was brought on by the obstinate and sober good sense of Berengar in the eleventh century. Berengar is represented by turns as an intellectual hero and as a vacillating trimmer.* He was hard pushed in debate, but not convinced, by Lanfranc. He was twice forced to sign a recantation, which he twice revoked. He argued his case before Gregory VII. (1079), and was put down only by a single vote, — by the ordeal, say some, of casting the consecrated wafer into a flame, where it remained unscorched. He was spared by the Pope's own word, and died in peace at a great age, leaving a memory curiously mingled of veneration and abhorrence. On the issue, we are told, Gregory felt that the very foundations of his power

* I regret to find myself inclined to the latter view of this noted free-thinker, — unless one should allege, in excuse, the strangeness of his position, when he found himself arrayed, without intending it, against the current philosophy of the time : he assents to his opponent's ground, but gravitates back irresistibly to his own. In short, he was *a nominalist before the time*, and without knowing it. But compare Peyrat, *Les Réformateurs au Douzième Siècle.*

rested; and for three days of the debate the earth swayed beneath, and the sky reeled above, till it was determined that the mightiest of miracles was verily in keeping of the Church.

A few words will serve to state the theory on which this overwhelming form of realism reposed.

It is one of the simplest propositions of metaphysics, that a material object can be known to us only by certain impressions on our organs of sense, as sight, touch, and the rest. Of the object itself, apart from these impressions, we know absolutely nothing. Now can any such object be said to exist at all?

A loaf of bread, for example, has a definite size, weight, texture (which may be known to the ear by the sound it makes when struck), color, taste, and odor. Are these all we know about the loaf? Has it, as the Schoolmen would say, any *esse* independent of them?

Suppose these properties removed. First, suppose the "secondary qualities" of color, taste, and odor to be gone, we may still easily enough conceive the loaf as having shape and weight, — as it were, a block of solidified air. Take these "primary qualities" away, and what remains? — what, that is, as an object of our thought? Nothing whatever, says the Nominalist. To him the question is a metaphysical quibble, or an unmeaning play of words. Nay, says the Realist, there is left the *substantia* of the loaf; that is, the "substance," or substratum, in which the properties reside. The material qualities are one thing, the metaphysical substance is another thing, The qualities are superadded to that: they inhere in it, so to speak, like pins in a pin-cushion. We may imagine any change we will in the latter; we may even imagine it taken away and another substituted for it, without in the least affecting the former.

Here is the miracle of Transubstantiation. The intelligent Catholic does not say that the Bread is changed into the Lord's body. That would be to contradict too grossly the evidence of the senses. The bread may grow mouldy. It may be (as it seems often to have been) nibbled by church mice. It may be made of poisoned dough, and then the poison will do its work. These ignominious and fatal accidents cannot befall a celestial body. It is not the bread, but the "substance" of the bread, that is changed by the sacramental word of the priest;* and to this change no possible evidence of the senses can, from that point of view, offer any contradiction.

All this, it is easy to see, is purely a logical fiction. Science knows nothing of the metaphysical Substance with its sensible Attributes, — a conception which vexed the philosophic mind down to the time of Kant. It knows only things with their properties, — properties that have absolutely no meaning, except as essentially in the things themselves. Logically, we have to distinguish them and give them names. This, to the mediæval mind, was to endow them with a real existence of their own, apart from the thing

* The earliest writer in whom I have noticed this distinction is Haymon (about 850). It belongs, apparently, to the more developed theology of the Middle Age. Paschasius Radbert is content to state dogmatically the mere *fact* of identity. The idea of *change of substance* (though I cannot find in him the technical word *transubstantiation*) is first clearly stated by Hildebert (about 1120).

they describe. This logical fiction it is, that makes belief in transubstantiation possible.

The dogma stands or falls in the pious mind with the philosophy it assumes. No ingenuity of logic could prevail against it throughout the Middle Age, or while the authority of the Church was sufficient to suppress dissent. It was not till the nominalism of William Occam had been received into a mind of the sturdy independence of Martin Luther,* that the dogma fell naturally to the ground. It is probable that Luther never grasped it in its purely metaphysical sense; and, in attempting to retain the dogmatic sense, he had recourse to the needless and incongruous subtilty of "consubstantiation," which asserts the substance of the bread, along with the spiritual body which is held to pervade it in the sacrament. A chemist might compare it to a saturated solution of one kind of gas, which is yet void and capacious to receive another kind. As the logic of Protestantism became clear and self-consistent, this weak compromise faded quite away.

Anselm, as he is the earliest, so he is the most distinctly typical, of the School theologians. He is thought in his later writings to depart from the positive and strict realism generally ascribed to him. At any rate, it is clear that such a challenge to the common intelligence must be taken up by somebody; nay, more, that the springs of strife and contention in human nature were sure to be reached by it.

Philosophy is full as intolerant as theology. Nom-

---

* Luther, as Melanchthon tells us, was a diligent student and admirer of Occam.

inalist and Realist, we are told, were literally at swords' points in their dispute. The finer the point, the better it could serve to goad and sting the antagonist. Of Roscellin, a disciple of Berengar, — whose rude and now conscious nominalism provoked the debate, seeming to make the Trinity three independent Gods,*—no writing is left but a letter discovered a few years ago,† full of insolent and virulent abuse of Abelard, who, it seems, met and cornered him in disputation while the fires of his controversy with Anselm were yet warm.

Now Abelard — restless, daring, speculative, intensely combative and vain — had entered the lists at twenty as a general antagonist of everybody. Like Launcelot in the tilt, he had only to touch his opponent with the tip of his spear, and horse and man went down, — to trust his own account, or to judge from his eager host of enemies. The letter to a friend, in which he tells "the calamities of his life," gives one or two specimens of his keen retort. In this letter it is hard to see which is uppermost, — complacent recollection of his old achievements, when he unhorsed those masters of debate, William of Champeaux and Anselm of Laon, and became the most thronged and admired lecturer of his time; or the irritated contempt with which he visits his old opponents, and his incessant complaint of the persecution he underwent from their wounded pride; or his frank and even somewhat cynical self-accusation

* This seems to be the logical result of nominalism allied with formal orthodoxy.

† Given in Cousin's edition of *Abelard*, vol. ii. p. 792.

in the wretched story of his relations with Heloisa; or his complete unconsciousness of having done anything to invite hostility, or to forfeit respect as an orthodox theologian.

Some attempt has been made to exalt Abelard into a sort of religious hero, as the champion of free debate. But he was as eager to convict other men of heresy as to prove his own orthodoxy. Far the largest part of his theology is matter of pure scholastic speculation, without a ray of religious or moral glow; while, in matters that come near him for judgment, he is hasty, choleric, and superficial. It is not easy to pardon a man who, after confessing the great wrong he has done to Heloisa, can remind her, brutally, how he subdued her reluctance "by threats and blows," or feel even ordinary compassion for him, until, a humbled and heart-broken man, he wins the kindly testimony of Abbot Peter the Venerable by his edifying end.

In the rivalry of parties, it is always hard to see which has the more comfortable assurance of being right in the Christian faith. Roscellin or Abelard can be quite as fervent, on occasion, as Anselm himself. The case seems to be, that Abelard had no very strong convictions either way. Nominalist and Realist alike, he strikes impartially at their vulnerable spot. So far as he has any genuine conviction at all, it seems to be that all truth is relative to the mind that holds it. The very titles of his books — "Know Thyself;" "Yes and No" — betray this subjectivity. In one, he argues that moral right and wrong lie not in the act, but in the motive. In the other, he sets each point of Christian faith between two opposing statements of the most revered authorities, without any pretence of reconciliation. His career, which is a marvel of precocious and audacious brilliancy, is in its moral and its end a dreary failure, as he himself felt it to be. To the last, he was the unmatched champion of debate. At the final Council which condemned him, Bernard never met him with argument, and never meant to, but charged him point-blank with heresy, so as to silence him by pure bravado and ghostly authority; while he never attempted to reply, but appealed at once to Rome from men who he knew, if they did not answer him, at least had the will, and probably the power, to burn him at the stake.

Abelard, then, may represent the restless, speculative spirit, as Anselm best represents the purely religious dogma, of the period in review. Moreover, his early career brings us right into the heart and focus of the debate as it then was raging in the Schools.

Besides the ordinary theological and metaphysical motive, another element of controversy was found, a little later, in the study of Roman Law from the Pandects lately brought to light in Amalfi, and of the Canon Law just codified by Gratian. This new legal temper stirred up fresh suspicion and dread. "Would to God," says Roger Bacon, chafing with eagerness to write out the fruit of his forty years' solitary studies, —"Would to God that I could see these quibbles and frauds of the Jurists banished from the Church, and causes decided as they were decided forty years back, without all this rattle of litigation!"

But the protest of the most ingenious and patient

of monks was not likely to stay the tide of the new
enthusiasm.   Twenty thousand students at once in
Bologna, almost as many in Paris and in Oxford,
made a great cloud of witnesses to the rising faith.
We are in the midst of that astonishing phenomenon
of the University life of the Middle Age, some of
whose earlier passions burn in the letters of Abelard
and his opponent Bernard, his virulent assailant Roscellin, and his hot-headed disciple Berengar.

Paris, south of the Seine, was a great hive of intellectual industry, — called " Latin Quarter " to this
day, in memory of those old glories.   Here the eager,
turbulent, quarrelsome student-life is found in all its
vigor.   Quarrels of town and gown once cost a few
students' lives; and then the University authorities
withdrew, and closed the schools till the town should
be starved into punishing the guilty.   Quarrels of
privilege broke out between the older authorities and
the invading preacher-monks, leading, in course of
time, to the fierce attack of William St. Amour upon
the Minorites, and a controversy that touched the
very life of the Church in those days.   A brilliant
disputer, like Abelard, might be carried by sheer ac-
clamation into his professor's chair: what an appeal
to the irregular ambition of young talent!   Great
multitudes who came to learn, at least to hear, found
it easier to rush into the pleasures and vices of the
capital.   Here a group might saunter or strut in gay
luxury.   Here, again, were numberless poor scholars
in very rags, counting no cost or hardship too dear to
pay for the few crumbs of learning that fell from
their masters' table.   One story is told of three poor

fellows who lodged together, having only one shirt among them, — presumably their entire wardrobe: a woollen shirt, fortunately, which came down to their heels. As they could not all wear it at once, and as etiquette strictly required that they should not appear in the lecture-room without it, they took turns, two staying abed while the other attended in full dress at meals or in the class. What poorest student of modern times has ever been put to such a shift?

It was in the midst of such throngs as these — eager, restless, intelligent, ready to do homage to genuine ability, and just as prompt to detect a sham — that the mighty Albert taught: the largest intelligence of the Middle Age; the great interpreter of Aristotelian logic, physics, and biology; a man whose more than eighty years gathered up all the learning of his time; whose busy hand wrote it out in the twenty-one gray folios where we find it garnered now. Passion for a studious life had sought and gained permission to lay down the burden of his bishopric at Ratisbon; and he taught in the great schools of Paris and Cologne, where he enjoyed for years the fame of the first philosopher, the first theologian, and the first scientist of his age. He was so skilful a mechanician, too, as to be held learned in magic. A walking automaton of his making was taken for an incarnation of the devil by a pious pupil, no less a person than Thomas Aquinas himself, who attacked it in holy rage, and in a few minutes had destroyed the ingenious labor of years.* In genuine learning,

---

* The story is vivaciously told in a curious legend or romance of the life of the great master: *Le Grand Albert* (Paris: Martinon).

and in ponderous technicality of phrase, he more than any other is the typical scholastic of his day. He is praised, too, as the special champion of the Virgin; and his little treatise on the Eucharist gives more plainly than I have ever found it elsewhere the Catholic doctrine of what we may call the physical efficacy of the Lord's body, as the germ in the believer of that immortal body in which he shall rise again at the last day.*

And to Paris, drawn all the way from South Italy by his fame, came the big, smooth-faced, silent youth, whom his schoolmates — because he was always ruminating — nicknamed "the dumb Sicilian ox," † but whom we of a later day know as Saint Thomas Aquinas, the most orthodox, revered, and voluminous theologian of the Roman Church. The master was thirty years older than the pupil whom he outlived by six years. Thomas of Aquinum died under fifty, gently falling into a dreamy sleep, as it were, under the mere pressure of his unceasing, unwearying, unfinished work.

That work is his famous *Summa Theologiæ*, or "Summary of Theology," recognized as the most

---

* See above, p. 21. The statement next in fulness that I have seen is by Anselm (Epist. 107). Compare the illustration given by Mr. Froude in his essay on "The Philosophy of Catholicism," copied on p. 27. ("Short Studies," vol. i.)

† One of his fellow-students, taking pity on his supposed dulness, offered once to help him in his translation ; and so read on with him, till he came to a passage he could make nothing of, when Thomas quietly took it up, with the clearest and plainest exposition. The master understood him better, and was already proud of him: "When that ox begins to bellow," said he, "we shall hear the echo all around."

authentic and complete exposition of the mediæval
faith. It is in one sense a summing-up, and, so far
as may be, a final settlement of the discussions of
the long period we have reviewed. In form, it is a
commentary on the *Sententiæ* of Peter Lombard, a
standard text-book of " Opinions " on all points of
faith, and the stock-in-trade of numerous commenta-
tors. Its plan includes four Books, of which the last
was left unwritten, and is only filled out, in part, by
fragments from his other writings. Its method of
treatment is to state the point in the form of a query;
then give in brief the reasons or statements on both
sides; then close with an answer, or " opinion," delivered judicially, like the opinion of a Court.

If it is a weariness to think of reading the two
thousand folio pages in which this process is followed
out, what shall we say of the indefatigable industry,
the imperturbability of temper, that made the writing of it possible ? I cannot exaggerate the effect
produced on one who attempts a slight exploring of
it, of that busy, almost mechanical, serenity. The
movement is as regular, and seems as passionless, as
the unceasing lift and revolution of the *cam* in a
modern printing-press, and turns off its work with
the same monotonous regularity. The way, too, in
which the whole system of church dogma is quietly
assumed, just as a mathematician assumes his first
principles, — rather, perhaps, as an astronomer assumes the calculus, which it never occurs to him to
demonstrate, or as an engineer assumes his logar-
ithms, — is astonishing to one used to the radical
and restless temper of our time, which insists on

running back by the low *posteriori* road to the origin of all things, to explain so simple a thing as a pebble or a flower. Truly, one feels the advantage here of having "some things which the Court may take for granted."

It is needless to go, even in outline, over the long series of topics thus taken up and dealt with : theology, Christology, the trinity, the creation, the fall, angels, demons, sacraments, moral duties, and the conditions of the future life, — a vast topical encyclopædia.* But it is worth while to mention the sweetness, gravity, serenity, patience, good faith, which characterize this remarkable treatise. Observe that none of the topics mentioned are introduced as points of controversy : all that debate is hushed before we pass the threshold. The questions that occupy us here are not so much the *what*, but the *why* and the *how*, — questions which modern science dismisses without a glance, as unsolvable to the human mind.

No such doubt ever troubles our gentle Summarist. He discusses, with the same placid sense of satisfaction in the result, questions the strangest to us, — whether angels or beatified spirits occupy space ; or whether more than one celestial body can be in the same spot at once ; or whether God can command a thing that has been done not to have been done ; or whether it is as God or as Man that Christ sits on the right hand of God ; or whether the dove in which the Holy Ghost appeared was a real bird or not ; or whether, if the state of innocence had continued, all

* More than six hundred topics or queries ; more than three thousand articles ; more than fifteen thousand arguments.

Adam's children would have been boys ; or whether
a mouse that has nibbled the consecrated wafer can
be said to have partaken the Lord's body,* — as the
doctrine of Sacraments or Indulgences, so interesting
in an historical point of view, or those other questions
of the plain moralities of life, as to which we may
here find even now some hint of instruction and help.
The questions are to him not only solvable, but, in
his imperturbable and patient way, he means that
they shall be solved.

It could not occur to this serene and gentle dogmatist that a dissolving process was at work, making
dust and ruin of his foundations, and leaving his
carefully-built structure very literally a castle in the
air. But so it was. In the first years of the fourteenth century, that strange philosopher-errant, half-
genius, half-adventurer, Raymond Lully, — who had
learned Arabic for the sake of converting the Moors,
and was stoned to death in Tunis, at eighty, in bravely
carrying forward his pious crusade, — happened in,
gray-headed, threadbare, dusty and travel-stained, at
one of the schools in Paris, where a brilliant young
Scotchman was holding forth on some high question
of philosophy. Some gesture of dissent caught the

* These questions, which sound to us rather profane, are very
gravely treated also by Saint Bonaventura, who, to his credit, de-
cides that in Paradise there would have been about as many girls as
boys. He answers the last by an analogy : no one, he says, if you
were to baptize a mouse in the name of the Holy Trinity, would say
that it had received true baptism, or, in fact, anything but a duck-
ing, — the creature not having a soul capable of receiving its sacramental efficacy ; so a mouse which nibbles the consecrated wafer
has not, in reality, eaten the Lord's body.

lecturer's eye, who sought the traveller out when the hour was over, and asked him, abruptly, "What part [of speech] is *the Lord?*" "The Lord is no part, but All," answered the old man, reverently, — the first grave word of that mystic Pantheism, into which the great structure of Scholastic Theology was soon to be dissolved.

The young lecturer was Duns Scotus, clearest and ablest of so-called Realists, born the year that Aquinas died, and destined after his own premature death * to give his name to the "Scotist" school of Platonic theology opposed to the sect of "Thomists." His central point of ethics and metaphysics was the doctrine of Moral Liberty. His followers were the special champions of the dogma of the Immaculate Conception of the Virgin, then a disputed point of orthodoxy. Following the established method of his day, he span out the old yarn of Peter Lombard into a thread of such amazing length and tenuity that he was called "the Subtile Doctor;" and those whose thought was too deep or else too slow for their fellow-men have been named from him "dunces" ever since. Another Englishman, William of Occam, followed with hard good sense, knocking away those ideal corner-stones, choosing that theology should stand alone on its own merits, as revelation pure and simple. And, within the century, the spiritual gospel of Master Eckhart had sublimated the entire fabric into the semblance of a glittering mist.

* Or, by a very shocking account, premature burial. It was in Cologne, in 1308, at the age of thirty-four.

IX.

RELIGIOUS ART.

IN the boundless field of Art there are only two
points which we have to consider: namely, art
as the expression of religious belief or feeling in the
age under review; and art as the means by which
the Church made its powerful appeal to men, working
through the senses upon the imagination, emotion,
and conscience.

These two limitations lead naturally to a third.
The period of Christian Art with which I deal may
be taken as extending from the end of the tenth century till early in the fourteenth. I take the former
date, because it is generally held that a certain resurrection and buoyancy of feeling is manifest at the
moment when the shadow of a great dread passed
away, and the world seemed to have entered on a
new era of life and hope, — which showed itself in
a sudden blooming-out of creative skill in religious
edifices and the like; so that to this time is to be
assigned the *aspiring* character of mediæval church
art. I take the later date, because at this time —
that is, just after the age of Dante — we find, in the
pictures of Giotto and in monumental art particularly, an aim at *beauty for its own sake,* independent
of symbolic or conventional form ; and this, again,

marks the dawn of a new era, which is known more precisely by the name of The Renaissance.

My motive is as far as possible from that of an artist, or even an art-critic. Anything that might possibly savor of connoisseurship must be understood as taken, once for all, at second-hand. I do not claim to do more than hint, very broadly, the line in which our study should proceed. To narrow it somewhat more precisely, it will help us if we take into view an outline of what are commonly reckoned as the several spheres of Art, ranging from pure intellect to daily use. In such an outline, or schedule, we have —

1. Art that appeals purely to the imagination: of this the type is Poetry, which needs absolutely no aid of sense to its full enjoyment;

2. Art that addresses the sense of physical beauty: of this the chief types are Sculpture and Painting, which are called, conventionally, " the Fine Arts ; "

3. Art whose chief appeal is to the Emotions: of this the type is Music ;

4. Arts of Construction and Decoration : of these the noblest type is Architecture, especially that devoted to religious or public use; but they include also all that belongs to the beauty, comfort, and refinement of life, and is known as Household and Decorative Art.

Any of these, again, may evidently be degraded by base use, so as to serve merely sensual and corrupting delight, — which is what the New Testament means by " the lust of the flesh, the lust of the eye, and the pride of life."

Now, as we look back upon this scale, we see that
the religious Art of the period with which we have
just now to do occupies the middle portion,— neither
the highest nor the lowest. Its most characteristic
expression is in Music of organ, song, and bell; or
else in Architecture, which has been called "frozen
music," — the same sense of emotion, harmony, and
aspiration fixed in stone. Without dwelling on these
fancies, we easily recognize the *religious* motive of
early mediæval art, and see that it aims much more
at the complete expression of the feeling than at any
grace of outer form. It hardly ever trespasses into
the region of sensual beauty, which we look for in
painting and sculpture. We are tempted even to
think that it preferred ugliness for its own sake, lest
it might be suspected of any carnal charm.* Splendor of color and infinite patience of workmanship are
the only hints it gives of a reaching towards fine art
in one direction, or mere decoration in the other.
But, again, that early art is infinitely full and rich
in symbolism,— that is, the visible types and expres-
sions of belief. Ideal and typical figures — saints,
angels, devils, monsters, symbolic beasts — are set
forth with rude and clumsy skill, but with a wealth
of fancy that often runs riot, and with a downright
grossness which (we are told) modern notions of decency have compelled to be trimmed away.† This

* Look, for examples, at the abundant remains of the early Mid-
dle Age in engravings, or at the pictures of the so-called Byzantine
School; and compare those in Quarles's "Emblems" and the New
England Primer.

† "At Rouen, a pig plays the violin; at Chartres, a donkey holds

symbolic character is the first thing to be noticed in mediæval art.

This is easiest seen, again, in Architecture, in which the symbol is recognized and insisted on from the first.   The main foundation-stone, marked with a cross and consecrated by special ceremonies, signifies the Lord himself, as the twelve subordinate ones at the angles of nave and transept denote the Apostles. The walls, four-square, represent the people, gathered from north, south, east, west.   The columns are saints and martyrs.   The square building-stones betoken the four cardinal virtues; they are polished, to signify the purifying of the disciples by affliction.   And so on, to great weariness.*   The entire edifice has been represented as symbolic of the agony and passion of Man: the ground-plan — nave, choir, and transept — the human form outstretched upon the cross;† the crypt, his grave; the spire, the man himself erect, as

a sort of harp ; at Essonne, a bishop holds a jester's bauble.   Elsewhere are images of vices and sins sculptured with all the license of a pious cynicism." — Michelet, *Histoire de la France*, l. iv. ch. 9. Some of these may be seen in the crypt of Canterbury cathedral.

Here the satire is mild.   Sometimes it is more keen and pungent : as in an English cathedral, where a fox in priest's robes is preaching to a congregation of geese, from the text (parodied from Paul), "God is my witness how greatly I long for you in my own bowels!"

* This formal symbolism, it must be understood, is not in the motive of the builder, but in the mind of the monastic writers (it is ascribed to Hugh St. Victor), who sought to interpret everything allegorically, as they did the Scriptures.   Much of what follows is doubtless mere romantic, even morbid, fancy.

† It is said, even, that the choir or apse sometimes deviates from the main line of the building, as if to indicate the Sufferer's head upon the cross (Michelet : See his chapter, *La Passion comme principe d'Art au moyen âge* in *Histoire de la France*, before cited.)

it were, in his ascent to the higher life; the gorgeously-stained windows, in crimson and scarlet, as if to typify the blood of martyrdom; bestial and monstrous forms in the decoration, to denote his spiritual enemies subdued by grace; gargoyles, or rain-spouts, in the shape of dragons, to signify the devils escaping every way from the power of the Spirit within.* It is quite possible, in this style of exposition, to exaggerate and mislead; yet it is not possible to overstate the sincerity of the religious feeling shown in these structures, or the ingenuity of the ways in which it is exhibited.

And the motive is quite natural. At an age when few could read or write, when the master-builders themselves were most likely unlettered men, they must put their thought into the work of their hands. In our sense, it was not Art at all. It was a Bible, a Creed, a whole popular Mythology, written out in stone. Not only the style and proportions of the work, but the smallest details of decoration, have to be judged from the same point of view. It is not beauty we look for in them. Sublimity, perhaps; harmony, wealth of fancy; but, instead of vain de-

---

* As a type of another sort, a grain-dealer had been hung at Rouen for cheating. Half his property was given to the poor, and with the other half a portal to the great church was built, with sculptures portraying the wicked merchant's life from the cradle to the grave. At Rheims, a heavy tax had been laid on the people, and provoked resistance. At the base of a cathedral tower was a group of eight sculptured figures, representing the exactions and cruelties under which the citizens had suffered, — one taking money from his purse, another scarred with blows, others bearing the registers of taxation.

light of the eye, it is instruction, remembrance, terror, hope, awe, compassion, reverence, that are first of all to be appealed to. And these are touched by images which tell plainly, rudely, grossly, just as if they were put into words, the things men hated, feared, loathed, hoped, or worshipped, — the Bible stories or the martyr agonies, with which the Church through her teachings had made them familiar.

The one sufficient merit of such art is to tell the story plainly, — whether of the rich man in torment, or Lazarus in Abraham's bosom, or Saint Lawrence on his gridiron. The main pillars of the church of San Zeno at Verona rest on sculptured Griffins — monsters, that is, having the form of lions with the head and wings of eagles — which symbolize the two-fold nature of Christ; and so illustrate the text, "Other foundation can no man lay." "I have trodden the wine-press alone," says the prophet. The mediæval artist represents Christ as crushed literally by the wine-press, while his blood, as it gushes out, is caught in cups, and becomes the sacramental wine of life.

Again, we have to recognize the popular and (so to speak) spontaneous character of the work. If architecture at that day can hardly be called an art, still less was it a trade. It is not till 1133 that builders are known as a distinct class. Up to that time they are the humbler lay-brethren of the monastery, working each man at his trade. The task, planned by zealous monk or priest, was carried out by whole populations. Not far from the date just given, as many as a hundred thousand persons are said to have labored on the cathedral of Strasburg in the course of thirteen years.* Of course, we understand that skill in construction of a very high order must have come into play before the great wonders of Church architecture could be achieved, — the Strasburg spire, for example, climbing to its dizzy height of four hundred and ninety feet, with its marvellous open stonework at once ponderous and delicate, and its spiral stairways as part of its tower-decoration to the very foot of the needle that soars above. But these vast and daring elaborations belong to a later time. While the body of that superb minster was finished in 1275, the spire was not erected till a hundred and sixty years later, in the era of developed art which was the precursor of the Reformation.

Aside from the elaborate symbolism and the enormous scale, — both which mark the ecclesiastical, not

* The following description, written in 1145, refers to the work upon the abbey-church of Diva: "It is astonishing to see men of rank, proud of their birth and wealth, used to softness and luxury, fasten themselves to a cart with ropes, and drag stones, mortar, timber, and all the materials for building the sacred edifice. Sometimes a thousand persons, men and women, are harnessed to the same cart, — so heavy is the load ; and yet there is such perfect silence that you do not hear a breath (*mussitatio*). When they stop on the way they talk, but only of the sins which they confess with tears and prayers : then the priests exhort them to suppress their hate, to pay their debts, etc. If there is one so hardened as to refuse to pardon his enemies, or yield to their pious exhortations, he is loosed from the cart and driven with great shame and disgrace out of the holy throng." At night, the writer adds, lighted candles were set about the carts, about the church that was building, while the people kept watch, singing hymns and chants all night long, with prayers for the sick who were brought to the sacred spot. The letter is cited in Migne, clxxxi. 1707.

the artistic, motive, — the elements of these noble structures are very simple, almost rude. Even the typical pointed arch, which we are apt to think of as a symbol of aspiration, was most likely a matter of simple convenience. It is, in fact, the earliest and rudest existing form of arch, in one of the Egyptian pyramids. It is far less noble and graceful in itself, and needs far less scientific skill to build, than the round Roman arch: the Gothic vault is in itself a far feebler thing than the imperial dome. The same age which built the wonders of Gothic art, thought that the structures of Roman antiquity were "the handi-work of fiends, constrained by poets of bygone age and spells of power to move hell from its centre. . . . It was believed that demons and magic had sus-pended those gigantic vaults in air." *

The pointed arch is, in its elements, a makeshift to support the heaviest downward pressure at least risk and with least constructive skill. Its immense strength of vertical resistance was what invited its builders to pile it up in slender pinnacles, and scale the sky with its soaring tracery, and to make of the entire building, by the breadth and height of its win-dows, one vast transparency. Only in its magnificent repetition and multiplication, in the great upward development it reached, leaping boldly from the top of enormous columns, themselves set at distances so great, with so far-reaching perspective, and with such wealth of decoration, that they have been, fitly enough, compared to the sombre aisles of a great for-est, — only in this vast and crowded magnificence of

* Symonds : Renaissance in Italy.

carrying-out, does it become our example of perhaps
the very noblest style that architecture can attain.
We do not take from its glory, but only define just
where its glory lies, when we speak of the simple and
popular elements out of which it grew, and remember
that it was originally not a scientific construction or
an artist's plan, but the creation of a spirit which
slowly felt its way.

In the earlier (that is, the monastic) stages, the
walls were built clumsily, of small stones, embedded
in a great quantity of mortar,* and with beams of
wood worked in here and there to stiffen them, —
which, again, would decay and leave great gaps or
weak spots in the wall. At its best, the style did
not aim at the solid strength of the ancient orders.
Those tall columns carried no weight; or, as in Notre
Dame, of Paris, a ceiling some three or four inches
thick, as light as could be made. The ponderous
roof rested on the massy outer walls, and these again
were buttressed from spreading by a whole system of
outside props and supports ("flying buttresses"),
adding so much straggling breadth and intricacy of
plan.† The great structure grew in a certain spontaneous fashion, like a forest; and was not, like a
Greek temple, the carrying-out of a clearly grasped
and proportioned plan.

In all this, of course, I am speaking of the earlier
period, and not of the time when the Gothic style
had been carried out to the wonderful completeness
and splendor of its grandest monuments. The thing

* Schnaase : *Geschichte der bildenden Künste.*
† See Introduction to Michelet's *Renaissance.*

in it that interests us most at first is its fresh, spontaneous, popular character. One of the very curious records of the day is the account, given by the Abbot Suger, of the abbey-church of St. Denis near Paris, which was rebuilt and enlarged under his care about 1140. The old shrine, built some five hundred years before, had been a marvel of splendor with its silver roof, and of sanctity with its martyrs' bones; but had come to be far too small for the crowds which pressed to it on festival days. At such times it was packed to suffocation; the throngs could neither stir nor see; the officiating priests were fairly driven to escape out of the windows from the press; women screamed and fainted, or would be lifted up bodily by the sturdy, good-natured crowd, and so walk barefoot on their heads, — like a pavement, the good Abbot says. And he goes on to tell of the cargoes of fine marble fetched round by sea, sometimes by Saracen crews drafted to the service; and the supply of noble building-stone happily found in a quarry that had been deserted by mill-wrights; and how by diligent search through the forest he found twelve indispensable great trees, which the Lord himself must have kept hid for his own uses when the stoutest timber had been felled by the feudal baron hard by for military towers; and how, when the half-built wall was racked by a great wind-storm and in danger of falling, one of the priests prayed stoutly and unceasingly, with many gesticulations towards the threatened spot, and as the crisis grew imminent held out vigorously the arm of Saint Simeon, their holiest relic, and so by Divine aid saved the wall, — which remained the shrine and tomb of

the French Monarchy, till the storm of the great
French Revolution finally flurst it in.*

We have, too, many other curious illustrations of
the popular spirit which honored and thronged the
sacred pile.   It was before the great division of
classes that came about afterwards, long before those
classes were sundered in faith as they were in interest.   There was no grim solemnity, no puritanic
temper, in the respect paid the shrine: all the ecclesiastical pomp, doubtless, that could be mustered, and
all the superstitious reverence that the priestly order
could command.   But that very system of church
authority itself rested on the popular faith, — on the
swaying, boisterous, tumultuous ocean of the popular
heart.

We have just seen what turbulent, good-humored
crowds thronged to the exhibition of relics at St.
Denis.   The great festivals of the Church were,
doubtless, times of grave and solemn ceremony.   But
there was the Feast of the Innocents, when the children chose their boy-bishop, and parodied the holiest
offices without rebuke.   There were the popular holidays which filled the body of the church with feast
and dancing, with booths, tumult, and jollity.   There
was the Feast of Fools,† when the priests burned
leather instead of incense, sang vulgar songs, and
made a banqueting-table of the altar.   There were
Saints' days when they put on their vestments wrong-
side-out, cast bran in one another's eyes, and threw
hard biscuits to crack each others' pates; and other

* See the document in Migne, clxxxvi. 1239.
† See Du Cange, — Article Kalendæ.

seasons, when they trailed herrings on the floor in mockery of Lent, and tried to trip one another up.

Then there were the seasons of blessing the domestic creatures of farm and household, when cattle, sheep, and horses, like good Christians, paraded the sacred courts. "Suffer these innocents to come, and forbid them not!" said the kindly priest. There was the famous Procession of the Ass, — which patient beast was not cudgelled and bruised, but held in honor as the creature that had stood by the manger at Bethlehem, and carried the Babe into Egypt, and borne the King in triumph as he rode into Jerusalem on the first day of the Holy Week. A part of the ritual in his honor is still extant, with a long Latin hymn reciting his services and virtues, and ending in a vigorous chorus of brays. This was a time when rude humor and boisterous fun were held no desecration of the Lord's house.

In short, to understand how the temper of the time was felt in Christian Art, we must remember two things. Heresy had not yet taken such a shape as to make the Church tremble for its power, to beget that mingled terror, rage, and hate, which afterwards declared war against whole populations; while the line had not yet been drawn, except in the dignities of the priestly class, that afterwards separated so sharply the sacred and profane. This line was indicated by the chancel-rail, which the laity might not pass, and which marked the choir as the portion reserved to priests, the altar as a holy spot of religious ceremony. But we must not suppose that the great cathedral itself was in our sense of the word an exclusively "sacred" building. The body of the church was the people's gathering-place for any occasion of state and ceremony.

We do not at first thought realize what a noble feature of mediæval life was this free use of the noblest and grandest structures. In some dim chapel, or some low, damp basement made to serve the purpose of a Sunday School, I have sometimes thought in contrast of what you may see in the stately aisles of St. Peter's in Rome, — troops of school-children brought in there for their morning lessons, and trained among those costly splendors to their duty as faithful children of the Church. These superb structures are never once thought of as too costly or too good for the humblest uses. This most attractive feature modern Romanism has inherited from a day when all the popular life — its business, its passion, its turmoil, and its sport, as well as its austere and fervent piety — had a home beneath that spreading roof; when Courts of Justice as well as religious assemblies were held in its thronged aisles; when its ample spaces embraced everything that goes to make up both senses of a popular holiday.

The time of which I speak in particular exactly coincides with the first passion of the Crusades: the time when the popular heart and temper were probably in most absolute unity with the ecclesiastical faith. As nearly as such dates can be safely given, we may say that this phase of mediæval life culminates about the middle of the twelfth century. This was before the crusading ardor had spent itself, or begun to lapse into despair. It was the epoch of full splendor of those Military Orders which enlisted to the defence of Palestine. It was while the Monastic spirit found its most eminent representative, and the culmination of its power, in Saint Bernard. It was when the Church felt herself strong enough to repudiate the contract entered into with the Empire at Worms (1122), and plunge into her hardy and obstinate struggle with Barbarossa, to win by force of arms the prouder than imperial crown worn by Innocent III.

The visible glory of the Mediæval Church is greatest in the century beginning at this date. And, as in all times especially great in Art, wealth flowed away from private uses, to devote itself to the noblest public works. There is at this time nothing of private luxury, or personal comfort, measured by the standard of our day. There is splendor of armor, equipage, and costume, delight in bright color and the glitter of polished metal, delight in waving banners and caparisoned horses; but of the softness and indulgence which we know by the name of comfort there is nothing. Whatever that might cost, went to the channel of what, by comparison at least, we may call noble use. The town dwelling was cramped and poor, the castle gaunt and bleak, the banquet lavish perhaps, but rude and plain. And so, in a time whose wealth and skill were not to be reckoned beside ours more than the strength of children against that of men, public works were produced on a scale of lavishness and splendor which the wealth of the nineteenth century could never once afford to similar uses. The expensive things with us are not cathedrals, but warships, gunpowder, steel cannon, strong drink, improved drainage, railways, and household art.

The proper illustration of what has now been said of the symbolic and popular character of early Christian Art, would be a museum ·of monuments or drawings, especially photographs, of its fast perishing remains. But, at the date before given (1150), the subject begins already to connect itself with a very important revolution in society then going on, which gives it a new character. Up to that time, speaking generally, the Monastic Orders are in the ascendant. The most splendid and costly works were undertaken by them, — full of the rude symbolism and lavish decoration already spoken of, and wholly religious in their motive. The abbey-church of St. Denis, so magnified by the good Suger, is the glory of this very time. In vain such harsher spirits as Saint Bernard protested against the riotous fancies, which they might check to-day, but which streamed back in full flood to-morrow.

There was another power, too, which they dreaded even more, — the encroaching and tyrannous temper of Feudalism, that old rival and counterpart of the Church, then in its chief glory, and just reinforced by crusading adventure, by the enthusiasm and romance of Chivalry. A new splendor belonged to the profession of arms. Saint Bernard, in his harangue to the Templars, tries to make this new enthusiasm count for the Church, in summing up the virtues of the Christian warrior. But he also saw and dreaded the same temper, as it crept into the hearts of the consecrated order. "How incredible and strange," he writes to our friend Suger, "that the same hand which has struck with the sword of violence should give in God's name the blessing of peace!"* This active jealousy against the pomp and pride of the Feudal Order is one motive in the social revolution now impending. The royal power, too, has taken the alarm; and a few years later we find it, under Philip Augustus, embarked on the steady, unrelenting policy which in time will put that proud Nobility in complete subjection to a centralized, despotic Monarchy. Thus Church and State combine to bring about the revolution on which we have now to fix our eye.

Coincident with the first stages of it, and for half a century or more keeping even pace with it, we find that most astonishing growth of all periods of creative art, the simultaneous erection of the ten or twelve great Cathedrals which represent most completely the splendor, wealth, and perfection of the Gothic style. The period of this growth has been more strictly limited to the sixty years, from 1180, the year of Philip's accession, to 1240. What went before was comparatively feeble and poor; what followed, however elaborate, was tied by artificial and formal rule, and lacked the free fancy, the vigorous life, of this great age. And, what is still more striking, this growth is suddenly arrested at the latter date; the great impelling motive is somehow crippled; the vast structures already begun are left stunted and incomplete; the climbing spires had to wait for a later day, to be taken up in another spirit. Not one of the great works of this period was ever finished.

* Not literal: the passage is a long one (Epistle 78).

A few words will tell us the reason that lay behind this curious phenomenon. Previous to 1150, it will be remembered, the great architectural works were built by the Monastic Orders; and until 1133 there is no knowledge of a separate building class. Till 1150, the cathedral was inferior in size and splendor to the abbey-church; the Bishop was a less important person than the Abbot.* The same Abbot Suger, who after Saint Bernard was the highest ecclesiastic of France, was also the adviser, or what we may call consulting architect, in building the first of the great French Cathedrals at Noyon. A few years later, the whole great tide of popular and creative enthusiasm is turned to that one channel; and all over the North of France these vast structures begin to rise, with a rapidity of construction which in a day of so rude mechanical skill is literally amazing.†

We must understand, then, that the suppression of feudal privilege, which the King had taken in hand, called out in response an immense popular enthusiasm. The King's cause was the people's cause. The intolerable weight of a minute, insolent, and vexatious tyranny was lifted off, in part at least, and the popular energies had free play. This was chiefly seen in the great Towns. A change like that a century or

---

* Thus the official correspondence of Louis VII. while on the Crusade is addressed to Abbot Suger, and not to the Metropolitan bishop (Migne, vol. clxxxvi. col. 1365). Of him it was written by Hildebert of Mans, —

"Ille regens regem, rex quasi regis erat."

† See Viollet-le-Duc : *Dictionnaire raisonné de l'Architecture Française*, vol. ii. pp. 280-85, — Art. "Cathédral."

two earlier in Italy developed a similar commercial splendor and pride, though not political independence, in the great towns of France and near the Rhine. It was here that the elaborate system of modern industry took root, and was developed in trade-guilds, and became an intricate organization of training, privilege, and self-defence; as a little later, and a little farther north, it grew into the stormy democracy of Flanders and the Dutch towns. In France it was still subject to the central power, and in alliance with the King.

And here, as ever, the Church found its opportunity. Bishops became leaders, guides, spokesmen of the new spirit. The same municipal pride, the same intense consciousness of liberty, wealth, and power, that in Ghent, Bruges, or Louvain cropped out in the superb Town Halls, — purely secular in motive but hardly inferior to the glories of ecclesiastical art, — here joined forces with the clergy. The vast and noble municipal structures which sheltered and glorified the new life took the form of those magnificent Cathedrals of Amiens, Rheims, Rouen, Chartres, Paris, — the very noblest creation of Mediæval Art.*

These cathedrals were the City Halls of the period. They were the symbol of a rising nationality; they were the Church's recognized defiance to the Feudal Castle. They were not the property of an exclusive "sacred" class, or shut up to exclusively "sacred" uses. The Choir was still the place of worship; but the Nave, the body of the structure, arched over by

---

* Viollet-le-Duc, in the passage before cited, gives a list of twenty-five French cathedrals whose structure belongs to this period.

those exalted roofs of stone, and flanked by the pil-
lared aisles, and lighted by the splendor of colored
windows unspeakably gorgeous in the generous day-
light, belonged to the people. Here their multitudes
thronged for neighborly meeting or for holiday; here
their Courts of Justice were held, sheltered under the
same roof that covered the altar and the saints.

The Courts, too, as well as the Altar, were under
Church control. Bishop and priest were interpreters
of the Law. As guides of the people's conscience,
they claimed the right: for did not points of personal
duty or abstract justice — that is, heaven's justice —
come into every transaction between man and man?
Besides, the Canon Law which they administered was
on the model of the Civil Law, and so might stand
for impersonal justice, while safe from jealousy of the
State. It was more merciful, too, than Feudal Law,*
and so might well stand to the people as a rule of
equity and mercy. So, in the consent of those three,
— the King, the Church, the People, — the great era
of Mediæval Catholicism had its strong foundation;
and its grandest creation was in those magnificent
structures, its glory and its monument.

But here, as elsewhere, the Church forfeited its
actual strength and its splendid opportunity by its

---

* Of which the two most characteristic methods in judicial investigation were Ordeal and the Wager of Battle. Of the nature of
the "rights" recorded in the Feudal Code some hint has already
been given (above pp. 33–37), and more may be found in the intro-
ductory chapters of Taine's *Ancien Régime*. A very interesting
account of the way in which the influence of the lay barons was
suppressed in the royal courts of Louis IX. is given in Sir James
Stephen's "Lectures on the History of France."

incessant, insatiable, all-grasping ambition. Its genius was, never to be content while any source of authority was outside its own control. The audacious challenge of Hildebrand, the obstinate struggle of Alexander III. against Barbarossa, the towering ambition of Innocent III., the unrelenting animosity of the war upon Frederick II., the Church's apparent success in this campaign of near two centuries,* must alarm all the powers of the earth,— the more, in proportion as they really sought to enforce and sustain justice in their own sphere.

The " holy king " St. Louis, who in temper was the humblest subject of the Church, and in spirit a true saint as well as champion, sided strongly with the free-thinker Frederick against the monstrous encroachment of the Papacy. And now — bent as he was to be a righteous and God-fearing king in his own dominion — he watched jealously the rising ambition of the Priesthood. A conference of bishops complained to him that, as the age grew undevout, men neglected to pay their church dues or seek the Church's absolution ; and begged him to enforce its claims by royal authority. " We will do justice to every man," said the pious king, " and whom we find guilty of default will compel him to render you his due." †

This was not the jurisdiction the clergy demanded : they claimed, besides, to be judges of their own right. But the Crown was too strong for the Mitre. The people chose the king's part and not the priest's, surer of his equity than theirs. The alliance of the Church with the popular heart was broken. The

* Reckoning from 1048.   † Joinville.

"Pragmatic Sanction," charter of the Gallican liberties, made a few years later (1268) the first breach of Catholic unity; and from that time forth, we are told, the work on the great cathedrals paused, and those towers and pinnacles were left unfinished, arrested as it were in mid-air. Thus, by the middle of the thirteenth century, ecclesiastical power has already passed its noon.

But we may look back once more and try to conceive, if we will, what was its appeal to the imagination while still unchallenged. We may guess it, if we can, by what still remains of it at the command of Rome to-day, — incomparably more brilliant, imposing, and august than any military or state show with which it might possibly be compared. For tenderness of appeal nothing of the sort I ever saw approached the religious procession of *Corpus Christi*, as it wound by the hour among the uneven and narrow streets of Avignon, or for imposing grandeur the stately solemnities of Saint John's day at the Lateran. The secret of that power was never possessed so fully by any other body or authority upon earth: it is not likely that any other has so many avenues to men's enthusiasm and reverence to-day.

For, we have to remember, all we have seen or learned of the glory of the outer temple is but playing upon the surface of a tide of power, whose real depth is far within. The symbolism sculptured upon walls, or built into corbel and capital, or blazoned in the arches of stately windows, is repeated in innumerable ways, — in creed, song, litany; in priestly robes and swinging censer and lighted candle; in the tone of silver bell, or the deep mellow peal that steals down from the church tower like an enfolding mist, or the chime that rings out on the air at change of hours; in the chant sung by one powerful voice or answered by the harmonies of the cathedral choir; in the melody of hymns, whose tenderness we feel in the *Stabat Mater*, as we feel their terror and their awe in the *Dies Iræ;* in the uplifted Host which multitudes adore as a literally present and visible deity; in the diversities of sound and pomp of color that belong to the procession on some festal day.*

All these are only the various language in which that Church is continually preaching to eye and ear her awful mysteries, the symbol and accompaniment of the Real Presence, which she claims to hold only in her keeping. Whatever the human mind has yet conceived of terror and pain, of awe and majesty, of gladness, reverence, and hope, is shadowed forth in that language of picture and music, with a power scarce diminished to this day.

The change by which this splendor began to be visibly diminished may be held to date from about the time now indicated, the middle of the thirteenth century. The visible advent of the power that is destined steadily to encroach on its domain and introduce a different era is first made clear early in the fourteenth. We shall soon meet the symptoms in

---

* The night-procession of gorgeously attired priests, bearing lighted tapers, and winding in long array among the lofty outer galleries and the wide spiral of the balustrades, while the crowd stood in the darkness of the street below, is conceived by Michelet as suggesting to Dante the scenery of his descent to the Lower World.

politics, in the growth of opinion, in the weakening of faith, in the rousing of new animosities and fears, which accompanied this change. That mediæval life, gathered up and rayed out upon us in the works of Dante, is long before his death essentially a life of the past. Two symptoms of the change, in the region of Art, are all that belong to my purpose now. Instead of creative energy, we have formal rule; while Beauty begins to take the place of Truth, as the aim of the artist's skill. A few words on these two points will finish what I have to say.

Along with the other trade-guilds or associations of workmen in the great towns, the craft of architects or builders had a very important place. It did not differ in the principles of its organization from the others. Each trade must protect itself from competition as it might by arbitrary rules of fellowship, making of it something of a "craft" or "mystery." All this was very hostile to the spirit of free-trade, and the expansion of modern life has swept most of it away. The craft of Masons, or Builders, differed from the rest in being not a stationary trade, like that of the forge or loom, but from its nature a wandering one.* The mason must carry his skill where it was wanted, — that is, where the building was going on.

Hence, two consequences occur. In an age when few could read or write, he must be known to his craft by a greater intricacy of pass-words, or signs, which, alone of the mediæval "mysteries," seem to have survived in modern Free-Masonry.

* Schnaase.

The other result was more important. It was the development of a higher mechanical skill, and the forming of a large body of associated workmen, competent to carry on in detail the work which the great age of Christian architecture had created. The skill was no longer under the control of the inventor, of the man of genius, or of a few masters of the art; it must be shared by a great multitude of average men. The symbolism was no longer to grow up piecemeal, spontaneously as it were, or by instruction of monk or priest; it must be reduced to rules of proportion and symmetry of parts.

It is now that the most daring and astonishing structures of the whole Gothic period are found, — such as those at Strasburg, Antwerp, and Cologne. The last, in particular, which was absolutely suspended for nearly six hundred years, and was not completed till 1880, is a miracle of richness, grandeur, and proportion : all its dimensions, it is said, are studied to the last detail, so as to make it an ideal and final type of the utmost mechanical perfection that can be achieved. But it is all, say the critics, the work of rule and compass, by circle and triangle, — quite bare of the free luxuriance, the genius and the joy, to be found in older and perhaps ruder examples.* The criticism may be sound or not. At any rate it is true that the qualities just spoken of mark the change we have to note. They are, in short,

* Such a criticism certainly seems noway justified to one standing amidst the overpowering splendors of the finished work. To understand it, one should compare the rigid symmetry at Cologne with the unconventional freedom of style in earlier examples.

the qualities of the fourteenth and fifteenth centuries, not those of the twelfth and thirteenth.

And again, this craving for beauty and symmetry of form is what we shall have to see in the extreme formalism of Dante's verse; just as his wealth of symbolism reflects the mind of the earlier time. In literature, the stern composition of Dante was one of the first essays in the almost untrodden field of the modern, popular tongue; and its rigid lines soon gave way before the new invading sense of freedom. But, side by side with it, was the first growth of what was to ripen in another century to the Italian Renaissance. Italy had already outgrown the true spirit of the Middle Age. The stones of Florence were getting laid in those orderly, solid courses of her new cathedral, which were the outward token and anticipation of a new era of scientific construction.*

In the search for beauty, Art no longer aimed at visible utterance of truth. Not the Symbol,— which only pictures, no matter how rudely, some fact, fancy, or belief, as an alphabet might give it in written words,— but the Form, which satisfies the eye by its own grace or coloring, was what the artist sought to give. With this change, the era of old Belief was passing away, and the modern era of Taste was fore-shadowed. Giotto was the friend of Dante. And while some of his pictures at Padua † are purely symbols, even painful caricatures and grotesques, in Florence you see that superb Bell-Tower, the perfection of formal design wrought out in variegated stone;

* Michelet : *La Renaissance*, Introduction.
† In the Arena Chapel.

and pictures, too, of his, in which the faces of saint
and seraph are as delicately drawn and as brightly
colored as in the grander and richer wonders of a
later day.

These symptoms, quite as clearly as those in the
field of doctrine or politics, warn us that we are approaching the boundaries of another great historical
period. The thought, the art, the struggle, the adventure of the Middle Age have at best a foreign look
to us. Our interest in them is nearer than antiquarian; but neither the ideas nor the passions they
exhibit are shared by us. They are still far off, and
strange. It is different, as soon as we have passed
that great headland which marks the period and work
of Dante, and is known to us by his name. We are
now in the ranges of modern literature and modern
art. Boccaccio was a boy of eight when Dante died,
and in manhood became his first expounder to a generation that already found him strange. Seven years
after, Chaucer was born, who brought the modern
spirit fresh from Italy and the South of France, and
made it the perpetual possession of our own tongue.

These voices in literature and art are heard long
before the same modern spirit begins to penetrate
the religious belief of men. Two centuries and more
must pass, from Dante to Luther. Intellectually,
they are not so much centuries of movement, as of
rest and germination. A single cursory view is all
that we shall be obliged to take of the influences at
work; and this will best be had by a study of the
phenomenon known as the Italian Renaissance.

X.

DANTE.

CHRISTMAS of the year 1300 marks the best boundary-line from which we look back and forward over the field of the Middle Age. That line parts two divisions in the field, of which one slopes as definitely towards the wider spaces of modern life, as the other is covered thickly with monuments of a life already passing away. The Mediæval system of government, thought, and faith, kept so long by so hard a struggle to so proud a level, breaks as suddenly, right there, to find its new conditions, as at its great Cataract the Nile comes from the Nubian highlands to the fertile plains of Egypt.

The obstinate conflict of Church and Empire has just ceased in the literal extermination of the proud house of Hohenstaufen, hunted to their death by the unrelenting enmity of a long line of Popes. The daring structure of Scholastic theology shows but a fading twilight splendor since the death of its four greatest masters, all in the last six and twenty years ; * and is already undermined by unsparing analysis, or else sublimed to a pious mysticism.† The

* Thomas Aquinas and Bonaventura died in 1274; Albertus Magnus, in 1280; Roger Bacon, in 1294.

† Duns Scotus died in 1308; Eckhart, in 1329; William of Occam, in 1347.

vast pretensions of the Papacy, maintained with extraordinary vigor for nearly a century since Innocent the Third, are asserted in a form more daring and arrogant than ever by the old man Boniface the Eighth, who appoints this very year for a universal Jubilee, to celebrate the Church's triumph over all her foes.

It is the "last great day of the Feast." For months together Rome has been thronged by a continual crowd of strangers, reckoned as many as two hundred thousand at once, — thirty thousand coming and going in a single day, — whose endless procession, passing and repassing on the broad bridge which separates the western from the eastern city, seemed to Dante as he gazed upon them (then an envoy from his native Florence) no unfit comparison to that "great multitude which no man could number" of spirits whom he met in his pilgrimage through the world below. This year, which he reckons the half-way station of his own life, is the moment also of that appalling Vision, in which his inward eye swept the whole spiritual universe; and then he conceived the vast plan of a Poem that should embrace it all, — its Paradise, its Purgatory, and its Hell.

It has often happened that the thought and life of an historical period have been impersonated in some one man of genius, who has been its type and embodiment for later times. Thus — to take the best-known cases — the speculative genius of Greece is summed up in Plato, and the scientific in Aristotle; the romance and passion of the Renaissance are mirrored in Shakspeare, the ideal side of Puritanism in Milton, and the eighteenth century in Goethe. There are only two examples where a single life has in this way taken in and reproduced an entire period or phase of civilization, so as to stand alone as its sufficient monument. As Homer represents to us the pre-historic age of Greece, and as his verse bears down to us the melody and splendor of a time which we are only beginning to see by glimpses from other directions, — so in Dante we have a transcript or reflex, curiously complete, of the many phases of Mediæval life, in a form at once ideal and intense. All the glow of its romance is behind the transparent veil he has woven about his own "New Life." All the ardors of its faith are seen in the visions of un-utterable glory that crowd his "Paradise." All its subtilties of speculation are found in the arguments and comments of his "Banquet." The terrible or re-volting realisms of its creed fill the thronged circles of his "Hell." Its whole scheme of redemption is displayed in the steep ascents of his "Purgatory." Its partisan passion, its capacities of pride, wrath, and hate, come to a hot focus in some of his "Epis-tles," or are reflected in the incidents of his career. Its fond dream of universal sovereignty, its allied ideal Empire and Church, has its completest expres-sion and defence in his treatise on the Divine right of "Monarchy." There is no other name in literary history which is, in anything like so large a sense, a representative name.

There are two lives of Dante to be studied: one of the Man, as given by his biographers; the other of the Poet, narrated by himself.

The first gives us the details, at least the outline, of the events. This life we can very highly honor in its kind; but there is no need that we should idealize it, or disguise the grievous faults which he himself deplores, or make virtues of them, as many do. It shows him as the student, the politician, the soldier, "fighting valiantly on horseback in the front rank" at Campaldino; later, as the party leader, the magistrate, the exile, — banished with a vindictive wrath that threatened burning alive as the penalty if he should be taken; an exile from choice, passionately eager to return but as passionately proud, disdaining the least concession which might hint that he had possibly been ever in the wrong.

It shows him, in his two-months' term of power, "making himself his own party;" banishing impartially the chiefs of both factions, his own near friends; and, when sent on some mission to Rome, asking haughtily, "If I go who stays? If I stay who goes?" then, undermined in his absence, finding the gates of Florence barred against him by the implacable decree of exile.

It shows him for nineteen years a banished man, beggared by confiscation, finding brief rest anywhere in his austere pilgrimage; climbing (as he says) the steep stairs that lead to other men's houses, or tasting how salt the bread is on strangers' tables; resting his hope awhile on some princely house of Verona, Ravenna, or Milan; hailing with eager triumph the crowning of a new Emperor from beyond the Alps, whose fatal delay he chides, while proud in the same breath to kiss his feet; writing a letter of tempestuous defiance to his native city, and invoking upon her the curse of a conqueror's revenge; buried at last in the hospitable city of Ravenna, which proudly holds his monument, and where by a strange chance his bones lay safe — not one of them broken or perished — to be rediscovered and photographed in their first resting-place, in our own day.

Perhaps no figure of the remoter past is so familiar as that of the exile-poet: the Mediæval cap and robe, the pressed lip, the steadfast look, the sad, stern face, the head wreathed with the traditional laurel chaplet, — the same shape which his contemporaries thought had literally walked through hell; the same features which they thought were swarthy with the glare of its fires, — so that women, it is said, would shrink back, and point him to their children as the man who had been among the damned. That is the form and pressure of the outward life.

The other is the life of which he has written the first chapter in his *Vita Nuova*, — a life of vision and romance and contemplation, separated it would seem by an impassable barrier from the sharp passions and hard incidents of the first. There was never, I suppose, a story of childish experience so quaintly, so frankly, and so sweetly told, as in this "New Life." * It would be a pity to mar that tale of innocent love and romantic homage by any repetition or abridgment. I do not know any parallel to it except the little romance of Oriana and the Child of the Sea which I copied once before from *Amadis de Gaul* to

---

* Happily, the singular charm of style as well as spirit and form is preserved for us in Mr. Norton's version.

illustrate the sentimental side of Chivalry. It seems
almost grotesque to bring together that high-flown
romance and this naïve confession. But, without
some such hint, it is hard to show how completely
what is finest in the spirit of Chivalry is transfused
into the early poems and the waking dreams of
Dante.

We have, too, to bear in mind that the glow of that
young dream never faded out of his heart; that it
literally made the guiding-star through the shadows
and pains of his life ; that the little girl of eight in
crimson, the fair maiden whose chance greeting made
him tremble with timid ecstasy, the young bride at
whose early death it seemed strange to him that all
the world was not in mourning, became very truly
the glorified Presence of his pilgrimage, his guide to
Paradise, and his type of celestial Wisdom. So that
in very truth those words were wonderfully fulfilled
which he wrote at the end of his confession : —

" After this, a marvellous vision appeared to me, in
which I saw things that made me resolve to speak no
more of this blessed one, until I could more worthily treat
of her. And to attain this I study to the utmost of my
power, as she truly knoweth. So that, if it shall please
Him through whom all things live, that my life shall be
prolonged for some years, I hope to say of her what was
never said of any woman. And then may it please Him
who is the Lord of Grace, that my soul may go hence to
behold the glory of its lady, namely, of that blessed Beatrice, who in glory looketh upon the face of Him which
is blessed for evermore" (*qui est per omnia sæcula bene-
dictus*).

I must return to this ideal side of Dante's life, when we come to review the work he did. But, first, it is necessary to bring it into its right historical bearings. The point of view from which we have to look at it is the Italy of the Middle Age, especially that city-life, with which all the incidents of his own are so intimately bound up. A slight notice of this is necessary, also, to complete the outline of the period previously given.

The two parties to the conflict which raged so sharply, from the middle of the eleventh century till near the end of the thirteenth, were the Church and the Empire. Our attention is mainly taken up with them, and our sympathy or hostility is apt to be engaged in the fortunes of the main battle; so that we forget perhaps, a third party, quite as fit to enlist our interest as either.

Italy was the stake for which the campaign was fought, and Italy was the field of battle. Sovereign of Italy, the Pope had a broad territorial base for his political supremacy. Head of the " Holy Roman Empire," the Emperor must not only assert his divine right to sovereign rule, but must claim Rome for his capital, and Italy as the most essential part of his dominion. And so, in a very special way, the liberties of Italy were staked upon the quarrel; and we have not felt the heat of it, till we have seen how deeply the passions and the fate of Italy were involved in it. The party lines were nowhere else so sharply drawn; and no party cries divided cities or citizens with such bitter passion, as the names of Guelph and Ghibelline, — the party of the Pope and the party of

the Emperor, — which ring through all the history of
the time.

This point of view is the more important, because
the period we are considering is the age of early
Italian splendor.   They show you in Florence the
stone seat where Dante used to sit watching the walls
of the great Cathedral then building.   That most
glorious of bell-towers — two hundred and ninety-two
feet in height, and so delicately wrought that the
emperor Charles V. said it ought to be kept under
glass, like a mantel toy — was built by his dear friend
Giotto.   The same palaces and ranges of dark stone
which give such dignity to the streets of Florence,
were long before this the stronghold of rival houses
and the rallying-place of street factions.   The bloom
of her rich and haughty rival Pisa came still earlier.
That superb group of structures in white marble
which stands so bright and fresh to-day on her green
plain — the Cathedral, Baptistery, and Leaning Tower
— was begun long before the first Crusade, and completed soon after the second.   Through the twelfth
century Genoa was a powerful State, and with its
independent navy carried on single-handed several
important enterprises of the Crusade.   The plain of
Lombardy was dotted with strong, rich, and splendid
cities, able either to hold out singly against a siege,
or, united in the " Lombard League," to bring the
most powerful of Emperors to terms.   In 1295 Marco
Polo returned to Venice — then and for more than a
century before a superb and powerful capital — from
his twenty-four years' sojourn in the East, bringing
home to Italy his tale of wonder from Tartary, China,

and Japan.* The heroic age of the Italian towns and their age of tragedy were the two centuries just before the time of Dante.

The people of Italy, ground so long between the upper and the nether millstone, — imperial tyranny below, the sweep and whirl of barbarian tribes above, — began at length to rally from their dispersion and to fence themselves in towns. As early as the ninth century, Italy was a country of walled cities. The civic fortress was stronger than the feudal castle. Here the people began to be prosperous and safe. They tilled the fields; they diked the rivers. Agricultural wealth grew apace. Manufactures of cloths, furs, jewelry, armor, were as natural a growth of industry within the towns. From these came trade, and with trade increasing wealth.

The war of Investitures between Pope and Emperor — a war in which the country was so often at once the victim and the prize — was the people's opportunity. They had, at worst, liberty to choose between their masters, and their alliance with one or the other party had its price. Forced often to fight in self-defence, they came to have an intense local and military pride. The great wagon (*carroccio*), or platform on wheels, drawn by oxen, holding the flag-staff with the city's broad standard flying and the

* Nothing better shows the clear intelligence of the Italians of that day, and their long lead in civilization, than a comparison of this sober and authentic narrative with the wild fables of Sir John Mandeville, which passed current in England in the fourteenth century, just as in the fourth they had turned up in the vague historical speculations of Saint Augustine.

trophies of former fights, became the rallying-point of battle, and the heart of the most desperate defence.

The City must have its military as well as civic organization, and might want its military leader. Some noble house, beaten or impoverished in its old feudal estate, would migrate to the town ; and its chief, by boldness, tact, skill, or the force that runs in fighting blood, would come to be practically the master of the little State. Such is in brief the story, told over and over, of the rise, power, and splendor of the Italian towns, down to and during the time of the Crusades.

The early struggles of Pope and Emperor had increased the independence of the cities, and the Crusades had marvellously increased their wealth. A century of growth had thus prepared them for the twenty years' war which made the heroic era of their history, and which laid the foundation of the Italian liberties.

When Frederick Barbarossa came to the German throne, just after the disastrous crusade preached by Saint Bernard, his first care was to give order and prosperity to the German States which had suffered such calamity. Soon all Germany north and south was united under him, with a loyal and enthusiastic attachment such as it had never had for a sovereign before, and has never equalled since. The old local jealousies, the old family war-cries of *Welf* (a rival house) and *Weiblingen* (one of his own estates),* were hushed. Intelligent, resolute, inexorable, Frederick

* *Guelfi* and *Ghibellini*, as the southern tongue caught the German vocables.

believed as firmly in his divine right of empire, and doubtless as piously, as the Pope believed in his. Rome was his seat of empire, and Italy part of his imperial estate. The free Cities must own their master. He would deal righteously ; he would respect any established bounds of justice, — but sovereignty complete and full, such as he conceived to be his right in his hereditary dominion, he must have in Italy. And the terms of it, interpreted under the newly discovered forms of the old Civil Code, were defined at the Diet of Roncaglia, in 1154.

For some nine years, in the pride of her municipal independence, Rome had maintained the forms of a Republic under the brave but heretical enthusiast Arnold of Brescia. But he was made captive by Frederick and delivered to the Pope, who at once put him to death.* And when, with much boasting of their ancestry, the citizens of Rome magnified the honor of the imperial crown they now freely laid at the conqueror's feet, he sternly told them it was on his own right and his own sword he rested, not on any authority they could give.†

This campaign in Italy was the occasion of the famous Lombard League, and of that obstinate, eventful, heroic war in which Frederick was compelled at length to the reconciliation with Pope Alexander III. in Venice (1177), and to the Treaty of Constance, six years later, whose terms the Emperor and his house honorably kept. Through the greater part of the struggle the Pope had given the weight of his sacred

* See *ante*, p. 175.

† See the story in Greenwood's *Cathedra Petri*, vol. v. pp. 69–72.

office and his indomitable temper to the cause of the
League ; while terror, and possibly honest choice,
brought to the Emperor's side near half the cities
of North Italy.   The Bavarian house of Guelph,
holding by marriage large estates in Tuscany, proved
the Church's faithfulest ally ; and now Guelph and
Ghibelline had a new meaning, as the party of Pope
or Emperor.

The first was, in the main, the party of the people,
of Italian liberty ; the second, the party of the nobility, nowhere more haughty and cruel than here, in
whom the Emperor found his natural allies.   And
so the names Guelph and Ghibelline came to have
another meaning, as those of the popular and the
aristocratic party.   In this sense, Florence had held
to the popular tradition.   Dante himself, like his
family, was a Guelph in earlier life ; then, independent of both parties, he banished the contentious
chiefs of both ; then, in his exile, he was an ardent
and bitter partisan of the imperial side, to which he
looked vainly for twenty years for the restoring of
peace and the establishment of right.

A notice of these party names, with the change
of meaning in them, is necessary to understand the
barest outline of the story.   But Dante was born
amidst other conflicts, and in the very crisis of a
deeper tragedy.

The thirteenth century was not only darkened by
that obstinate and bitter struggle with the second
Frederick, which ended in the literal extermination
of his house ; * it was also stained by two great and

* His son Manfred, the gallant prince of South Italy, fell in

grievous crimes, each of which cost the people of Italy more blood and misery than almost any single cause. One was the crime of the Emperor, the other of the Pope.

In the stress of his endeavor to maintain Sicily and the South, Frederick gave over his subjects of North Italy, bound and gagged, to the able, vigilant, jealous, vindictive, merciless control of his fierce partisan Eccelino da Romano, whose name is infamous to this day for the vast scale and diabolical ingenuity of his cruelties. Eccelino was a small, pale, keen, wiry, indomitable man, who never knew love or pity to any living thing, — the express image of the Devil, said his contemporaries, even as Christ is the image of God. As an example of his barbarity, he set a guard over a defenceless house, and left the whole family to starve slowly to death ; and once, having captured a town, he cut off the feet and put out the eyes of every man, woman, and child, and left them so to perish.* Frederick, more mercifully, cast his mutilated captives into the flames.

A few years later, to crush the heroism of Manfred, Frederick's valiant son, successive Popes gave over all of South Italy to the insolent, wanton, unscrupu-

battle in 1266; his grandson Conradin was beheaded at Naples in 1268.

* It is pleasant to record one good trait of this demon in human shape. Crimes with a political motive he did not shrink from ; vices which had no such motive, he could not tolerate. Seeing a German noble once attack a woman, he instantly drew his sword and struck off his head ; and when Frederick rebuked him for acting hastily, he replied, " So I should have done to your Majesty, if I had seen you attempt the like."

lous adventurer Charles of Anjou, and turned loose upon that fair land the hordes of ruffians mustered from all western Europe and waiting for a new crusade to Palestine. So Sicily and Naples, like the South of France, were devoted to the horrors of a holy war till the great revenge of the "Sicilian Vespers" in 1282, which in one month swept the island clear of every French invader. When this appalling deed was done, Dante was a boy of seventeen.

The vast two-fold tragedy, in which the two parties were equally guilty, must destroy the moral hold of either upon the loyalty of common men, and reduce the struggle more and more to a mere war of passion and persons, in which the names of Guelph and Ghibelline are little else than unmeaning battle-cries, — a war whose chaos of interests, ambitions, and crimes fills circle after circle of Dante's "Hell."

It is from the depth of this political disorder, and in the despair which seemed to come upon all patriotic souls, that Dante seeks passionately for deliverance, by calling back the mind of his country to the sublime ideal of Church and State, co-equal and independent each in its own sovereignty. His treatise "On Monarchy" is the most complete existing statement of that ideal. It is even our one chief authority for knowing the best thought of the Middle Age on the theory of Politics.*

That theory is fantastic and impossible, as applied to human things. The moment of its realizing, if such a thing could be, — and indeed it had seemed to be, once, with Charlemagne, and again with the third

* See Bryce's "Holy Roman Empire," p. 264.

Otho, — would be the moment of fresh rivalries, and of a new irrepressible conflict. But our fervid and generous idealist cannot see it so. He is a true Catholic, none more so. He fully believes in the Church's divine universal rule in things spiritual, and will tolerate no heresy. But it is just as clear to him that the Empire has a like divine universal rule in things temporal. To Cæsar must be rendered the things that are Cæsar's, as well as to God the things that are God's.

The argument is very plain to him. First, for the sake of justice and peace, there must be one Government, sacred and impartial, over all mankind. Secondly, that government belongs by divine right to Rome, whose just sovereignty Christ himself declared by being born under Roman rule, and dying by sentence of a Roman court. Finally, this power is held by Rome immediately from God, — " whatever the Decretalists may say," — just as much as that of the Church itself; it is therefore an original Divine Right, and quite independent of the other.

These are the three stages of his argument. It is not the strength of that, so much as the earnestness and pathos of his plea for peace in the weary, bitter, and hopeless storm of party strife, that moves us in this essay. We see in a clear intellectual statement (to his mind, doubtless, unanswerable) the motive which governed him in his long exile, — the motive at once of unpardoning wrath at those who would perpetuate the struggle for baser ends, and of eager hope when any ray of light broke upon him: from beyond the Alps, in the coming of Henry of Luxem-

burg * upon the scene ; or from beyond the Po, when
a patriotic ambition seemed for once to move his
noble protector Can Grande della Scala, of Verona.

During his long exile, that Vision of Dante, which
he first saw as in a dream, standing on the Bridge of
St. Angelo at Rome, was growing clearer and more
profound, and was shaping itself in the hundred can-
tos of his " Divine Comedy."

The name " Comedy " (which in its first sense is
" village-song ") was given it, he tells us, first because
it begins in pain and ends in joy, like the conventional comedy of the stage ; but also because he wrote
it in " the vulgar tongue," — the same tongue, he
says, in which simple women say their prayers and
talk with one another. So that his own explanation
of the title reminds us that we have passed the noon
of the Middle Age, and have come into the era of
modern literature. For an understanding of the time,
Dante's writings are the first we have to read in a
modern dialect, and not in the Mediæval Latin, which
has been our only resource so long, and in which his
own more formal treatises are conveyed. So dignified,
vast, and learned a topic as he had chosen, seemed to
him at first to demand the stateliness of that language, and his first essays were in it. With good
fortune as wonderful as the skill and power it shows,
he wrote it out in the perfect melody and exquisite
chime of the most musical of tongues, then as sinewy
and strong, if not so liquid and sweet, as it ever afterwards became.

* The Emperor Henry VII., father of that blind old John of
Bohemia, who fell fighting at Crecy, in 1346.

For perfect mechanical execution, for skill that
never hesitates or falters, for absolute control of dic-
tion by faultless accuracy of ear, it is probably not too
much to say that there is no other poetic structure,
in any language, that can be set in comparison with
this. In the elaborate interweaving of its triple verse
not a rhyme halts, and not a word, he tells us, was
chosen for the rhyme's sake which he would not
have chosen otherwise. In complete symmetry, and
in curious fitness of all the parts, no other poetry so
naturally as this suggests the superb architectural
image of Mr. Longfellow : —

"How strange the sculptures that adorn these towers !
    This crowd of statues, in whose folded sleeves
    Birds build their nests ; while, canopied with leaves,
Parvis and portal bloom like trellised bowers,
And the vast minster seems a cross of flowers !
    But fiends and dragons on the gargoyled eaves
    Watch the dead Christ between the living thieves,
And underneath the traitor Judas lowers!
Ah ! from what agonies of heart and brain,
    What exultations trampling on despair,
    What tenderness, what tears, what hate of wrong,
What passionate outcry of a soul in pain,
    Uprose this poem of the earth and air,
    This Mediæval miracle of song !"

It is no more than we must say of all poetry worthy to be read, to say that its melody must be known
and felt in its original tongue.* Translations, at best,

* No possible manipulation of English can give the peculiar
melody of Italian, where almost every word ends with an unaccented
vowel. One may well imagine, on the other hand, that Dante himself would often have been glad if he could put the firm English

are but so many far-away copies from so many points of view. If they keep the harmonies of form, they obscure or break the sense. If they are rigidly true to that, they turn, it may be, exquisite verse into bleak and arid prose. With some moderate knowledge of the language, one may do best, perhaps, to take some clear and faithful version as guide (or more than one, if possible), feeling, as he goes, that no great poet can be known at second-hand.* The difficulties may be far too great for him to master them alone; but with such a guide, with the indispensable leisure and calmness of spirit too, he need not weary at the long ascent. And at the end of it his feeling will be like that of one who has climbed a very high mountain, rising steadily, swell after swell, long after it seemed impossible to go up higher: a sense of wonder and glory, not at any sharply defined prospect about him, but at the width and depth of the Universe itself, which is suddenly revealed,—an infinite splendor, and a deep sense of rest. In that last proof of power, this great poem stands alone.

More, too, than any other excepting Homer and Shakspeare, Dante is not only a name in literature,

cadence in place of the incessant double rhyme. Cayley's version is a constant illustration of this contrast, which is as far as possible disguised in Longfellow's.

* Certainly this is no substitute for the competent study of the original; but it is a method of study which deserves more attention from educators than it has received. To be a Dantean scholar might cost the best labor of a lifetime: *non cuivis contingit;* but a month, to a thoughtful student, would be enough to give the inestimable first-hand knowledge of what is best in Dante.

but a department in literature. Within the century
of his exile and death, his works were the subject
of lecture and comment in six different colleges of
Italy, with professorships expressly founded for their
interpretation. This, I take it, was due not simply
to their merit as poetry or as science, but to the fact
that they pictured the life of an age already fading,
so that to comment on them was to expound an entire period of history. Except Shakspeare, again, no
author has had such blind admirers, such uncompromising champions. Societies of students, in various
lands, are devoted to this one study. Literary jour-
nals have been founded — one at least is in publica-
tion now — exclusively to propagate and increase
this lore. The unique attraction of his verse has
created a literary taste, and the widening study of it
has formed a literary school.

It is not, however, the poetical structure, but the
argument itself, that we have to consider; and that,
again, only as it exhibits certain features of the Life
we have been studying all along.

In form, the poem is the story of a pilgrimage, —
first with Virgil as guide through the nine vast circles of Hell, narrowing to the centre of the earth,
which is a core of solid ice; then, at the antipodes,
along the steep ascent, winding through seven circles
up the hill of Purgatory, until in the terrestrial paradise he is met by heavenly Wisdom in the glorified
form of Beatrice; then through the nine celestial
spheres of Paradise, among innumerable companies
of the just made perfect, into the very presence and
beatific vision of God himself.

Hell is crowded with images visible to the eye and sharply appealing to our sense of terror and disgust. It is a mirror of the passion and guilt of the age, and can be studied even with a sort of antiquarian interest.* The ascent through Paradise, with long arguments and pauses, seems (it must be confessed) weary and interminable as we go, but for its marvellous and unfailing melody; yet here, as still more on the hill of Purgatory, there are strains of the purest poetry, sweet and limpid as a meadow-brook, and bright as a green lawn spangled with flowers. All are needed, the weary spaces of dialectics as well as the horror and the charm, to fill out this picture of human life, — this poem, whose subject, Dante said, is Man.†

The imagery of the poem embodies the full belief of Dante's age, scientific and philosophic as well as theological. We need not ask how far it was his own belief. In some sense it was, no doubt. But he himself tells us that there are four senses to it, not one; and we are free to take which of the four we will. The *literal* takes it simply as a plain story of fact. The *allegorical* treats it as symbol and myth, to which our own mind must bring the key. The *moral* reads it as a practical lesson of life, a warning from its sin and an exhortation to its holiness. The *anagogic* finds in it a hint and inspiration of immortal hope. I shall only speak, briefly, of the symbol and the moral.

* "The inscrutable darkness towards which all men travel becomes a black and polished mirror, reflecting with terrible luminousness the events of the present and the past." — SYMONDS : *Renaissance in Italy.*

† HOMO, he says, not VIR.

We have seen before something of the intense and vivid realism of the Middle Age, as shown in its science, its philosophy, its dogma, and its art. We have the same thing, naturally, in what we may call its mythology of heaven and hell. The same rude popular fancy that could see the consecrated wafer as a bleeding finger, or find signs of wrath and pity in a wooden statue, busied itself with tales and images which set forth, with terrible distinctness, the doom of guilt or error. A peasant comes in a thick wood upon a party nobly attired as for a holiday, and seated at a sumptuous feast; but there is no joy in their countenances, and as he looks he sees that the viands before them are blazing coal. A monk returning from some pious errand shrinks back into a wayside thicket, where some friendly hand stops his mouth from any outcry, as he watches a gorgeous cavalcade of high-born knights and ladies, some of whom he can recognize as lately living in the flesh : every face is sombre, with a settled look of pain ; and he perceives that armor, stirrup, spur, and golden helmet are all glowing hot, and gleam with the flames of hell.* A famous lecturer — one whom Dante himself had heard in Paris and remembers in Paradise † — had been in earlier days a free-thinker, and had led some of his young pupils into fatal error. He is crossed one day by the ghost of one lately dead, and bidden to hold out his hand ; as he does so, the tormented spirit drops from his finger-tip one drop of sweat into his open palm : it is the sweat of the

* See the story at full length in *Ordericus Vitalis.*
† *Paradiso,* x. 136.

agony of the damned, and falls like a drop of molten
iron, boring its way sharply till it comes out at the
back of his hand.*

These are the tales and images which burned themselves upon the fancy of that time, which Dante must
have been familiar with from childhood. The circles
of his Hell are nine vast galleries filled with such
lurid pictures, each made more vivid and intense by
some touch of his strangely realizing art. Fire-flakes
drive against his naked ghosts like snow-flakes in
a winter storm. Snakes wreathe themselves about
them, locking them in horrid coil. ·They wallow in
the filth and stench of sewers. They groan under
leaden cloaks so massive that those with which Frederick crushed his prisoners to death were but straw
by comparison.† They are bitten and stung by demons, whom they strike at, blindly, as a dog in sunshine snaps at wasps and fleas. They are turned to
trees, that hiss and bleed when their twigs are plucked
away. They stand, head downward, in little pits of
burning sulphur. They are confined in fiery tombs,
whose lids, now open, will be shut down on them
forever at the Day of Judgment. They float in frozen
lakes, their faces masked and blinded with gathering
crusts of ice.

It is said that when these ghastly images were first
published, in the earlier years of Dante's exile, they
so seized the fancy of the Florentines, that a theatre
was built against one of the bridges of the Arno, gal-

* This whole subject is well illustrated in Ozanam's "Dante."

† For this understanding of the passage compare Kington's
"History of Frederick II.," vol. i. p. 475.

leries and pit, where crowds gathered to see a spectacle of the torments of the infernal gulf. "Here," says the narrator, "was made the semblance and figure of Hell, with flames and other pains and torments, with men dressed as demons, horrible to see; and others had the shape of naked souls; and those gave unto them divers tortures, with exceeding great crying and confusion, the which seemed doleful and appalling unto eyes and ears: till the galleries broke down, and numbers, both actors and spectators, perished in the stream; and, as the crier had proclaimed, so now in death went much folk to learn news of the other world."

There is no one feature of the poem by which Dante is generally so well known as by these horrors of his Hell. What we have to see is, that, while the artist skill is his, the symbolism it portrays is not. It is the dark side of the popular creed that fills his canvas. These pictures were furnished him out of the vast Pandæmonium of the Catholic mythology. These horrors all breathe and burn in the tortured imagination of his age.

Without passing on to symbolism less terrible and less familiar, such as abounds in the later divisions of his poem, it will serve our purpose best to look at it briefly as a whole, and consider the type of Religion which we find in it.

Of the type of theology I need say nothing. That is simply the common pattern of his age. The difference between religion and theology is that the latter can be taught, and stereotyped, and kept in unvarying form, and taken at second-hand; while religion, to be religion, is the immediate growth of the man's own nature, or else the immediate inspiration of God.

Now Dante believed himself to be an inspired man. His creed did not make it difficult for him to believe this. His long dwelling in solitude among the Hebrew prophets had deeply persuaded him that he was of their company. His illusive predictions of peace to Italy, and of the triumph of the righteous cause, he doubtless believed to be of divine revelation, as fully as Saint Bernard did those promises and exhortations that a century and a half before drove the Crusaders upon their ruin.

Moreover, Dante was a loyal subject of his Church; and his austere imagination was not daunted by those very real horrors which prefigured the doom that Church menaced to the damned. He had seen men burned alive, he says. Saint Dominic is among the glorified spirits in his highest heaven. The blood and ashes of Languedoc do not prevent his receiving into Paradise one of the chief agents of that desolation. All this we must remember, if we would know how his sublime panorama of the religious life could exhibit it in such lurid and appalling forms.

And now, to conceive its lessons in a way to be of instruction and avail to us, we must think of Religion as he did,—as all great religious teachers and inspired men have done, — as having its springs in the moral nature, and its foundations in the moral law. If we take his picture-gallery simply as the transcript of his creed,—that is, of his theory about religion,—we find it simply a mythology childish and grotesque.

With us, as with Farinata, the terrors of his Hell may invite only defiance and contempt. With us, as (we may fear) with a majority of his readers, the splendors of his Paradise may seem more unspeakably weary than any sorrows or any toils of this sorrowful and toilsome life.

Take it, on the other hand, as a transcript of what he had seen and known of human life itself, — its guilt and misery, its hopes of pardon, its celestial peace, — and what a Vision of Life we find in it! how full of pictures that speak as plainly as those on any cathedral wall! Austere and sad we may feel the dominant tone of them to be; but out of what austere and sad experience he spoke! and then, what dreams of celestial beauty, of pure blessedness and peace!

But, first of all, his lesson of the religious life is a moral, not a theological lesson. The two poles it turns on are not so much pain and joy, as sin and holiness. Nay, the very joy he tells of, but for holiness, would itself be weariness and pain. His keen eye saw, his great heart felt, those awful, those sublime possibilities of human nature. So vivid and real was his thought of them, that — as in the profound glimpse of a tyrant's soul which in one moment of vision we find in Plato* — those coiling serpents, that storm of fire-flakes, those pits of mud and stench, mean only the misery and corruption which successful guilt can never hide. Eccelino, tearing off his bandages and starving himself to death in prison, makes a picture (if you look to the soul of the man) as tragical as

* See "Gorgias," chap. 36, *et seq.*

where Dante shows him in his vision, his black head
floating in a lake of boiling blood. Those painful
climbing steps of spirits in Purgatory, bent under the
anguish of great weights that seem to crush them like
the figures crouched in the corbel of a massive wall
of stone, are yet taken with a certain grave gladness
and hope, because they are upward steps — they are
forward steps—towards the still joy of that terrestrial
paradise, where, like Bunyan's Pilgrim when he sees
the Cross, we shall find that the burden has already
fallen from our shoulders.

The three great portions of which the poem is
composed we may consider, then, as three stages in
the religious life,—the stage of Fear, of Hope, of Joy.
It is common with us to speak as if, theologically, we
had outgrown the stage of Fear; at least, as if it were
one that belongs to a low and unworthy conception
of the religious life, and of God himself, the author
of it. But not so thought Dante; and his thought
about it we may find, after all, to be deeper and truer
than ours is apt to be. "The fear of the Lord is the
beginning of wisdom." Do we fancy that that fear
is only the mild awe — thin phantom of the vigorous
and real fear the bravest souls on earth have felt —
with which we calmly contemplate the equal government of God ? Nay, rather, there are dark terrors,
horrible phantoms, which we can never dissociate
from our thought of human life, — moral, social, political ; and it would not be well for us if we could.
The stern lines which Dante puts on the portal of his
Hell may well startle us, not so much by their vivid
antithesis as by their everlasting truth : —

"Through me ye enter to the City of Pain ;
  Through me ye enter to eternal Grief ; *
  Through me ye enter in among the Damned.
Justice moved Him on high who fashioned me ;
  Divine Omnipotence created me —
  The highest Wisdom and the primal Love.
Before me was not anything created
  Save things eternal : I, too, stay eternal.
  All hope abandon, ye who enter here."

The wisdom and the love which work among the moral conditions of our life are not such as hide or forget its unsparing judgments. Unless the pilgrim to the Celestial City shall have the nerve to face all those terrors, and see every sort of evil in its own worst shape,—unless he conceive the depth of the Pit and the sharpness of its agony to those who have lost their light, or made themselves wilfully blind, — it is impossible that he should bear with patience the necessary burden of that sad weight, or that his eyes should ever be unsealed to the glory of the Beatific Vision.

---

* In the Latin languages Pain and Grief are the same word,—Old English, *Dolour*. The Italian in these two lines is *città dolente*, and *eterno dolore :* "a repetition of sounds," says Mr. Longfellow, "like the tolling of a funeral bell, —*dolente . . . dolore*." Shakspeare uses "Grief" in the same double sense : 2 Henry IV. i. 1.

XI.

THE PAGAN REVIVAL.

THERE is an odd paradox of Michelet something
to this effect. The Middle Age, he says — that
is, the system which we have known as the "Empire
Church" — had really perished before the time at
which we have now arrived; but it could not die yet
for two hundred years, *for it was already dead, and
you cannot kill a corpse.*

Like many another paradox of that brilliant writer,
this has one side of glittering falsehood; but another
side, also, of sober truth. Still, the figure which
Michelet presents to us is not the best we can have
to represent the change that was going on during
those two centuries. An historical era, or a great
secular institution, does not perish like a corpse, by
a process of mere corruption and decay. It is rather
like a great forest tree, which has had the vigor to
undermine and overtop all the surrounding growth,
and so to thrive at their expense. They are puny
under its shadow. They are stunted and dwarfed,
because its prodigious vital force has starved their
roots. Still, while it flourished, it was the glory of
the forest, and the life of the earth was a grander
thing for its predominance. But its roots are with-

ered now by failure of the nether springs. As its branches shrink and its foliage drops, sunshine streams in; and the same vigor which it absorbed before goes now into the life of other kinds. It is they now that overflow with sap, and put forth new branches. They must increase, and it must decrease. But it is long before they rival the actual majesty of its growth; and whole generations pass before a voice is heard bold enough to say: "Cut it down; why cumbereth it the ground?"

We have taken the year 1300, and the pontificate of Boniface VIII., as the point of time from which to date the process we are now to follow rapidly, to the dawn of the Protestant Reformation. In fact, what strikes us most of all is the suddenness with which the change becomes apparent. Dante, whose career as seer and poet may be said to begin at this date, really opens, without knowing it, the gateway of modern life. He himself has no suspicion of the impending change. His symbolism is wholly in the mythology of the past, which he devoutly accepts without demur. His dream of the age to follow is simply the ideal which five centuries have been spent in the vain attempt to realize. To fulfil that dream he appeals to the same force of arms from abroad, which has desolated Italy more than once, and will for five centuries more wreck her liberties and welfare.

For a century the splendid spiritual empire held by Innocent III. has been kept in the grasp of his successors, almost without loss, possibly with apparent gain, of strength. Gregory IX. and Innocent IV.

have more than held their own against the ablest sovereign of the time, Frederick II.; while Alexander IV., Urban IV., Clement IV., and Martin IV. have ruthlessly and successfully carried out the same line of policy, to the extermination of the imperial house. Rodolph of Hapsburg has accepted the Empire on terms which concede to the Church complete victory in the struggle going on now for just two hundred years (1073–1273). So that Boniface VIII. might seem well justified in the exceeding arrogance of his triumph, in that year of Jubilee, when, with an ostentatious splendor never seen before, he celebrated the final triumph of the Church over all her enemies, and asserted that strict submission to Rome was absolutely essential to salvation for every individual of the human race.

Within three years Boniface himself was dethroned, imprisoned, and died insane. In less than another year his successor had been murdered by poison; and, in the jealous policies of the time, an intrigue with the French king brought about the election as pope of a French cardinal, who (as Clement V.) removed his court to Avignon, where for seventy years the enormous pretensions of the Papacy were still asserted by a series of dependants on the crown of France. Wrath and humiliation at this affront on the pride of Italy break out in Dante's objurgation* at the Gascon who has done this thing, and his successor of Guienne (John XXII.). Italy for those seventy years was delivered from the deadly struggle of Pope and Emperor, only to be delivered over to native despots, who vexed

* *Paradiso,* xxvii. 58.

her still more cruelly. And when at length Urban VI. was installed in Rome (1378), a rival pope was chosen in France; and for forty years the Catholic world was divided by the "Great Schism," with two supreme pontiffs hurling anathemas at each other, or else, with the cunningest diplomacy, evading the schemes and pledges contrived to bring about religious peace.

Thus we come down to the early part of the fifteenth century, amid scandals and divisions which it might seem impossible ever to heal. They were healed, however, at the famous Council of Constance (1415). John XXIII., who began life as a privateering adventurer, and escaped the doom of hanging suffered by his fellows, was confronted with charges of shocking crimes and enormities, drawn up in seventy counts, and forced to abdicate the sacred office. The peace of the Church was confirmed by a solemn act of human sacrifice. The pious reformers John Huss and Jerome of Prague were burned at the stake for heresy. To insure their doom the Emperor Sigismund was obliged to violate the passport, or safe-conduct, given to Huss; and to relieve his qualms of honor, the same Council invented and formulated the celebrated dogma, that no faith is to be kept with heretics.* Thus the Church had rest from her alarms, and breathed freely again for another hundred years.

It cannot be supposed that this monstrous process, or the monstrous terms on which security was bought, could escape the judgment of braver and better men.

* The form of this dogma may be seen in Mansi, xxvii. 799.

Five of the popes, whose iniquities he has known,
Dante puts in hell,* — a vigorous symptom of the
style of criticism the Church system must now expect. William of Occam — the clear-headed ration-
alist I have before spoken of, who lived to near the
middle of the fourteenth century (1347) — was a
pious and fervent monk of the Order of St. Francis.
As a young man, studying theology in Paris, he came
out in a vigorous pamphlet taking the French king's
part against the enormous pretensions of Boniface ;
and afterwards, with equal vigor, defended the Franciscan doctrine of the "Poverty of Christ" against the
discreet but unevangelical manifesto of John XXII.
His assaults on the Realism, which was the foundation of the old Catholic theology, were the visible
stroke that caused the downfall of Scholasticism.
His pious, sturdy, independent English temper he
bequeathed to his young countryman John Wiclif,
who at Occam's death was twenty-three ; † and so
was developed that serious, devout, rational form of
Christianity, which has made the best element in the
religious life of England ever since. Chaucer was
but four years younger than Wiclif, and an eager
listener to his words.   And along with the fresh,
romantic spirit which Chaucer brought over from
France — where he was a soldier in the "hundred-
years' war" begun by Edward III. — we know what

* Namely, Anastasius II. (*Inf.* xi. 8), Celestine V. (Ibid., iii.
59, as generally understood), Nicholas III. (Ibid., xix. 70), Boniface
VIII. (Ibid., 53), Clement V. (Ibid., 83), — the first for heresy, the
next for desertion, and the others for simony.

† Born, it will be noticed, just a century after Thomas Aquinas
(1324).

appeal there was to the popular mind of the period in the contrast between the poor Parson of his tale and the bloated prior or the beggarly monk, in whom he lashes the sins of the Church.

Perhaps, indeed, no symptom of the time is more formidable than the way in which the most pious of the fraternities of monks now confronted the degenerate Church with its own forgotten ideal; and the unrelenting animosity with which the Church resented and repelled their protest. I have mentioned before the fate of four Puritan seceders from the lax Franciscan Order, who for their sturdy adherence to the older ascetic type were burned alive at Marseilles, early in this century (1318), and the horrible extermination of the Order of the Templars a little earlier (1312). Most likely the Templars were examples of the abuses, as the Minorites were of the antiquated fervors, of monastic life. The fate of those four, however, was only one incident in a bitter and unrelenting persecution of a form of piety that had grown, legitimately enough, from those old ideals. After long wrangling they had been allowed to form a separate Order; but this was abolished by Boniface VIII., and many of them were in open revolt from Rome. Before that secession was suppressed two thousand of them had been burned at the stake.

The Fraticelli, as these fanatical seceders are sometimes called, were a single group in a great swarm of pious and extravagant heresies. Master Eckhart, one of the most fervent of religious writers, whose sermons you may still read in their quaint old German, was sharply stigmatized as a heretic, a pantheist, a mystic, a leader of the dangerous enthusiasts passing under such names as Beghards, Beguines, and Brethren of the Free Spirit, who held, some of them, that the Christian dispensation itself must pass away before the new revelation of Divine Love.*

That there was pernicious extravagance, with real danger to good morals and social order, we need not doubt. A like fanaticism, we know, took horrible shapes in the era of the Reformation, and under the Commonwealth. But it is interesting, at least, to see that the earliest protest against the Mediæval system was not from intellectual unbelief, but from an excess of religious fervor. It is the same old lesson. The new dispensation of faith is heralded, far away, not by the construction of any dogmatic scheme, but by the heat and light of conscience. The "ethical passion," often vague and astray but always loyal, is the one thing with force enough to make men forget the horrors of Languedoc, and brave the spies and torments of the Inquisition,† obedient to the vision of what seems to them a holier life.

But side by side with that great political degradation, and that great outgrowth of pious fervor, ran another line of development, which from its most characteristic symptoms we may call a Pagan Revival. In reality, it is the wakening of the mind of Europe to a new intellectual life; and is shown just

---

* The year 1260 had been set by the Abbot Joachim as the date of the new dispensation. See Rev. xii. 6.

† The Inquisition was formally established in France by the "good" King John, about 1350. For illustrations of the temper of this period see Hauréau, *Bernard Délicieux et l'Inquisition Albigeoise.*

as much in the Christian Art of Giotto, and in the
Romance introduced by Chaucer into England, as in
those properly pagan features which belong especially
to Italy, and to a class of the more scholarly and cultivated minds.   But it is these pagan features which
we have chiefly to attend to: first, because they show
most plainly by contrast the change from the strict
theological domain of the foregoing centuries; and
then, because they include so much of what has gone
into the best thought of modern times.

Moreover, the term Pagan is meant for distinction,
not for disparagement.   It is true that a great amount
of pagan cruelty and looseness of morals came in with
this new tide of life and culture, and that it ran out
into excesses quite worthy of the times of Tiberius
and Nero.   As to these, we may say simply, just
here, that, as the Church had been a leader in everything else, so now she adopted in full the new pagan
spirit, and exhibited in the very highest degree every
phase of its enormity, down to the very crisis of the
Reformation.   So that, in dealing with it, we are
dealing in very truth with the Spirit of the Age itself.   And it is the spirit of an age, not any outward
form or pressure of events, that makes the real matter
of our study.

The first thing we have to notice is the frankness
with which this spirit meets us on the very threshold
of the era we are entering.   Open, for instance, the
Latin correspondence of Petrarch,* — just as we have
had to use the Latin correspondence of Abelard and
Bernard, of Abbots Suger and Peter the Venerable,

* Contained in three charming volumes : Florence, 1859–1863.

and even of Dante, to get at the spirit of their age,—and at once you find yourself in another atmosphere. One does not know how to account for the immense difference, in hardly more than a single generation. For Petrarch was a youth of seventeen when Dante died,—old enough to have shared with him some of his obsolete passions and hopes for the regeneration of Italy. But Dante and Petrarch lived in two different worlds. As truly as the mind of one was a mirror of amazing brilliancy and depth, turned towards the stormy life of the past, so was the mind of the other a glass clear and radiant, through which he looked toward the larger and calmer life of the future.

I have nothing whatever here to do with the sentimental and artificial style of poetry of which he was such a master, and by which he is generally best known. The name of Laura does not occur once, I think, in all his correspondence,— even where it might so easily, when he speaks with a delight half childish of the laurel chaplet he is to receive in Rome. It is simply as the scholar, the man of letters, the traveller, and the friend that we see him here ; something, too, of the patriot, when he presses upon the Emperor Charles IV., with modest urgency, the claims of Italy to her sovereign's care.

The one thing we care to notice in these Letters, besides the easy purity of their style, is the cheerful sense that he is living on friendly terms with the great minds of pagan antiquity. His companions are Cicero, Virgil, Horace, Socrates,— even Homer, a gift of whom (a sealed book to him, since he can read no

Greek) he accepts from a friend in Constantinople
with a sort of pious joy.   Cicero, it is true, has done
him an unkind turn; for a heavy volume of his Letters, which Petrarch has copied out with his own
hand, has caught once, twice, thrice, in a fold of his
study-gown, and so, falling to the floor, has grievously
grazed his shin.   But a gentle remonstrance is enough.
To all these good friends of ancient days Petrarch addresses himself in familiar epistles,—nay, to Virgil and
Horace and Lucan in their own style of Latin verse.
The simple joy he has in knowing these august names
wells over, as it were, in such holiday recreations.

Even more: on occasions when he would seem to
have most need of the conventional resources of his
Christian faith (and in his creed Petrarch is a serious Christian believer), in the letters of consolation
he writes to several of his friends under bereavement,
his tone and phrase are simply those of Cicero, of
Seneca, and of the younger Pliny.   It does not occur
to him that this new fountain of fresh waters, from
which he drinks daily, may not perhaps be sufficient
for all the needs of the better life.   The tone may
be a little formal now and then; the words, at least,
look stereotyped and conventional to our eye; but on
the whole the impression is of something quite spontaneous and hearty, though by any sound judgment it
is certainly rather shallow.   The fresh, hearty, genuine intellectual life which Petrarch imbibes with
such serious and cordial satisfaction is wholly from
the antique pagan source.

In short, almost before we are well out of hearing
of the thunders of Boniface, before the smoke of that

grim sacrifice of Templars and Minorites has drifted quite away, the spirit of the Pagan Revival is already here. And this is so far from being a choice or caprice on Petrarch's part, that he himself is alarmed at it, and says, "Julian the Apostate is risen from the dead!" We are perplexed to account for the sudden apparition. Something, it is likely, is due to the simple transfer of the papal court to Avignon. Italy was free from a presence and a pressure which had long held back what might have broken out much earlier. Even Papal Rome had kept something of the state and tradition of the Pagan Empire. And Italy at large had never cut the cord that bound its most familiar recollections to a Past which we call "Classic" to this day.

The Christian Art of the Middle Age never fairly got root in Italy, where a score of cities could show monuments of a grandeur and skill which men were content to imitate without hoping to rival. It was not till the new era had come to its full growth, that Michael Angelo could boast that he would lift the dome of Agrippa's Pantheon into the air. Such names as Consul, Senator, and Patrician show how powerfully men were still controlled in public things by ancient names. We have seen how the old republican fire broke out in Rome — at least, a blaze dangerously like it — when Arnold of Brescia brought there the flame of his religious and patriotic zeal. In this very century, a tavern-keeper's son at Rome, heated with crude fervors taken from hearsay of antiquity, and gifted with a popular and impassioned eloquence, could raise a storm of revolution which drove out both noble factions; and, as the Tribune Rienzi, could exhibit for three years a rule of peace as brilliant as it was brief (1347–1350).

It was more a travesty than a revival of the old Republic. But it showed at least that there were hot embers and even live coals, where there looked to be only ashes; and that, a breath let in or a pressure taken off, there was likely to be a fire, possibly a conflagration. There was not enough of public life in Italy, or sense of national unity, to create a new political era as Dante hoped. But no sooner was the visible presence of the Papal Court gone, than what life there was — at least, what was not consumed in the feuds of the petty States — rushed at once into the channel most completely opposite to that which had confined its tides so long.

It was thus that in a very special sense Italy became the field of the new movement, and the leader of intellectual life to the modern world. It lay, so to speak, nearer the boundaries of the old Empire, and caught most readily the perfumed airs that drifted over, as soon as the artificial wall of separation became ruinous. That wall was what we know as the Mediæval system of church dogma and church life. How opposite it was to the spirit of pagan antiquity, and how the opposition was confirmed by four centuries of valiant fight against it, we have had abundant occasion to see.

Since its first great victory under Constantine, the ecclesiastical system had lasted now just a thousand years. A thousand years are a very long time for one type or ideal of life to predominate in human things;

and the restlessness of Europe is not like the contented quiet of Cathay.

Besides, from the necessity of its position, and in obedience to its higher law, the Church had made war not only upon Paganism, but upon that human nature itself out of which Paganism grew ; nay, upon those very forms of literature and art which were the fairest fruit of that elder religion. It was impossible that a system which declared human life under a birth-curse, the very earth itself stricken with blight for one man's guilt, the soul of every man doomed from its conception to an eternity of horror unless redeemed by ecclesiastical spells, should be honestly held much longer. The very genius of the South was a living protest against it. That fair land, so gracious and dear to the heart of Virgil; that blue sea, so glorious in the verse of Homer; that bright sun, which in the pathos of Greek tragedy stands for all the gladness and hope of life, — the world of old mythology, the home of ancient faith, — were always tending to revive the memories, to re-create the structures, which had been so pitilessly destroyed. We need not go over again the arguments that show how needful that destruction was. But at least we can see how slippery and uncertain must be the hold by which a system of ascetic, austere, and formal piety could maintain itself against the new invasion of that spirit.

However that may be, as the Church dominion waned in the fourteenth century, there came a strange sense of emancipation. The Mediæval system — which we at this day can study as a variegated and gorgeous cloud, shot through now and then with sharp lightning — was still close about men ; but it seemed to be lifting and drifting, like a great mist that has long overhung plain and valley. The memory of it was as the memory of an oppressive dream. Its bright visions faded into unreality ; its terrifying spectres fell back into the world of dreams. The very vividness with which they had been grouped and painted out by Dante must have had its share in making them seem mere hauntings and phantoms of a perished mythology. What had been once the atmosphere in which men lived and thought, was in their memory a nightmare and an incubus.

The recoil was not only from the thing, but from the names and associations which recalled the thing. And thus, as the new spirit found its way within the boundaries of the Church itself, it began to color the official language of the Church, and to create for it the semblance of a Pagan creed. God the Father becomes Jupiter the Best and Greatest. The Eternal Word is born from him, like Pallas springing full-armed from the brow of Jove. The Holy Spirit is a celestial Zephyr. The Muses of Helicon are invoked to sing the birth of Christ, and Proteus foretells his advent to the river-god of Jordan ; while the foes that bring about his death are Gorgons, Hydras, Harpies, and Chimæras, the whole phantom-brood of the Greek mythology.

Just how early the beginnings of this Pagan Revival are to be dated, it is not easy to say. Like all great secular changes, it was most likely imperceptible in its coming. Men say, Lo, here ! or, Lo, there !

when it is already among them. To use our former figure, it was a part of that thick undergrowth, never quite killed out, which sprang into sudden vigor as soon as the foliage of the great overshadowing tree began to be thinned away. To quote the image of Jesus, men go on eating and drinking, marrying and giving in marriage: then comes the sudden flood, and all their little world is swept away.

These images apply, of course, not to the visible institutions of the Middle Age, — which to all outward seeming may have been as strong as ever, for yet two hundred years; just as it was four hundred years before the flood came, described in the homely but sublime prophecy of Jesus. The change was in those thoughts, those motives, those ideals and dreams of men, out of which institutions grow. And this change is best seen not in the vague imagery which we have been employing, but in looking more accurately at two or three definite symptoms of the time.

The first of these for us to notice is the change that has come in the spirit of Literature. The three names most familiar in the time immediately after Dante are those of Petrarch, Boccaccio, and Chaucer, who all died before the end of this century, — Chaucer at its very close. It is not of the slightest consequence which of the three we take for a type of the new movement, — except that the last shows better than the others how widely the spirit was diffused. If we take as a type of the earlier time the ponderous, painful, formless labors of Thomas Aquinas, whose death was just a hundred years before that of Petrarch, and compare him with either of the three, we shall get a notion of the vast change in the direction and temper of the intellectual life. I will not press the contrast; but only speak of a feature or two in the later period.

The familiar companions of men's thought, as we have seen in Petrarch's correspondence, are the orators, poets, and historians of pagan Greece and Rome. The Mediæval formality of style gives way before a new and ardent literary passion. The Gospels, the Prophets, and the Fathers, who have been cited with astonishing frequency and readiness through the entire mass of earlier Christian writings, are set aside for another class of authorities. Cicero and Seneca, Virgil, Horace, and Lucan, begin to be the familiar names. We know well enough the spell which these and other great spirits of antiquity have always held upon the cultivated mind, through a certain fascination in their writings which has never been completely analyzed. From Jerome—who was reproached in a dream as more Ciceronian than Christian, and so vowed in that same dream to abjure the Classic writers — to the last English bishop who earned his see by editing a Greek play, that subtile and deathless charm has been the same. I do not think it is accounted for by beauty of form or style, which many critics have absurdly exaggerated. Still less is it due to wealth of thought, — for, as compared with many modern writers, almost all the ancient ones are lamentably thin: Demosthenes, for example, one of the very first in value and noblest in tone, is inconceivably meagre, to one who judges by such a standard as Webster, Burke, or Gladstone.

Part of the charm, no doubt, is due to the curious suggestiveness of a tongue so foreign to our mood as Greek or Latin, as its obscurities yield before the brooding study we spend upon them in school-days. But a larger part, I should think, is from the directness with which the ancients dealt with the matter in hand, — a directness unattainable to any educated modern. They wrote, as they thought, without precedents and without authorities. This directness in dealing is seen in perfection, of course, only in the earlier Greeks, with whom the very forms of speech and the first principles of style are purely matters of experiment, — feeling their way as they did (take Thucydides as an example), with many a blunder, among the intricacies and pitfalls of human speech; so that in Greek we have the almost unique phenomenon of a literature springing, like wild flowers, literally from the very soil. Virgil and Horace, it is true, and even Cicero, claim merit as elaborate imitators of reputable models. There was, for them, something like a standard of form, but no such thing at all as a standard of thought. Natural Science was not; and what we moderns call a Creed, or formula of fundamental beliefs, was to their mind a thing inconceivable. Except for moral sympathies or antipathies, Platonist or Aristotelian, Epicurean or Stoic, have an equal right to fair hearing. The most radical heresies — philosophical, moral, religious — are discussed in Platonic dialogue with the calm freedom of after-dinner talk. Cicero himself appeals eloquently, a thousand times, to the Immortal Gods whose existence is a fair open question to his mind;

and his intellectual master, Plato, leaves us in doubt whether his finest speculations go beyond a form of words.

In the great writers of antiquity, then, the pagan revivalists of whom we speak found that one thing which they craved with exceeding hunger,—the complete emancipation of the mind from dogma. We have been so long wonted to this, at least in matters that come closest home to us, that we do not at first conceive what an emancipation it was. When we call to mind, however, the immense machinery of the Confessional and the Inquisition, — the secret espial and the fiery doom of the faintest hint of heresy ; when we compare the faltering and defeated effort of Abelard for mental independence with the vigorous free thought at the "revival of learning," — we come to a nearer estimate.

Perhaps its most interesting illustration, however, is seen in the devout zeal with which the old pagan authors are welcomed back, and their writings are revered as a new order of sacred books. Nothing so justifies the name "Pagan Revival" given to this period, as that resurrection of antique life, that sudden familiarity and reverence felt towards the old masters of thought and style. Nothing less than this pious ardor of the new faith could have inspired the prodigious labors of exploring, comparing, and copying-out of texts, which now became the task of scholars. The preliminary labor was done with infinite toil by generations of copyists, before the invention of printing — for which the world had another century to wait; and it was quickened by dread of the Turks, which sent troops of learned Greeks into Italy from threatened Constantinople, with treasures that suffered no scholar's hand to be idle. The process I speak of may be reckoned to have been going on about a century, spite of ecclesiastical jealousy; when in 1447 it was formally sanctioned by the Church in the election of "a little, ugly, bright-eyed, restless-minded scholar" as pope, — Nicholas V., the first pontiff avowedly of the Renaissance.

The second symptom we have to note is a craving for fleshly beauty, — beauty of color and form combined. The older Greeks, as we know, had made a religion of this; and the Romans, or the later Greeks, had deeply degraded it. The Middle Age had delighted in bright color, in golden decoration, and in exuberance of life in sculpture: many of its buildings are overrun with quaint forms of lower animal life, and its costly manuscripts are splendid with the formal patterns of its illumination. But the spirit of Pagan Art was a deep offence to the serious temper of the Church, and was repelled at every point by the monastic spirit that ruled in the Church. Where ornament was admitted, the outline was rude and stiff, and its figures were wrapt in clumsy drapery, to hide all possible loveliness of form.

We have ourselves known something in our own day of the Puritan protest against many styles and, essays of modern Art; and we may conceive the shock which Mediæval prudery must have felt at the frank nakedness of those works of pagan antiquity now beginning to be eagerly sought and prized. To the Greek, nothing was so comely or so noble as the naked human figure; and the wealth of antique sculpture now brought to light may be almost said to have created a new sense, which abhorred the monastic restraints, and craved the delight of an ever widening freedom. Grace of form, or vigor of movement, was no longer to be confined by characterless and flowing draperies. The saints, even, of the Christian Calendar, who filled to the imagination the place once held by the gods and goddesses of the Roman Pantheon, must rival them too in visible charm. They must have carnal beauty as well as spiritual grace.* So sacred art, as well as secular, came to be taken possession of by the new pagan spirit.

It would be easy, but it might be pedantic, to multiply illustrations out of the immense range of Italian Art. It is better worth while to note that the intellectual phase we have been regarding is mostly confined to Italy. Mind and morals were much more serious in the North. The same revolt of intellect which carried the grea Italian scholars to Homer or Plato, opened up to the Germans and English the grave, diligent, and devout study of the Scriptures. While Petrarch is in rapture over a version of the Iliad, done by Boccaccio into wretched Latin, Wiclif is zealously carrying out his great task of giving his countrymen for the first time a Bible in English. While the brilliant group of Platonists in Florence are reviving whole systems of pagan philosophy, grave

* Thus, Saint Sebastian, a beautiful youth stripped naked and pierced with arrows, became a favorite subject of religious composition. A picture of him by Fra Bartolommeo was found to have such an effect on the emotional Italian ladies that it was ordered to be taken from the church.

German students devote their lives to a mastery of Hebrew, and are laying the foundations for learned criticism of the New Testament text.

What is very strange in our eyes, it was not the Pagan Revival but Christian Scholarship that roused the jealous animosity of monk and priest. Hebrew and Greek, they taught, were heretical in essence : Greek was a new-fangled invention of the Enemy; a student of Hebrew would infallibly turn Jew. Doubtless, the instinct of monk and priest was right. The critical study of the Bible — much more, the popular knowledge of it — was the foe the Church system had most to dread. And it was not long before the Inquisition racks began to turn, and the fires of martyrdom to blaze, if by any means this new learning could be extinguished. The purely pagan movement that rose and swelled about the very centre of church authority went on, meanwhile, unchecked, and, as we have seen, was definitely adopted into the Church itself, in the person of Nicholas V.

So far, however, it was not distinctly mischievous, nor, in a broad way, was it an evil. On the contrary, Humanity is largely indebted to it for whatever freedom of thought and beauty of life we now enjoy. The very name "humanity" belongs in a special way to this epoch : the promoters of the new learning are known as "Humanists," and polite letters are "the humanities." I need not enlarge on this view of the matter, — to us, perhaps, the most interesting view. Looking back as we do from the modern world, which has been so greatly brightened, instructed, and charmed by the labors of this splendid period, we are in no danger of doing it injustice. Especially, now that something like a pagan reaction is taking place among us in a new worship of Art and a powerful recoil from Puritan austerity, we may very well let the Italian revival plead its own cause with us.

But there is another side of it, which from the point of view of Christian history is far more important for us to see. At first sight we can well pardon it, even admire it, because it shows itself as a new delight in life, a fresh and spontaneous enjoyment of natural things. It is an age of progress, of hope, of abounding confidence; an age when it seems a new privilege to live. I cannot point to any illustrations of this fresh romantic spirit so charming at once and so familiar as we find in the smaller poems of Chaucer,—the sunny content in living, the delight in such simple daily joys as skylarks and daisies. All the senses were open thus to a world of innocent delight.

We know how this spirit had been dwarfed and cowed by the ascetic gloom of the Middle Age, — a gloom that was felt far more, since that divorce took place between the church creed and the popular faith; especially since the horrible persecutions by which the Church attempted to keep its hold. The thoroughly morbid view of life into which that old asceticism had grown, is seen very strikingly in a tract by Innocent III. "On the contempt of the world," which is simply a study of it in the graveyard or the dissecting-room. Against such pathology as this, it was time for the healthy animal nature to assert itself. And, so far, all our sympathy lies that way.

We find, too, a physical vigor, a boldness, a type

of beauty, which made the Italian of the Renaissance, it is said, the most splendid race, physically and mentally, that has ever existed, — unless, possibly, the freemen of ancient Athens. The hardy out-door life, the passion and adventure of the time, had their part in shaping out the strong personal traits which we admire. The struggle for existence—not in dingy shops in the sordid way of competition for gain, but in city streets for political eminence — was never anywhere more keen, or more brilliant in its effect. That fulness of sensual and intellectual life was the one great phenomenon of the time, and has given it, in distinction from all other times, the splendid name of Renaissance.

But with all this was the one fatal thing, that the Church alone had the keeping and interpreting of the Moral Law; and, in the reaction against the Church, men lapsed at an appalling rate into what was worst in the inhumanities and debaucheries of the old Pagan world. We allow near two centuries before the last degradation has been reached. Then the old Paganism has come back, with seven spirits more wicked than itself, and has taken full possession of the Christian Church. "The corruption of Italy was only equalled by its culture; its immorality was matched by its enthusiasm." You may see in Rome a portrait by Raphael of Cæsar Borgia,* which we may take as a type of what the Pagan Revival had now reached — a man in the prime of life, of entire physical beauty, of perfect physical vigor, able, self-collected, deadly — just such as Domitian or Commodus may have

* Or, as the critics say, not of Cæsar Borgia, and not by Raphael.

been : a man so cruel that he put out his prisoners' eyes with his own hand ; so strong that he could fell an ox with a blow of his fist ; so lustful that he kept for his private spoil forty ladies from the sack of a single town. His father, a man of the same splendid physical traits in his youth, was the wickedest of all the popes, — Alexander VI. The horrible scandals of his reign it will not do even to mention ; but two anecdotes may serve to show the strange travesty which the papal religion had now become.

Some years before, under Sixtus IV., there was to be a duel to the death between two squads of the papal guard. Hearing of it, the Pope posted himself at a window looking down on the closed yard from which no man was to escape, gave his blessing to the combatants, and crossed himself as a signal for the massacre to begin.

In Alexander's time the revel of crime was at its height. His son Cæsar had by great craft made peace with the powerful enemies of his house, and sealed it by a banquet at his castle of Sinigaglia, where after dinner he strangled them all, — one, as a dying request, beseeching absolution of the Holy Father, whom he knew to be the instigator of this monstrous murder. Alexander himself, it was universally believed, was poisoned with the wine he intended for a guest. At his death, said the popular legend, he was heard to say faintly, " It is right, I come ; " and seven fiends were seen in waiting to carry his soul to hell. For he had made a compact with the Devil to reign as pope for twelve years, and then that his soul should be Satan's slave forever.

The serious thing in all this riot of blood and debauchery — of which it is impossible to give more than the barest hints — is that it was the legitimate fruit of the Pagan Revival, as soon as ever it threw off that yoke of the moral law which the Church had made so grievous to be borne, and such an affront to the freedom of human nature itself. In one sense it was worse than the older Paganism, which Christianity had once — and, it might seem, once for all — overthrown. The grossnesses of that were (until its later degradation) like the grossnesses of the Old Testament, — not voluptuous but simply coarse, perhaps even childlike and unconscious. Like Adam in the garden, it was naked but not ashamed. It is impossible that it should be so any longer, when there has once been a wakening of moral consciousness. "I had not known Sin but by the Law," says Paul; "but when the Law came, Sin revived."

That is the real lesson, and the last word of this Pagan Revival. It had to be followed by a Christian Revival, which we term the Reformation, — or the last state of mankind should be worse than the first. Culture and refinement can never take the place of the strenuous thing we call Virtue. Whatever we hold to be the source of the Moral Law, — of Christianity, not as a creed or ceremony, but as a spirit and life, — it is the only salvation mankind has found as yet from those horrors of ancient society against which its first revelation was made; horrors to which Learning itself may open the door, and Art can only decorate the way.

What is called the irony of history has no more

tragic example than the condemnation of the last great preacher of ecclesiastical righteousness by the most profligate of popes. Savonarola was tortured, strangled, and burned by sentence of Alexander Borgia (1498). His short-lived theocratic State, with its quaint police of children, and with Jesus Christ formally proclaimed King of Florence; his eloquent but futile predictions of a Divine judgment upon Italy in the French invasion; his helpless protest against the corruptions of the Papal Court, — are the expiring effort of Mediæval faith to assert the authority of Divine Right in secular things. The world itself has suddenly expanded to new dimensions, and demands a different ideal. Discovery and Invention crowd hard upon the domain of Dogma. The religious life which is to survive this great change must express itself in other phrases, and clothe itself in other forms. Sacerdotal Christianity is fatally dishonored; and the forces are already in training which, in the next generation, will deliver their assault under the new banner of Salvation by Faith.

CHRONOLOGICAL OUTLINE.

N. B. — Names of Popes are in SMALL CAPITALS; names of Emperors in **heavy type.** The mark † denotes the year of death.

800.   Holy ROMAN EMPIRE : **Charlemagne** † 814.
795–16. LEO III.   814–40. **Louis I.** (the Pious).
817–24. PASCAL I.   819. Marriage of Louis and Judith.
828–44. GREGORY IV.   833. "The Field of Lies."
858–67. NICHOLAS I.   843. *Partition of the Empire.*
872–82. JOHN VIII.   858–86. Affair of Photius.
885–91. STEPHEN VI. (Last of good Popes).
        843–877. **Charles II.** (*the Bald*). — FEUDAL PERIOD.
        871–901. Alfred the Great (England).
900.   *Free Cities in Italy. — Magyar Invasions.*
905–11. SERGIUS III. (of Counts of Tusculum) : Corruption of Papal
            Court ; Theodora and her daughters ; Marozia and Theodora.
914–28. JOHN X. (Son of Theodora) : League against Saracens.
931–36. JOHN XI. (Son of Sergius III. and Marozia).
        936–73. **Otho I.** (the Great) : in Italy, 951.
        936–54. Alberic (Son of Marozia), Consul.
956–63. JOHN XII. (Octavian, son of Alberic).
        John deposed by Otho : "*Pactum Ottonis.*"
973–983. **Otho II.**   983–1002. **Otho III.** (Regency of Adelaide).
990–998. Crescentius (Son of Theodora) rules in Rome.
1000.   *Splendor of the Caliphate of Cordova.*
999–1003. SYLVESTER II. (Gerbert).
            Saintly Kings : Robert I. (France), 996–1031.
                        Stephen I. (Hungary), 997–1036.
                        Henry II. (Germany), 1003–1024.
        House of Franconia : **Conrad I.** 1024–1038.
                        Henry III. 1038–1046.
1033. BENEDICT IX. (a child of ten ; abdicates in 1044).
1044. GREGORY VI. (deposed).   46. Henry III. in Italy.
1048–55. LEO IX. — *Hildebrandine Reform.*

1050.   *Berengarian Controversy.*   1053. Norman alliance.
    1056–1106. **Henry IV.**
1058–61. Nicholas II.   59. Rule of Papal Election.
1061–73. Alexander II.   65. War against married clergy.
1073–85. Gregory VII. (Hildebrand). — Controversy of Investitures.
    1076. Humiliation of Henry IV. at Canossa.
1988–99. Urban II.   94. Council of Clermont.
    1096. *First Crusade:* Peter the Hermit; Godfrey.
1099–1118. Pascal II.   Kingdom of Jerusalem established, 1099.
1100. 1106–25. **Henry V.**   1111. Concessions of Pascal.
1119–24. Calixtus VII.   1122. *Concordat of Worms.*
    1125–38. **Lothair II.** (*homo fit Papæ*).
1130–43. Innocent II.   1138–52. **Conrad I.** (*Hohenstaufen*).
    1139. *Second Lateran Council.*
1145–53. Eugene II.   47. *Second Crusade* (Saint Bernard).
      1152–90. **Frederick I.** (*Barbarossa*).
1154–59. Adrian IV.   1154. Diet of Roncaglia.
1159–81. Alexander III.   *Lombard League.*
    1163. *Council of Tours.*   64. Constitutions of Clarendon.
    1170. Death of Becket.—77. Submission of Barbarossa at Venice.
    1179. *Third Lateran Council:* decrees respecting heresy.
    1190. *Third Crusade:* Death of Barbarossa.
1198–1216. Innocent III.   1190–98. **Henry VI.**
1200.   1204. *Fourth Crusade* (to Constantinople).
    1208–29. Albigensian War.
      Founding of Dominican and Franciscan Orders.
    1215. *Fourth Lateran Council.*
1216–27. Honorius III.   1212–50. **Frederick II.**
1227–41. Gregory IX.   1218–27. *Fifth Crusade.*
    1226–70. Louis IX. (Saint Louis, France).
1243–54. Innocent IV.
    1245. *First Council of Lyons:* excommunication of Frederick.
    1247. *Sixth Crusade.*   1251. Ravages of Pastoureaux.
1254–61. Alexander IV.
1265–71. Clement IV. — French in Sicily.
    1268. *Pragmatic Sanction* (France).
    1274. *Second Council of Lyons:* Affair of Greek Church.
      1273–91. **Rudolph** (of Hapsburg).
1281–85. Martin IV.   1282. Sicilian Vespers.
1294–1303. Boniface VIII. (abdication of Celestine V.).

1300.   Boniface VIII.   1302. Bull *Unam Sanctam.*

1305–14. Clement V.   1307–12. *Process of Templars.*

    1308–13. **Henry VII.** (of Luxemburg).

    1309–78. *Popes at Avignon* (Babylonish Captivity).

    1314–47. **Louis IV.** (of Bavaria).

1316–34. John XXII.   1334–42. Benedict XII.

    1338–1444. *Hundred years' War* (England and France).

1342–52. Clement VI.   1347–50. Rienzi, Tribune.

    1348–78. **Charles IV.** (of Bohemia).

    1348–51. The Black Death: 25,000,000 said to have perished.

Flagellants. — Persecution of Jews. 58. *Jacquerie.*

    1356. *The Golden Bull*: independence of Germany.

1378–1417. The Great Schism   1378–1400. **Wenzel.**

    1383. Wiclif's Bible in English.

1378–89. Urban VI.   1378–94. Clement VII. (French Pope).

1389–1404. Boniface IX.

    1394–1424. Benedict XIII. (Peter de Luna, French Pope).

1400.   Statute *de hæretico comburendo* in England (1401).

1404–06. Innocent VII.   1410–37. **Sigismund.**

1406–10. Gregory XII.

    1409. *Council of Pisa* (elects Alexander V.).

1410–15. John XXIII.   1414–18. *Council of Constance:* elects —

1417–31. Martin V.   John Huss burned July 6, 1415.

    1420–34. *Hussite War in Bohemia.*

    Wars in France: Jeanne d'Arc burned, May 30, 1431.

1431–47. Eugene IV., deposed in 1435 by —

    1431–49. *Council of Basel:* elects Felix V.

    1439. *Council of Florence:* Terms with Greek Church.

1447–55. Nicholas V.   1453. *Constantinople taken by Turks.*

    Sovereigns: 1461–83. Louis XI. (France); 1479–1512. Ferdinand I. (Spain); 1485–1509. Henry VII. (England).

1471–84. Sixtus IV.   1481. *Spanish Inquisition established.*

1484–92. Innocent VIII.

    1492. Conquest of Granada; Discovery of America.

1492–1503. Alexander VI. (Borgia). 1493–1519. **Maximilian I.**

    1494. Republic of Florence restored; Charles VIII. in Italy.

    1498. Torture and Execution of Savonarola.

1500.   *Splendor of Italian Art.*

1503–13. Julius II.   1510. Luther in Rome.

1513–22. Leo X.   1517. Luther's Theses on Indulgences.

EMINENT NAMES.

Scotus Erigena † 883.
Wala † 835.
Agobard † 840.
Ebbo † 851.
Haymon † 853.
Radbert † 865.
Anschar † 865.
Gottschalk † 867.
Hincmar † 882.
Avicenna, 980–1037.
Damian † 1072.
HILDEBRAND † 1085.
Berengar † 1088.
Lanfranc † 1089.
ANSELM, 1073–1109.
Peter of Bruys † 1120.
William of Champeaux † 1120.
Roscellin, 1050–1121.
Abelard, 1079–1142.
Abbot Suger † 1152.
BERNARD, 1091–1153.
Arnold of Brescia † 1155.
Peter the Venerable † 1156.
Peter Lombard † 1164.
Thomas Becket, 1117–1170.
Averroes 1126–1198.
Abbot Joachim, 1130–1203.

Stephen Langton † 1228.
Alexander of Hales † 1245.
Robert Grosstête (Lincoln) † 1263.
Albert (the Great), 1193–1280.
Bonaventura, 1221–1274.
Thomas Aquinas, 1225–1274.
Roger Bacon, 1214–1294.
Raymond Lully, 1234–1315.
Duns Scotus, 1274–1308.
Fra Dolcino (burned), 1307.
DANTE, 1265–1321.
Giotto, 1276–1336.
Eckhart † 1329.
William Occam † 1347.
Bradwardine † 1349.
Tauler † 1361.
Petrarch, 1304–1374.
Boccaccio, 1313–1375.
Nicholas (of Basel), 1308–1382.
John Wiclif, 1324–1384.
CHAUCER, 1328–1400.
John Huss, 1369–1415.
Gerson, 1363–1429.
Thomas Kempis, 1380–1461.
Erasmus, 1467–1536.
Copernicus, 1473–1543.
MARTIN LUTHER, 1483–1546.

257. The Italian Republics, 258. Frederick Barbarossa, 260. Guelph and Ghibelline, 262. Frederick II. and Eccelino, 263. The *De Monarchiâ*, 264. The *Divina Commedia*, 266. Dante in Literature, 268. Form of the poem, 269. Popular fables, 271. Symbolic imagery, 273. The lesson, 274.

XI. THE PAGAN REVIVAL, 278-303. — Papacy of the thirteenth century, 279. Boniface VIII. and his successors, 280. Council of Constance, 281. Wiclif, 282. Religious fanatics, 283. The new paganism, 285. Petrarch, 286. Rienzi, 288. The genius of the South, 290. New spirit in Literature, 292. Charm of the ancient classics, 294. Spirit of classic Art, 296. Serious temper of the North, 297. Era of the humanists, 298. Moral corruption of the Renaissance, 300. Savonarola, 303.

THE END.

University Press : John Wilson & Son, Cambridge.

www.ingramcontent.com/pod-product-compliance
Lightning Source LLC
Chambersburg PA
CBHW031019120726
47905CB00007B/1974